Praise for

Running in Silence

"*Running in Silence* is not just about eating disorders and recovery—it's a book that incorporates questions to help others begin dealing with their behaviors. Steil reveals the courage it takes to go to a place of pain and find the strength to heal. She breaks free on her own terms and shows the reader how to do the same. There is hope and compassion from a writer who cares about the reader.

We need more stories like this with guidance. It's a helpful book for anyone, especially to educate parents, coaches, and athletes. *Running in Silence* will encourage anyone to get that push they are looking for to not merely exist, but to live."

—**Suzy Favor Hamilton**, former Olympic middle distance runner and *New York Times* bestselling author of *Fast Girl: A Life Spent Running from Madness*

"Rachael Steil is a talented writer dedicated to sharing her journey, her struggle, and her most vulnerable moments to help others. Her courage shines through on the pages of *Running in Silence*. Rachael has an important story to tell and she not only shares it, she offers up actionable tools for those who struggle with disordered eating to begin unraveling their own stories and find their own courage."

—**Jennifer DiGennaro**, certified Intuitive Eating Counselor and founder of Nourished Energy

"Rachael's voice is no longer silent, but is now a guide to those looking to better their lives. Her honest and compelling memoir courageously sheds light on her fight with eating disorders and brings hope that recovery is possible. This story gives everyone a voice."

–**Brittany Burgunder**, author of *Safety in Numbers*

"Not all of us can identify with eating disorders, but *Running in Silence* gives a star athlete's perspective of what it's like. The decline and then the journey back is a compelling story that gives us hope that any of us can recover from our challenges."

—**Don Kern**, adventure runner and the director of the Metro Health Grand Rapids Marathon

"Rachael Steil has written a powerful book which began as a series of blog posts in the midst of her struggle with an eating disorder as a collegiate runner. Intended as a self-help guide, this book will also be useful to the coaching and sports medicine community which surrounds athletes, helping alert them to the important message that eating disorders are not just about weight. As Rachael tries one restrictive food plan after another, only to fail and blame herself for not being 'strong enough', she invites us into the mind of a highly competitive athlete, with a drive for perfection and a 'mind over matter' mindset which places her, and many others like her, at particular risk for disordered eating behaviors. *Running in Silence* also demonstrates how eating disorders flourish in an environment of secrecy and shame, for it is only by beginning to admit her struggles and talk honestly with others that she is ultimately able to heal."

—**Gail Hall**, LMSW, CEDS, Director of Comprehensive Treatment for Eating Disorders, and co-founder of the Michigan Eating Disorders Alliance

"*Running in Silence* is a poignant account of the author's struggles with disordered eating. In her memoir, she meticulously describes the development of her disease, moving from a coincidence between weight loss and faster times in competitive racing, to an exploration of raw food diets, an increasingly relentless hunger, and an epiphany about the relationship between food/weight and the self. *Running in Silence* is unique in its inclusion of questions at chapter ends about different aspects of the author's journey and her reflections about the variety of behaviors that can be associated with eating disorders. These questions, and the detailed description of the author's life, make the book an important contribution to the literature on this topic."

—**Susan Haworth-Hoeppner**, Professor of Sociology at Aquinas College and author of *Family, Culture, and Self in the Development of Eating Disorders*

"*Running in Silence* is a powerful yet haunting memoir that gives anyone reading an idea of what it's like to struggle with both an eating disorder and with the ultimately unattainable goal of perfection. With her poetic style, Rachael takes readers on a journey through various diets and lifestyle changes that eventually caused great unrest and put her health at risk.

Rachael's book is a pleasure to read, despite the difficult and sometimes uncomfortable topics she addresses. *Running in Silence* is unique and is truly a self-help book in that Rachael not only raises awareness about eating disorders, but she also invites readers to think about the ways in which everyone looks at food. Steil provides thought-provoking questions and exercises at the end of each chapter for those who want to explore their own relationship with food and body image, something that sets this well-written book apart from any others in the genre. Many books on the market that pertain to eating disorders are written like journal entries, but *Running in Silence* takes a much broader look at eating disorders and provides much-needed insight into the ways in which someone in the throes of the illness can recover.

By examining and then challenging her own beliefs around food and body image, Rachael was able to come to a better place in her life. She is a shining example of what life can be in recovery. If ever there was someone who walked her walk, it's Rachael. This is someone who not only courageously overcame her own battle with a potentially life-threatening illness, she then turned around and asked, 'How can I help others?' Her desire to reach those who might be suffering by writing about her own life is only part of what makes Rachael a true heroine.

Running in Silence is a must-read for anyone who wants to better understand the causes and potential cures of eating disorders."

—**Lize Brittin,** former world-class mountain runner and author of *Training on Empty*

Running in Silence:
My Drive for Perfection and
the Eating Disorder That Fed It

by Rachael Rose Steil

© Copyright 2016 Rachael Rose Steil

ISBN 978-1-63393-340-8

Cover photo by Bri Goodyear Luginbill

Published by

 **köehlerbooks**™

210 60th Street
Virginia Beach, VA 23451
800-435-4811
www.koehlerbooks.com

Running
in Silence

My Drive for Perfection and
the Eating Disorder That Fed It

Rachael Rose Steil

VIRGINIA BEACH
CAPE CHARLES

This story is not just my own.
It is one story that reveals many unheard stories.
This is dedicated to those who are running in silence, who
feel that their situation "is not bad enough" to get help.
You are worthy and important enough to be heard.

Author's Note

This book is intended as self-help, but because it also shares my own story in detail, weights, numbers, and eating disorder behaviors are revealed throughout. This may be triggering to some. My intention is to show the change in my body weight in conjunction with my mindset and restriction and bingeing, and how some of these relatively "average" weights can hide an eating disorder based on the misconception that low weight indicates a high level of severity of the illness. Some names and identifying details have been changed to protect the privacy of individuals.

Table of Contents

"Be kind to your body.
It will speak for you or against you one day.
Remember."

~Unknown

Prologue

WITH A BUTTER KNIFE in one hand and the numbers on a scale in the other, I pulled the crumbs and rock-hard frosting of the frozen birthday cake up to my tongue.

And I clawed. I clawed deeper into the cake from my squatting position over the chilly kitchen floor, clawed desperately for any morsel I could chip off the solid block of sugar. All the while the hair on the back of my neck stood up for fear that someone would come by and catch me in the act, for fear that someone would walk into this cold, white kitchen and find good, sweet Rachael sitting before the open door of the refrigerator as a food thief.

I could have waited for the cake to thaw. I could have pulled the cover off the dessert to avoid cutting my wrist as my hand scrambled beneath the plastic. In fact, you could say that with proper discipline and control I could have avoided the incident altogether.

Only, I *had* been the epitome of discipline for the past two years. The girl who snuck into the desolate kitchen that night couldn't even recognize herself when she frantically opened all the cabinets and drawers only to find them bare, when she pulled at her face with desperation and want. The girl who had been eating cooked food all day when she seemed so adamant about her raw food *lifestyle* could barely believe she was now putting not just her *purity* in jeopardy, but also her running success. Nonetheless, she opened that refrigerator door to find the frozen cake sitting before her like a god on its chilly throne.

All-American.

I slammed the blunt knife into the stiff icing.

School record-holder.

Brown cake crumbs scattered everywhere.

Raw. Food. Runner.

I grabbed a chunk of frosting between my shaking fingers, all the while knowing this was not the first time I was putting my newest, greatest running career at stake. I could already imagine the confusion on my parents' faces when I crossed the finish line of the 5k in over eighteen minutes; how my teammates would shake their heads and mutter something about "her raw food diet" and the skeptical eyes that would trail up and down my growing body, how upsetting it would be to reveal the Rachael I had tried to push down for so long, the Rachael my new college friends and coaches never saw because I entered collegiate cross country and track with a body shrunken from my high school one—a body now equipped with a dark voice whispering its incantations, its reminders of how different I was, how I needed to exert more control because *something was broken inside of me.*

And as I continued to reach for the cake that night, I repeatedly told myself, *This is the last nibble, this is the last piece of frosting.*

I could feel the walls of the hallway just outside the kitchen closing in on me, tighter and tighter.

Someone is coming.

They will find you.

You will grow bigger.

You must stop this.

The very air suffocated me, fear electrified my body, and the lights of the small kitchen glared down at me until the butter knife slipped.

The knife slipped from my frosting-covered fingers and clanked to the floor. And I jumped, my heart pounding wildly as I wondered who could have heard, who would come running in and how I could possibly explain what the hell I was doing.

But the hallway outside the kitchen remained as silent as ever. And deciding this was a good chance to escape before anyone did come, I let the refrigerator door fall shut, slid my foot across the tile floor to remove all evidence of cake-thievery, and dashed back to my room.

The dark voice followed. It swept through the hallway with me, clung to my shoulder as I entered the guest room and realized with horror what I had done. Because the moment I entered the bathroom and looked down at the chocolate cake crumbs peppering my outstretched palms, my mind was screaming.

Calories.

Binger.

Thief.

I struggled to turn on the faucet, my fingers slipping with frosting residue, but not even the rush of cold water could flood out the voice. I tried to reassure myself that this mistake was fine because it meant I had come to a breaking point, and I promised everything would change from here.

But it was a promise I kept breaking that summer. Because even as I washed my hands vigorously, even as I promised again and again that this was the last time, the Rachael deep down burned with a passion, a hunger, a desperation that the raw food diet could not fix.

» » »

November of 2010, a year before this scene in the kitchen, I took sixth at the national cross country meet of the National Association of Intercollegiate Athletics (NAIA). I was fast, but I was not fast enough to win. At about the same time, a friend told me about what I later found to be the miracle diet for athletes. It was the raw food diet, and it had become all the rage for the most disciplined, health-conscious athletes, athletes, I thought, like me. Better yet, I knew I was perhaps the only college runner to take on something as daring as this.

But this raw food choice was more than just a new way of eating; it promised to solve all my problems with food and all my unhappiness. It did neither.

Running in Silence began as a series of journal entries when I first started focusing seriously on my weight and investigating all the different diets that promised success. At some point, I realized that my story was more than just my story and that by writing about the specific ways in which I got free of the trap of disordered eating, I could help other runners and people in general.

I came through my own eating disorder, and I want to tell others how that happened. It is intended as a study guide that will be most effective if you consider the questions labeled "Food for Thought" about each chapter and then let the "Mile Markers" guide you toward understanding and healing a possible eating disorder or addiction in your own life. You should also make full use of the worksheets at the back of the book.

The greatest lesson I learned in this long and confusing journey was that my body was never broken, my mind was never beyond repair, and I was never really as alone as I thought I was. You are part of my story, and I want you to share the same ending I did—that of recovery, redemption, and hope.

Food for Thought

1. The Prologue begins with a graphic scene in which the author is huddled over a frozen cake on the kitchen floor, shoving chunks of it into her mouth. Is there any experience in your life that is comparable? Is there any behavior that frightened you or made you feel ashamed?

2. In what circumstances have you felt your control and self-discipline slipping? Did it scare you?

3. Who is the "Rachael deep down" inside you whose voice demands to be heard? In what ways do you think you have kept her quiet?

Mile Markers: Running with a Voice

1. Treat yourself to a nice journal. Take your time shopping for it. If it fits your budget, splurge a little. This is a gift to yourself. Look for a cover you really like and plenty of blank pages.

2. Identify and admit your problem. Write about it.

3. Choose one person you think you'd be willing to share this with.

Chapter 1

Rawchael

"Alone, Deepening."
~Sylvia Plath

ONE HUNDRED AND EIGHTEEN degrees is the maximum temperature at which raw food could be cooked. It was also the number I saw on the scale at the beginning of my freshman year in college, a number, I hoped, that would propel me to a national cross country and track title.

"It's called a raw food diet," I told them—my parents and a few of their friends who followed the weekly emails I sent out during that first year of college. In those updates I often shared my excitement at having become a national NAIA cross country and track runner. That enormous step from taking twenty-sixth at the high school state meet to taking sixth at nationals in college marked the beginning of big changes in my schedule and my priorities and, finally, in my whole life. For the moment, I was on a winning streak.

And now, raw food would make me faster than ever.

Life moves very fast when you're heading toward trouble:

- September 2010: I got faster
- February 2011: I began research for a paper
- May 2011: I started to eat more raw foods
- April 2011: I tentatively, and not quite honestly, told my family about the diet
- April 2011: Dave responded

Aquinas College is a small liberal arts school located in a half-mile-long wooded section of Grand Rapids, Michigan. It is a beautiful campus and, even with the pressures of assignments and grades, a peaceful environment. Nonetheless, one month before the end of my freshman year and with some anxiety, I sent an email to my family and friends announcing my adoption of a raw food diet and explaining that the diet was for health, that my growing interest in nutrition since the summer after my graduation from high school had spurred the desire to learn more.

I lied. I did not tell them the real reason for going raw.

Dave, a good friend of my parents, read the raw food email update skeptically.

I always respected Dave as a friend and runner even though we were decades apart. He was well known in the master's age group (over 40), and he dominated the local and some national race scenes. Short with a muscular build, Dave had a loping, jagged gait, and he diligently put in the miles and strength work to be as good as he was. He had the face of a man hardened by training in the harsh elements of Michigan, looking much to me like tanned, grooved stone. When he was just in his shorts and T-shirt, you could see the bulging veins in his arms, and even his smile (when he gave one) was strained under his fierce, narrow gaze. If I had been a man in my sixties racing Dave, I would have gladly let him pass on by.

And it was Dave who responded to my raw food diet email immediately:

Rachael,

Normally I don't have too much to say about what you are doing. Radically changing your diet doesn't sound good to me. Why fix what isn't broke? You are mentally and physically super. You are a college champion in

*your freshman year running. Did you accomplish all
the things you have on a poor diet? One of your emails
mentioned how much you like and how well you run on
banana, peanut butter, & oatmeal. You have been very
successful as a student and athlete.*

*I have been strong & healthy all my life. I am not
going to make such a radical change in what I fuel my
body and mind. I just would like you to try the diet this
summer or after graduation or never. Give it some
thought.*

For Dave, both running and friendship were serious business,
and he had already questioned me closely months before this
raw food announcement email on a Christmas day run (no
rest on holidays!). Dave had known me since I was in grade
school, and he always wanted to stay updated and support my
running success.

The first question that Christmas morning, as we ran side-
by-side, was about our pace-per-mile. 7:30, I told him, a pace
that he declared was rudely interrupted by a dog who crossed
our path. The second question was about my sudden increase in
running success from high school to college.

"What has changed? What kind of workouts have you been
doing?" he asked.

The good thing about transitioning from high school to
college and suddenly smashing personal best running times
by nearly a minute was that everyone attributed it to great new
coaching and a tougher college running regimen. There was no
denying that Coach Woj had great workouts for the team and
I no longer felt burned out from running multiple high school
races in a week, but I knew that workouts were not the only
changes that had propelled me to the top.

Deep down, I knew I could not reveal—even to myself—how
broken I was or how I had to solve a problem I felt too ashamed
to admit.

Fraud.

Dave admired me as an athlete and clung to every word of
advice I gave him each time we ran. I valued his good opinion and
I knew he talked to my mom, so I always avoided "the secret." My

black spandex pants hung loosely from my legs as we coasted down the road, and I talked about how our team had more rest between meets, how we ran tempo runs, interval workouts, and long runs.

I was isolated by my problem.

Dave and I never talked much about food—until my raw food discovery in February.

The only thing that had compelled me to look further into the raw food diet after a friend had first mentioned it was a research project for a freshman writing class at Aquinas. I could choose any topic I wanted and, on a long list I had compiled of subjects all related to running, the raw food diet appeared somewhere near the bottom. But I hemmed and hawed between barefoot running, Kenyan runners, and, as a last resort, the raw food diet. Finally, the decision was taken out of my hands.

"I think raw food would be an interesting topic," Professor Winkler said decisively at our first conference to discuss the assignment.

I stared at "raw food" written on my sheet. *Really?* I had not expected him to encourage the pursuit of this one.

"I'm sure you would find a great deal of information on it," he said.

» » »

Still thinking the Kenyan runners would have been intriguing, I put off the raw food research project until the weekend. Finally, I dragged myself to a local bookstore; the raw food diet was nothing more than a class assignment.

From the first page of *The Raw Food Lifestyle* by Ruthann Russo, the raw food world spoke to me. Its careful, prying fingers reached out to my growling stomach and tickled my urge to indulge in enough food to satisfy me. I realized that this was a diet of *abundance*.

The raw food diet was not really a "diet" at all, the advocates claimed, but a *lifestyle*. Also called "living food," raw food burst with enzymes and rapid vibration, an indication of how "alive" it was, and how much more alive it could make *us* (Russo 2008, 3). I could witness these energy levels for myself by looking at what were called Kirlian photographs. One such example online showed cooked and raw broccoli side by side. The cooked broccoli looked as if a small white-hot fire burned from its limp branches, while the raw broccoli radiated with fierce lightning sparks, its energy shining larger and brighter (Russo 2008, 72). These photographs indicated energy levels of the broccoli and the energy the food would transfer to us.

I can run faster.

I can have more energy.

I can eat just raw fruits and vegetables and attain ultimate health.

I can be full.

Heating food above 118 degrees would destroy the enzymes essential for digestion, as well as about 30-50 percent of the original vitamins and minerals. Carcinogens, mutagens, free radicals, toxins, these words littered the pages that explained why cooked food was blasphemy, why cooked food destroys us, why we should all convert and convert others.

Protein hardens.

Fats are destroyed.

Sugars are caramelized.

Raw food was most *natural* because it had been around since the dawn of mankind—before fire—when our ancestors had to search in the wild for fresh fruits, nuts, and vegetables. The raw movement explained how humans were not born with a body adapted to attack a wild animal. After all, how could our tiny, bare hands rip into raw flesh? How could our flat teeth sink into meaty gristle? The raw foodists claimed that because of these characteristics and many more, we are, by nature, frugivores, people who are meant to consume a diet of just raw fruits and vegetables.

I learned that raw food was defined as whole, live, uncooked, unpasteurized, unpreserved, and unprocessed food (Russo 2008, 2). Still not quite converted, all I could imagine eating were stalks of celery, apples, and carrot sticks for breakfast, lunch and dinner. How could I get protein and calcium without meat and dairy? How could I adopt this diet and not run into injury?

The modern raw foodist knew the answer to that. When I returned home that night to conduct more research online, I saw photographs that were not of cooked foods, as I thought at first glance, but *raw:* raw "pasta," or spiralized zucchini strips drizzled in fresh tomato sauce; chocolate pies made of nothing but date sugar, coconut, and nut butters; green smoothies touting health and vitality in every sweet, banana-infused sip.

Raw food could be as simple as grabbing a pear for the road or concocting delicious, whole food recipes. And if I didn't want to go fully vegan, I could also follow the rare raw foodists who included raw, organic animal products. But according to most raw foodists, you could get sufficient calcium and protein from just eating fruits and vegetables. This was a revelation to a runner who reluctantly included meat because she thought it was necessary for an athlete (I say "reluctantly" because if given the choice, I would have simply eaten food with fiber, thinking it was the easiest way to stay full and lose weight). What a *wonderful* surprise that this runner could actually just eat fruits and vegetables, the ultimate fullness of fiber, and *thrive.*

And it was exactly this, an excuse to just eat fruits and vegetables, that sealed the deal.

I could eat more food lower in calories and avoid weight gain.

I could eat more and *lose* weight.

» » »

Over the following days, I began to look at the chicken in our school cafeteria differently. I ate it out of habit, making sure to first wipe off the questionable fatty sauces. I accusingly observed the limp, cooked broccoli that I always piled high on my plate. I drank cow's milk, questioning every sip.

"Did you know we don't need as much protein as nutritionists say we do?" I asked my teammate Elizabeth at practice. And, "Did you know that calcium doesn't have to come from milk?" to my teammate Alina on our jog to the track for a workout.

As I continued to soak in the information, I imparted my new wisdom here and there to my new friends on the track team. And finally I wrote the research paper, extending it over the limit. In fact, I kept researching long after the project. Something inside me could not stop until I gathered all the evidence, until I knew everything. Now that I felt there was more to learn, more ways to perfect a diet, the hunger for the information intensified.

» » »

I was at lunch in the cafeteria, chewing on a piece of chicken, when I made the first decision: I would become a vegetarian.

"You'll be so thankful!" said my friend Abigail, a vegetarian herself.

I felt invigorated as I walked to my next class. Vegetarianism sounded so intriguing, so elegant, so . . . superior.

And that's when it hit me. If I could be so bold as to try vegetarianism, why not go all the way? Why not become a *raw foodist?*

The final decision was not made without hesitation and fear. As I entered my world regional geography class that afternoon, I thought about how a diet of mostly raw food could change my life. It would mean strategizing, further research, and possibly a downfall in my running career if I didn't get the right information for my nutritional needs.

But you can eat until you are full.

You don't have to worry about weight.

You can be the best Rachael you've ever known.

I also began to think about how timid I had been most of my life, how I preferred to hold back and watch as others made grand, bold decisions, how I didn't make controversial leaps like this for fear of imperfection or actual failure. How I always maintained control. But if other people could experiment, why couldn't I?

I wanted to take the chance now.

I decided to record my thoughts and feelings about raw food in a private journal, thinking I would look back someday and see how raw food changed me, how it propelled me to an even greater running career, how I would begin to feel changes in my energy levels and vitality and reclaim a control over food and my body.

The dim voice of sanity in my life still mattered. I replied to Dave's email about my decision to become a raw foodist.

Dave,

I know it will be a radical change for me, but I'm going to take it slow. For now I'm going to stick with my normal breakfast of oatmeal, but I want to eat more raw vegetables and fruit throughout the day. I don't plan to fully transition until summer, where I can take some time to experiment for a week or two. I figure that if I feel better than normal, or if everything just goes well, I might try it out longer. But if I'm not happy with it, there's nothing that says I can't turn back to what I feel is right.

I appreciate your input. Thanks again for giving me your thoughts!

—Rachael

Or should I say, Rawchael?

Food for Thought

1. Rachael says that her much older and more experienced friend, Dave, admires her and follows her lead a lot. What is it about her that has inspired that admiration? Is it something real, or is she faking it?

2. So far, do you like this author, and why or why not? Do you identify with the complicated, often confused, thoughts she has and the decisions she makes?

3. Rachael identifies herself as "Rawchael" for this first chapter. What might this say about her relationship with herself?

Mile Markers: Lies to Hide the Shame

1. In this chapter, the subtle dishonesty of hiding her eating problem has progressed to something more direct as she tells her family and friends a lie about her reasons for trying the raw food diet. Consider situations in your life when keeping a secret somehow grew into real dishonesty.

2. Consider the reason for the initial dishonesty, was it because, like Rachael, you felt ashamed of something?

3. Where do you think this shame comes from? Write down the sources. It could be from societal pressures, family values, friends' comments, distorted perceptions of yourself, etc.

Chapter 2

Unraveling Raw

*"To refuse the dark side of one's nature is to
store up or accumulate the darkness; this is later
expressed as a black mood, psychosomatic illness,
or unconsciously inspired accidents."*
~*Robert A. Johnson,* Owning Your Own Shadow

122 pounds
One hundred and twenty-two pounds
55 kilograms
8 stone
One thousand nine hundred and fifty-two ounces
122 pounds

"ARE YOU A VEGETARIAN?"
"Rachael, the Veggie Queen!"
These comments bombarded me in the cafeteria within the first few months of my freshman year of college. I had arrived already thin, if only I had seen it, already thin from fifty-mile running weeks and an already veggie-heavy diet. Thus diving

into raw food months later didn't look too suspicious since eating raw fruits and vegetables was not a major shift from previously piling my plates with cooked vegetables, sometimes a fist-size portion of chicken buried beneath.

"That's why she's so fast," my teammates would say.

My cross country teammates might have thought I ate strangely, but I was just as uncomfortable with the way they ate. After a summer of carefully portioning out the correct foods in their proper amounts according to the rules I typed up and printed out in an organized binder, I was suddenly surrounded by my fellow runners grabbing small slices of pie, cubes of cake, or little bowls of ice cream every day. I sat there, my plate overflowing with broccoli and cauliflower, as I watched them celebrate with burgers and pizza. They ate hungrily, wolfing down their food amid laughter and chatter, while I sat thinking about whether the scoop of tofu stir fry I had taken was equal to a cup, about how to calculate the calories online later, and how to make sure I only ate one apple to avoid too much sugar and too many calories.

You are different.

You can't eat like they do.

I was jealous that my friends could eat their food without much thought. I missed feeling that way about food. I loved the food I ate now, but I also wished to eat more variety without guilt and fear of weight gain. I felt self-conscious that my teammates might figure out how much I thought about calories and weight.

I wanted to eat in my eating disordered ways without allowing anyone to suspect my problem.

I pretended to engage in conversation at each meal. I looked around the table, nodding and laughing at jokes, while everything inside me whirred and ticked away at numbers, while I measured out portions with my eyes, and wondered and worried: Had I made a mistake? If so, how could I fix it? And, always, how could I make my meals closer to perfection so that I could someday eat carefree like they did?

My mom was the first person with whom I had discussed the miracle of raw food. It wasn't until a few days after I told her about the diet that she remembered a woman who occasionally ran with her in the Grand Rapids Running Club and was a committed raw food advocate.

Jill and my mom weren't close, but they knew each other well enough for me to email Jill. She responded almost immediately and invited me to visit her at Harvest Health, a whole food store across town where she worked.

The moment I walked into the store, I knew this was where I would return often for raw food. The place sold everything from organic produce and sprouted grain breads to herbal medicines, kombucha drinks, and, of course, raw food products like seed crackers, kale chips, nut butters, and "Raw Revolution" bars.

"I'm so excited for you!" Jill said the moment she greeted me. Jill was around fifty, her face long and narrow and her body thin but well-muscled from miles of running. Her hair was a short, wispy, dirty blond, her eyes shrunken, her lips pursed in a tight smile. Jill seemed eager to have a raw-foodie friend, as I'm sure they were rare and few. In fact, I felt surprised to find even one raw foodist living anywhere close to Grand Rapids, let alone in the running group I had been a part of since childhood.

But I wondered if diving into the raw food realm had perhaps made Jill quiet. Was she one of those raw foodists I had discovered in my research on the Internet, the ones who were connecting with their "inner spirits"? I could tell she felt excited to have me in her circle at that point, but her excitement was subdued as she gave me a light hug and cautiously showed me toward the back room.

The room was dark save for a small window, but the light from the refrigerator revealed all too clearly the raw mango pie Jill offered me. It looked like a gooey, vibrant orange pudding in a pie pan. The edges were lined with something resembling dirt gravel made into a brown crumbly crust. Jill cut a messy slice decorated with white coconut "sprinkles" and set it before me.

"It is so smart of you to start a raw food diet right now," she said wistfully. "I wish I had started at your age."

I nodded proudly and smiled, carefully cutting my fork into the tip of the wedge of pie. The mango center had oozed into a blob on the plate, but the first bite made up for its odd appearance. It was like a sweet creamy pudding, and I was sure in that moment that it was one of the best desserts I had ever tried.

Jill began talking about how she started eating raw food and how much it seemed to help her aching left elbow, but I was too busy relishing the sweetness of this nourishing dessert. The mango center, smooth and creamy, created a moment of pure pleasure as my teeth bit into the texture of the sweet, nutty crust underneath.

I tried to eat the pie slowly to savor every bite, but it disappeared in what seemed like seconds. And although I pointedly eyed the large pie dish for more, to my disappointment Jill stuck the whole thing back in the refrigerator. However, she pulled out more raw samples. She lined up three tall glass bottles, one filled with green smoothie, one with almond milk, and a third with a raw electrolyte drink she made for her runs. Pouring a bit of each drink into a Dixie cup, she pushed the samples toward me.

The green smoothie had the consistency of thick tomato soup and I was hesitant, but, as with the pie, the flavor convinced me. "This . . . is amazing!" I said, swirling the thick, pulpy texture around in my mouth. The fruit overwhelmed the bitter greens in the drink, making it sweet.

"Oh, you like it?" Jill asked.

How could I not? What was she so baffled by?

I asked what she put in it.

"Banana, kale, apple, water, ice, agave nectar . . ." Jill listed off the ingredients, but I lost her at "kale" and "agave nectar." Fear of the unknown coursed through me. I wanted to feel more confident going into this diet, knowing that Jill, a runner, was doing it too. She had been thriving on it for years! I just didn't like how the calories had suddenly become like ghosts in the food; they were there, but invisible, pleading not to be counted. It was a new fear to overcome: biting into food that had no attachment to numbers in my mind. The raw food gurus reassured their followers that it was nearly impossible to get fat eating only raw foods.

But the fear lingered.

When Jill had to get back to work, I decided to walk around the store to see what I was getting myself into. I started with the first aisle near the refrigerators, where I found a small jar of sprouted, raw peanut butter. I smiled, turning the packages over in my hands to look at the ingredients, but my smile faded quickly when I found the price.

Ten dollars a jar?

I panicked. What if my parents thought the diet was too

expensive? What if this was too much for us, for me to handle?

Indeed, the organic food prices were higher than any vegetables I had seen at my local supermarket. As I continued to walk down the first aisle, I found a tub of RAW calcium supplement powder and felt my gut clench.

Will I need to buy this?

Will I risk breaking any bones if I don't include it?

The new information seemed endless, and I realized how ignorant I was about the world of raw food. Knowing I still had more research to do, the next day I put schoolwork to the side and stayed glued to the Internet for hours. I had to make sure I would get the right nutrients, since I didn't want to make any mistakes and ruin what I had worked so long and hard to achieve, more success in running than I had ever thought possible for a girl like me. In my mind, even one mistake could mean disaster.

I recorded everything I ate in my journal, thinking how I would look back on all of this and marvel at my discipline and courage, how I would see amazing changes in my body and energy levels.

"Eleven-mile run with the team," I wrote that Sunday. "Took a swig of the almond milk Jill gave me for recovery."

And then, lunch: "Ate a salad and two cups of fresh fruit. Afterwards I didn't feel tired, which could be because of my new uncooked eating habits!"

Dinner consisted of three large salads with salsa. I was aware that the tomatoes had been cooked to make the salsa, but I compromised with myself by saying that I could only do my best in a school cafeteria and that perhaps weaning myself off cooked food little by little was the best way to get used to this diet.

Food for Thought

1. Before she resumes her story, the author has included an odd list of weights. Why do you think this list is important? Does it reveal anything about Rachael?

2. Rachael isn't sparking attention from her teammates due to how *little* she is eating. She even says her plates are piled high with food (vegetables). How might this be one way to "hide" an eating disorder?

3. What do you think of Jill? Does she remind you of anyone you know? Does she remind you of yourself in any way?

Mile Markers: Recognizing Rituals and Habits

1. Keep a food journal and record what you eat for a few days.

2. Pay attention to your eating patterns. Are there habits you would like to break?

3. Rachael concludes, watching her teammates eat, that she is "different." Are there ways in which you feel different from your friends or family?

Chapter 3

Learning the Logistics

EATING A VARIETY OF fruit each morning in my dorm room, plums, bananas, oranges, and apples, I scrolled through Steve Pavlina's blog. This morning routine was the new norm. At the time, it seemed a significant change from my 7 a.m. mornings using a sample spoon to control the portions of hot oatmeal that I scooped out of a bowl, alone in the cafeteria.

Pavlina was a well-known blogger on personal development. His website reached millions of readers, and a quick Google search of "raw food diet" led my teammate and friend Elizabeth, a junior, to Pavlina's blog section where he described his 30-day trial with raw food. Elizabeth sent me a link to the blog, so I decided to get going on my research by reading from it each morning as I ate.

"I'm more interested in what fundamental diet we can all thrive on, not merely survive on," Pavlina wrote in one entry. "Just because we can tolerate a food doesn't mean we should. We *can* drink large quantities of alcohol. We *can* eat cooked food. We *can* eat goat's testicles if we want. But just because we *can* eat something doesn't mean we *should*" (2007).

This spoke to me strongly because for the past few years, family members and friends had encouraged me to eat desserts and high-calorie meals. They seemed set on convincing me that I *should* treat myself, that I *should* indulge, and that treats and indulgences could only be "junk food." I was never quite able to say why this didn't make sense; I just knew it didn't.

Then Pavlina's words said it for me and gave me the anchor I needed. I had an excuse, a reason to eat "perfectly" without worrying what family members and friends thought. As long as I had the raw food philosophy to justify my refusal of so-called "indulgences" and things like that creamy mango pie as treats, I did not have to worry about a thing. I had finally found people who thought like I did about food.

I felt relieved—until my team began to notice.

No one talked much about my raw transition at first, but I caught them staring more often at my large plates overflowing with sliced zucchini and summer squash, bits of sunflower seeds sprinkled over it all. I added red bell peppers for a sweet crunch and dipped the vegetables in fresh salsa. Plate piled high, my confidence soared.

These were the easy times.

Dinner was often when the desire for cooked food crept in. And even the nights when I didn't have cooked cravings, the voice in the back of my mind urged me to grab the available tuna for more protein after intense track workouts. I gave in to this fear about protein early on in the raw food experiment, but after a few bites into fish one night, I stopped myself and pushed it away.

"You can get sufficient protein from fruits and vegetables," the raw food gurus had explained. And it wasn't just their words that convinced me; they had science to back it up. They had studies to show that if we ate enough fruits and vegetables, we would naturally get enough protein, since the requirement for our bodies is actually quite low. They also explained how the food pyramid and its emphasis on protein from meat was USDA propaganda to get people to buy more meat. Greed, money, corruption, all of this was the root of the deteriorating health of America, and the raw food diet was here to help bring everyone back to vitality.

But what if I'm doing something wrong?

My greatest fear was breaking a bone or running into some other major injury, so attempting a diet few runners adopted both thrilled and scared me. Sure, Jill was all for it, but even I sensed some uncertainty in the way she obsessed over every little ingredient.

"I make sure to get my protein powder," she said, referring to a baby blue and purple container labeled "Raw Protein." She had given me sample packets of magnesium-calcium blends as well, which only made me worry more that I just wasn't getting enough calcium from the dairyless diet. If we had to ingest these powders and manufactured raw foods to run well, what was the point in even eating only raw food? Wasn't raw food in its whole, natural form supposed to be enough for our bodies if this was the way we were designed to eat?

A week after I started the diet, the stomach gurgling began. I loved stuffing myself with the low-calorie vegetable dinners, but once I added fruit for dessert, my stomach bloated uncomfortably throughout the evening. It expanded gradually as I worked at my laptop; my fine, well-tuned runner's body filled the room with gas. And the whole process started over: the bloating, the discomfort, the release. I crawled into bed nearly every night holding my aching tummy.

The stomach pain/gas/bloating went on for a little over a week. But after those first cramps, my body adjusted, probably because I was already eating a diet high in fiber.

The stress increased not only with the upcoming final exams for school, but also with a diet I knew I hadn't mastered perfectly. I felt I still had so much to research, so much to understand. It became a race against time, not only to keep up with my studies, but also to make sure I did everything right with eating.

I reassured myself that I was only experimenting with the raw food diet, but the deeper I dove into it, the more I knew I couldn't turn back. I couldn't just erase and forget about everything I had learned.

» » »

"You're supposed to wait ten minutes before you go up for seconds."

Kolin, the sly jokester of the guys' team, said this as I rushed through my plate of raw vegetables and nearly sprinted from my seat to grab more. Kolin never smiled when he cracked jokes like this, which often made me wonder if he actually was joking. My stomach jolted at any comment about my food, about how I was eating.

They must see what a glutton I am.

What made it worse was that I wasn't going up for seconds; I was on my *fourth* plate of salad and vegetables. I knew it seemed excessive. I disliked eating so much in front of my teammates, but I knew I had to eat enough vegetables so I wouldn't be too hungry later and cave in to the fruit I had stashed in my dorm. As healthy as fruit was, I knew it was higher in calories than vegetables, and I felt determined to keep the calorie count as low as possible while feeling full.

They will see you.

They will watch you.

They will know.

Another night, Elizabeth took one look at my plate of raw zucchini, summer squash, and beets, and held her stomach in disbelief as she made a comment about how she couldn't imagine "stomaching the fiber."

I focused on my plate of food, but I felt my face heat up. If Elizabeth couldn't eat this much, was that how everyone else felt? Was there really something wrong with me? Had I stretched my stomach too far? Had I become gluttonous?

Any normal person would eat much less.

The moment I left the cafeteria that night, I started to cry and called my vegetarian friend Abigail.

"I just feel so bad. I hate that everyone keeps bugging me about my food," I explained.

I didn't know how to tell her I hated how much I ate, too.

"Awe, Rach! I'm so sorry. You're right, what they're saying is so wrong. We'll straighten things out."

The teasing felt especially harsh because I felt that any focus on my food meant a focus on my body, and even though I ate in ways that would raise questions and skepticism (and I knew this), I still didn't want it to be the big show.

Abigail did provide some protection whenever she joined me

in the cafeteria by criticizing the guys' fatty foods, but it didn't faze them one bit.

"Here, Rachael, eat my burger!" Stephen said.

Stephen had tried since the beginning of the school year to get me to switch meals with him as a bet. I used to laugh it off, but after hearing it the tenth time, I had had enough.

"Come on, where's your protein?" the guys would ask, grunting as they wolfed down their hot dogs and steaks.

If only they knew the drawbacks of what they are eating.

I felt justified in eating the right food, but anger boiled within. I wasn't bothering anyone else about what they ate. They had no right to comment on my food like this.

"Rachael, you can't take all the fruit," my teammates said later that week, laughing as I stashed four bananas and two apples into a bag I had brought into the cafeteria. What they didn't know was that I had taken five oranges from the church social the night before, too.

I could only smile back, pushing the bag of fruit underneath my seat as I sat down with another overflowing plate of salad.

Food for Thought

1. Rachael seems all over the place in this chapter, changing all her eating habits, reading everything she can find to back her up, sure one minute, frightened the next, angry with her classmates, then intimidated by them. What are your feelings about her as you read this chapter?

2. What do you think about the raw food diet so far?

3. Does Rachael in fact "learn the logistics" of the diet in this chapter?

Mile Markers: A Raw Social Life

1. Rachael is really preoccupied with what her friends think about her eating. She feels terrible when they tease or even notice; she feels better at once if they support her. When you are trying something new, how concerned are you with what other people think?

2. In what circumstances have you felt caught between looking "normal" for the people you are with and wanting to give in to the urges of an eating disorder?

Chapter 4

The Battle of Olive Garden

"Not everything that is faced can be changed, but nothing can be changed until it is faced."
~Lucille Ball

121 POUNDS

AS I CONTINUED MY research into raw food, I couldn't help feeling intimidated by the vast array of extravagant raw food recipes. I wasn't sure how to get started on raw pizza, pie, or even the "simple" recipes like raw almond milk or green smoothies, so I asked Jill, the raw foodist runner, to show me the ropes. Jill agreed in our final email exchange (as we had become email buddies so I could ask questions), and she suggested we meet at her house to make the same raw mango pie she had me sample the first time I visited her at Harvest Health.

Jill was her usual self, an odd combination of nervous energy, constantly in motion, and a kind of shy reticence. She moved energetically around the house but stood back while I leaned in to look at all her contraptions.

We first came upon the dehydrator, which looked like a small portable oven with dozens of shelves on which to place food. I was in awe. I had only read about dehydrators, so seeing one for the first time allowed me to understand exactly how it heated up food at such a low temperature. It was a slow cooker that never went above 118 degrees so as to keep the food "raw."

"This is where I dehydrate my almonds, pumpkin seeds, and walnuts," Jill said, opening the glass door and pulling out a shelf of seeds. I peeked in, mystified and anxious about all that was required of a raw foodist. All I had learned at that point was that sprouting nuts was necessary to allow the enzymes to "awaken," but did you also need to *dehydrate?* I didn't dare ask about it, wondering if I had just missed something in my research.

When we walked into the kitchen to start the pie, Jill handed me two fruits a little larger than an apple. Their color reminded me of an orange sunset fading into a green pasture. "Do you want to cut these up?" she asked.

I stared at them. "What are they, and how do you do it? Sorry, I've never cooked much before, or rather, uncooked." I laughed.

"Oh!" she said, surprised. "Those are mangoes. You just cut off that tough rind and then cut away the flesh from the large pit inside."

Jill made it sound simple, but the slippery, flame-colored flesh of the mango was difficult to grip and I was afraid the knife would slip and cut into my unskilled fingers. I managed to finish the job unscathed and looked to Jill for the next task.

"Now we're going to blend those fresh mango slices with the dried mango," Jill said, pulling out a plastic bag of what looked like tiny orange elephant ears. She poured both the wrinkly and the fresh mango into her Blendtec blender, added water, and the contraption roared to life. I watched, mesmerized, as the blades cut effortlessly into the fruit, creating a thick orange paste.

"And now to the crust," Jill said, pulling out bags of walnuts and almonds. But she also pulled out something unfamiliar, something that looked like an oversized raisin. "Can you pit these?" she asked. "You can try one, too, if you'd like."

Dates, they were called. They looked similar to the color, shape, and size of a cicada bug, but their texture was soft and sticky. Biting into the first one, I smacked my lips as it stuck to my teeth and the roof of my mouth like peanut butter. But the natural sugars exploded on my tongue.

"This is so good!" I said, surprised at the sweet intensity.

Jill smiled.

I couldn't believe my parents hadn't introduced me to dates growing up. The only mention of "dates" in my life was my lack-thereof throughout high school. But I also recalled reading about an old man chowing down on dates at the bottom of an ocean whirlpool, a book called *The Merlin Effect* by T.A. Barron. There was nothing about the description of the dates in that book that inspired me to go out and buy them. How could anyone who has tried dates not rave over these fruity jewels, these caramel-like sugar-bombs? How could they not preach to the world, spread the word, and encourage everyone to try them?

Once Jill and I had blended the dates, almonds, and walnuts in the food processor, we used a spatula to scrape out the thick, sticky mixture and then pressed it into the bottom of the pie dish with our hands. We poured in the mango paste for the pie filling. I couldn't add the final touches of blueberries and kiwi slices for decoration until Easter, the day I would bring this pie to my family, so we set aside the mango pie and Jill showed me how to make other rawcipes.

We began with raw almond milk. Jill grabbed the almonds from her dehydrator and poured them into the blender with dates, water, ice, and agave nectar. I looked at the agave nectar with suspicion.

Do we really need to add in unnecessary sugary calories?

I made a mental note not to use agave nectar in my own future almond milk recipe.

After blending, Jill took what she called a cheesecloth to filter out all the gritty almond pebbles that had not been fully pulverized. Finally, she poured the almond milk into a large glass container, stoppered it, and stored it in the refrigerator.

Next up was the green smoothie. Jill assembled the ingredients, an eclectic mix of Udo's oil, nuts and seeds, agave nectar, frozen bananas, and berries. She finished it off by stuffing in loads of dark greens.

Surprisingly, the blender was able to chew it all up into a drink of a deep reddish-purple hue rather than the typical dark green I was expecting. I figured this new color was due to the blueberries and raspberries Jill added.

Jill dipped a spoon in to try it, looking nervous. "I *think* that tastes right," she said. She poured the concoction into two tall, clear glasses.

Famished and excited, I slurped down half of it before Jill even had a chance to sip from hers. I swirled the sweet drink around my mouth, feeling a bit of a grainy texture from some of the leaves not fully pulverized. But the smoothie was thick and refreshingly cool in my mouth.

"I'm so glad you're doing this raw diet," Jill said, sitting down near me with her green smoothie. This comment was a common expression of gratitude Jill repeated in our email exchanges. "I keep telling my daughter how unhealthy it is when she eats pizza, or I try to show my husband how I can make these delicious raw almond-walnut burgers instead of the meat, but he won't do it."

I simply nodded, but my stomach clenched. This is exactly what I didn't like about some of what I saw as fanatic raw foodists, the ones devoted to making the diet their entire life, softly condemning those who "just don't know any better."

"There's a Rawluck group you can attend in Grand Rapids to meet some others who eat this way," Jill added. "I'll give you the information for the next one, but I won't be going. I don't like crowds like that. It's gotten too big for my liking."

I smiled and expressed my interest in the Rawluck. But it was the green smoothie in that moment that had my attention.

"I can't get over how delicious this is!" I said, finishing it off. And it was true. The smoothie barely even tasted like what someone would call a "health drink."

» » »

I left Jill's house about an hour later to meet up with my team for a five-mile tempo run. Once we finished the workout, we left for Olive Garden to eat dinner together.

"What are you going to get?" Carly asked when we sat down to wait for our table.

"Well, my stomach is bothering me, so maybe just a salad," I said. I felt my face grow hot, knowing I had lied about my stomach hurting, but I needed a reason to order a salad without stirring up any questions from my suspicious teammates.

Just do it, Rachael. It will be fine.

I had already looked at the menu online: Pasta Ripiena at nearly eight hundred calories, Fettucini Alfredo at over one thousand, and the rest of the food was clearly not raw, let alone vegan.

Except for the salad.

When the server came, I felt relieved that she stood next to me so that I didn't have to yell my order across the table.

"Um, can I just get the salad? No dressing and no croutons?" I asked in the smallest voice possible, hoping she would still catch everything so I wouldn't have to repeat myself. Luckily she wrote down my order without further question, and I breathed a sigh of relief.

The worst was over.

But minutes later, as we all chatted together while we waited for our food, my roommate Jessica asked from across the table what I had ordered.

Ugh, Jessica, why now?

"Just a salad," I said, forcing a smile to make it look lighthearted. So far, the girls' side of the team hadn't said much about my experiment with raw food, and I wasn't about to start drawing attention to it now.

Ten minutes later, everyone's salad came; and mine didn't.

And then everyone's meal came; and mine didn't.

"Excuse me?" I called the server over, carefully raising my hand to get her attention. "I ordered a salad for my meal . . ."

"Well, we brought the salad out, didn't we?"

My stomach plummeted. I tried to explain to her that I had asked for salad *without* dressing and croutons, not the salad she had brought for everyone as a starter. The salad I had ordered would be my *main* meal, I said.

The server reassured me that I would get my salad soon.

I wanted to slump down in my seat. I felt self-conscious knowing that I would have to eat my dinner after everyone had eaten theirs, further drawing attention to the salad that was so unlike everyone's rich, heavy pasta meals.

» » »

A few nights later I checked online to find that Kolin from the cross country team had posted a link to the MyFoodPyramid calorie tracker on my Facebook page.

"I would like you to create an account and log your food intake for a week or so just to see if you are really getting all the essential nutrients that you need," he wrote.

I stared at the post, dumbfounded. It seemed particularly ironic since this was the same calorie counter I had used in the not-so-distant past, and Kolin seemed to think I knew nothing about it. I laughed to myself, but I was infuriated as I read through the post again. Why did everyone think I wasn't getting enough nutrients when they were the ones eating junk food? Why did everyone think they had the right to evaluate what I was eating?

I texted Elizabeth about the post, and she was on it in an instant: "The food pyramid is USDA propaganda," she wrote below the Facebook post. "It is used to increase capitalist gains from grains. Rachael's diet is her concern (and to some extent her parents' and coach's). Luckily for you, she has enough tact not to paste the consequences of consuming over-processed, greasy, fatty foods on your wall."

I wanted to hug her.

My younger sister Angela decided to chime in as well: "Just because you 'researched' the proper diet by Googling 'healthy' or something and getting a 'government approved' diet pyramid, you think you have the right information. If you want the real facts, actually do the research, and you'll be blown away by how misinformed you really are and have been in the past because of the government. I'm sure Rachael thanks you for your concern, but she's got a better grip than anyone I've ever met."

But Kolin's post made me realize that perhaps my teammates were observing more than I had thought, that maybe they were whispering behind my back about my "strange" new eating habits.

I called Carly to ask.

"Well, they have been concerned," she said. "Especially when we went to Olive Garden, and you only ordered a salad after a long, tough workout."

My stomach plummeted. No one had said anything about my meal, so I thought I had gotten away with it. But I realized now that of course they wouldn't say it to my face!

I tried to reassure Carly that I was trying the raw food diet, and it was difficult to eat anything raw at the restaurant. She finally seemed to understand and messaged me about it later:

> *I have to admit that I was a little more concerned than I let on when we talked, but seriously, now I know you're not concerned about weight, and you are getting all of your nutrients. You really just want to feel good and be the best athlete you can be! Hardly anyone is as dedicated as you to feeding their body well, and I think people may be somewhat in awe of your discipline and dedication. I just wanted you to know that I fully support you now, especially after our conversation tonight.*

This situation scared me though. I didn't want them to see my intense concern about my own body; that I had to discipline myself because I was such a glutton. It made me feel more visible, bigger somehow, to draw this attention to my food.

» » »

Little by little, I found myself eating more, and seemingly more than I had eaten in a long time. It scared me to feel this ravenous hunger again, but raw food's promise of weight loss somewhat eased the voice in my mind. Still, my appetite had grown almost too unbearable to ignore. It scared me to *want* this badly, to sense even a gradual loss of control. And it seemed like the more I ate, the stronger the urge became.

I went back to what made me most comfortable: research.

I could investigate why I had suddenly become so voracious. I could understand why eating so much food caused me to suddenly want to eat even more. And in researching online, I found other raw foodists who also felt this strange, ravenous hunger. Further research and suggestions by raw food peers led me to the conclusion that by eating raw food, we were simply eliminating toxins. Thus, our bodies searched for food to heal the internal wreckage done by cooked food. Another source suggested that, after consuming so much dense, cooked food for so many years, our bodies were simply not used to the lighter load of raw food.

Food for Thought

1. What are your thoughts about Kolin's comment on Rachael's Facebook page? What did you think of the responses to it from Rachael's friends?

2. Rachael isn't supposed to worry about calories since she's eating mostly raw food, and the *lifestyle* promises abundance without this anxiety, but she still seems unable to let it go. Why do you think this is so? What does this say about eating disorders?

3. Why do you think research makes Rachael feel most comfortable? What does it say about her relationship with her body?

Mile Markers: The Approach

1. Write down what you think would be the best way to approach someone with an eating disorder. Remember it is an illness that goes deeper than appearance. Also consider that the triggers, the comments, and the recovery process might differ from person to person.

2. Look online or read books on eating disorders for other alternatives and suggestions. Do any of these suggestions match your own ideas? If you have an eating disorder, think about your own situation for guidance.

3. Since eating disorders often provide a false sense of control, someone has to *want* recovery to begin that process. What made you "want" recovery if you have already been seeking it? If you haven't made that decision yet, what do you think it would take? In what way does disordered eating help you feel in control?

Chapter 5

Not Enough Protein

I DIDN'T OFFICIALLY MEET my college cross country and track coach until near the end of my senior high school cross country season when he came to a dual cross country meet on a chilly, rainy Wednesday afternoon. I had finished first in the race, only to jog out of the chute back onto the course to cheer on my teammates.

Coach Woj (short for his last name, Wojciakowski) introduced himself to me soon afterward. He was a young man just over thirty with a gentle voice and smile. I humored Woj, listening to what he had to say about his beloved Aquinas, but I already had my heart set on a NCAA Division II college.

Only, his next few words spurred a change within.

"I love that you went back to cheer on your teammates after you finished," he said.

I hadn't decided to cheer for my teammates that day to impress Woj. I had always wanted to cheer for them after I finished. I enjoyed their success, loved finding the right words to say that would cause that switch to turn on in their minds to beat the person in front of them.

I liked seeing others excited and happy with their hard work and feeling like I helped them strive for that achievement.

But to realize that something I was so passionate about, both running and helping others, was recognized by someone who had just met me, made me feel special beyond my times and athleticism.

I meant something more to Woj than just a fast runner.

"I just wanted to thank you for the opportunity to watch you run and to get a chance to talk with you," Woj wrote to me in a letter days later. "I left Kentwood and realized I had not only met a great runner, but also a great person. The qualities and maturity you possess will lead you very far in life. When you get some free time, I'd love the chance to show you and your family what Aquinas College has to offer, both academically and athletically."

It was a coach from a larger college division who told me he didn't think I would reach my potential at a small school like Aquinas. I had brought up Aquinas in conversation when this coach asked about my college choices, and his words concerned me. I *did* want to become a great runner. It had been a dream of mine since I was a child. Would taking a risk at a small school flush that dream away? Would I have enough of a challenge? Would I ever become as great as I had always hoped?

I felt I had been in a "running rut" for years since my times were improving too slowly for my liking. I wanted to stand out from the crowd, to be one of the best. I felt I had put in way too much work to still be running high eighteen-minute 5ks, when the top girls in the state ran the 3.1 miles in seventeen minutes. There were girls who had been running for just a few years and winning state championships while I had been running since I was five years old. I spent the summers going into each high school cross country season hammering speed workouts, sweating up quarter-mile-length hills, lifting weights three times a week, going to physical therapy to keep my body injury-free, and eating fruits, vegetables, lean meats, and pasta. How could I *not* feel that I deserved more than what I was getting from my performances?

Bigger schools, I thought, had the running secret, the way to ultimate success, until Woj's words echoed in my head. His enthusiasm for who I was as a person made me feel valued and appreciated.

In February of 2010, four months after I had met Woj, I sent him an email.

"See attached," I wrote.

I had set a self-timer on my camera, posing in my dad's old Aquinas uniform for a picture of myself in a frozen running stance with a big grin and two thumbs up.

This is what I had sent to Woj. This was what my destiny held.

I would run as an Aquinas Saint.

» » »

I raced proudly for Woj as a freshman. I wanted to make him glad he had recruited me, glad that I would not only be a great teammate now, but also a fantastic athlete. I had proven myself by running personal bests by over a minute, leading my team to a conference cross country title and earning my place as an All-American that fall with a sixth place finish at the national NAIA meet.

And now raw food, I thought, would make me even more successful in the track season.

A few weeks into what I still called my "experiment" with the raw food diet, Woj took a small group of our distance team to Hillsdale for a big 5k race on the track. When we arrived and sat in the stands hours before our race, Woj pointed to the limp flag. "The wind is at a standstill," he said. "Perfect conditions."

I couldn't have agreed more. As the sky darkened and night rolled in, I felt something good coming.

It would be my first 5k at night, a chance to run under the lights and on a blue track! And at this point I had what I saw as a possible advantage: the raw food diet. Would it give me more energy, more power and speed? Would it make me lighter?

As I ran my warm-up in the infield twenty minutes before the race, the stadium lights surrounding the track went dark. The announcer called out a delay, and I sat down on the grass, for the moment unsure of what to do. I had already completed my warm-up and felt ready to race, but there was no way to predict whether the 5k would start in fifteen minutes or sixty.

"They don't know when the lights will be back on again," I heard coaches tell their athletes around me. Some runners slumped in frustration; others sighed with relief.

"Sounds like it's going to be a while yet," Woj confirmed as he approached me on the infield, hands in his jacket pockets.

"All right," I sighed, picking up my sports bag. I felt chilled and decided to join the other competitors in a building nearby.

Halfway down a long, white hallway, I could hear the hum of dozens of runners, chatting with coaches and friends, laughing, relaxed in the tentative way of serious athletes who are waiting to perform. I found a spot along the wall and joined them. I was one of them; I was at home here.

Stomach growling, I grabbed my bag and pulled out a Larabar, a nearly-raw energy bar consisting of just dates and almonds. Ripping off a piece with my mouth, I chewed slowly, taking large gulps of water here and there. I normally wouldn't have eaten this close to a race, but I figured that we had to wait for a while now, and my stomach couldn't hold out any longer. No one else was eating.

The moment I finished my snack with a large swig of water, I heard the boom of the announcer from outside the building: "The lights are working again so we will resume racing in fifteen minutes."

Fifteen minutes?

Crap.

I looked down at my stomach, now heavy and bloated with food and water. I had thought the race wouldn't start for another hour, but that clearly wasn't the case now. How would it be possible for me to race "light" anymore?

Sighing, I got up from the tile floor, knowing I had to get outside and jog for another warm-up. The race would start whether my stomach felt ready or not.

I had wanted so badly for this race to prove to everyone that the raw food diet would help me, not hurt me, and now that chance seemed lost. I wanted to show them that I meant business, that I knew what I was doing, and that I was indeed "getting enough protein." Not only would this Larabar and water-filled stomach weigh me down, but it had the potential to give me a terrible stomachache, too.

Then problem number two arrived.

When I pulled on my spikes and jogged around near the start, my orthotics, the layer of stability for my shoes, rubbed uncomfortably against the arches of my feet.

Stupid, I thought. These new orthotics had arrived just days before the race, but I had failed to try them out due to pure laziness and false confidence that they would work. And I couldn't run *without* that support either, so they had to stay in my shoes.

I tried tightening the laces, which helped a little, but my left foot still rubbed like sandpaper against the rough orthotic and sock. I would have a large blister by the end of the race, but like the bloated stomach, there was nothing I could do about it.

What will my teammates think if I bomb this?

How in the world will I be able to stick up for the raw food diet?

I could already picture Kolin smirking about my downfall.

It's probably because of what she's been eating, he would think.

But I had to shake his voice out of my head. The starter announced my race, and I had to get to the line, ready or not.

Pulling off my warm-ups, I approached the start suddenly calmer than I expected. At this point, so much had gone wrong that all I could do was run my best.

"Good luck," I said to the women around me with a small smile. I took a deep breath.

I'm the only raw foodist at the line, I thought. *If anything, that ought to be an advantage.*

The moment the gun exploded, so did my legs. I took off, free of worry, free of any hindrance or doubt. I flew away from my concerns. Heavy stomach? I had less than twenty minutes to deal with that. Pain in the feet? Just a little.

A smile slowly spread across my face. I was only 200 meters into the race but I suddenly knew it would be a great day. The race felt fast as I dashed under the lights at 10 p.m. and my shoes slapped hard on the concrete-like surface. The push-off was effortless.

Woj clapped his hands enthusiastically at the first corner. He seemed pleased with where I positioned myself in the race.

He said I looked strong and relaxed. And he was right. I *felt* strong and relaxed. Meanwhile, the stadium lights brought the track to life, and everyone on the infield screamed at the women around me.

"C'mon, Anna! Stick with these girls!"

"Let's go, Jen! Relax, relax!"

I didn't worry about time or the number of laps. I fell into a trance as I circled round and round, repeatedly passing and being passed by other women.

But I was right about my foot; with each lap my left orthotic rubbed harder and harder against the soft flesh. I could picture it forming into a red, raw blister, but I knew I had to make this race worth the pain. If I didn't race well, the blister would be a hindrance. If I raced my best, the pain of the blister would be worth every step.

Twelve minutes came and went, and I felt tired and defeated. "Just five more minutes!" a coach yelled to an athlete near me.

I didn't like hearing this. Five more minutes? It seemed like an eternity. But after a moment's frustration, I shook it off and pulled ahead of the woman next to me.

Coaches hovered over the track, screaming out splits and pacing and mechanics. But I could hear Woj's voice over all the others, perhaps because it sounded strong and sure—just the way I was racing.

With only three laps to go, I picked up the pace and passed the pack of ladies I had been staying with. I felt tired, but my body found another gear. I rounded the bend of the track, and with a lap to go I read the clock at 15:44. I knew this meant a best time to come; I just had to finish the race the right way.

Three hundred meters.

Two hundred.

The final stretch.

I watched in those last hundred meters as 16:59 clicked by. I was so close to breaking seventeen minutes, but I passed the line four seconds later, still a personal best by ten seconds and an Aquinas school record.

The moment I crossed the line, I found my dad outside the gate. He reached over the fence and embraced me with a huge grin and tears in his eyes. Having heard me talk about the raw food diet so much recently and all the flack I had been getting for it from my teammates, I pulled back from my dad with an "I-told-you-so" smile, pointed my finger, and said, "Now *that's* for 'not getting enough protein!'"

Food for Thought

1. Even though Rachael is a people-pleaser, she doesn't just run to please her coach and peers. There is great joy in her speed and freedom in the run. How does running speak for Rachael? What would it mean for her to lose her speed?

2. Do you think the raw food diet gave Rachael an advantage? Have you ever taken on a diet where you feel how you ate affected your performance in any sport or task in your life?

3. What do you think about Rachael's teammates and their skepticism?

Mile Markers: Beyond Numbers

1. Rachael is very focused on achieving her goals as a runner, but when Coach Woj recognizes who she is as a teammate, she feels a sense of peace. When have you felt someone recognized you beyond the physical work you put out?

2. Write down a list of the people in your life who you feel value who you are as a person. Do they bring out the best in you? How do they do this?

3. In what ways do you help others to see their value in who they are?

Chapter 6

A Morning of Mono-meals

ONE MORNING, I GRABBED eight bananas.

A mono-meal, it was called, a meal consisting of only one type of food, which, according to the promoters of raw food mono-meals, was an ideal way to eat. It required the body to break down only one type of food, saving digestive energy and leaving more energy for daily activities. And I hoped that a mono-meal could help me to know when my body was truly full. If I grew sick of the one food I was eating, then it meant my body was no longer hungry, of course!

When I first learned about mono-meals, they seemed absurd. But they seemed less absurd when I read how in nature, animals only eat one type of food in a meal. And the more I thought about it, the more it made sense. Lions *did* eat just gazelle in a meal, and monkeys *did* eat just bananas.

Mono-meals sounded like an easy way to read my body. I had strayed from intuitive eating—basically, how I had eaten as a kid and throughout most of high school—for so long that I no longer understood what it meant to feel full or hungry.

Now I lived by rules.

The morning of my eight-banana mono-meal, I reached for the first soft banana, peeled it, and bit into its soft flesh. I swished the creamy, sugary baby-food texture around in my mouth and swallowed.

One down, seven to go.

I munched away. A sip of water here, a bite of banana there, and one empty peel on top of the other soon led to a small pyramid of banana peels before me until, yes, I finished eight bananas. I felt sick of the fruit by then, but I had done it.

I tried the banana mono-meal again the next morning with another eight bananas, while Elizabeth, who happened to be eating breakfast in the cafeteria as well, watched in stunned silence.

I was not as successful this next time, because after six of the spotty brown bananas I couldn't stomach any more. They had grown too sickly sweet for my liking, so I grabbed a pear and an apple to switch up the taste. My body thanked me for it, but my mind told me it would just take more practice.

However, I quickly dismissed the idea of mono-meals when I realized I couldn't build up my tolerance for that many bananas at one time or any fruit for that matter. One morning I had tried to munch through eight apples, only to find my jaws aching, my gums sliced up from the way I bit into the apples, and once again my stomach bloated.

It was a fine experiment, but I didn't see another mono-meal in my immediate future.

Between meals that began with pears and ended with large plates of mushrooms, red peppers, sugar snap peas, and summer squash, I had numerous downfalls.

Near the end of that spring semester a guy from the cross country team sat with me one night in the cafeteria. The place had cleared out by then, as almost everyone had already eaten and left while I still sat chewing my food. I had more than enough times accidently bitten my cheek in my furious chomping of the crunchy vegetables and had done so even more now that the cheek was large and swollen.

After an hour of chewing, I still didn't feel full. I felt relieved my teammates had finally left so they couldn't see how much more I wanted to eat, but I still had *this* guy sitting with me, trying to keep me company.

"So I heard you're trying to do a raw food diet?" he asked.

"How'd you find out?" I had just sat down with my third large plate of broccoli. Cooked broccoli this time, though, with cooked tomato sauce poured all over it.

So much for raw food.

The more we continued to chat, the more irritated I became. Binge mode had taken hold, and I wanted more than anything to be left alone with my soggy, soft broccoli, to be able to eat more cooked food and stuff my face to my heart's content.

You are invading my privacy.

Food for Thought

1. Rachael writes, "If I grew sick of the one food I was eating, then it meant my body was no longer hungry, of course!" What possesses Rachael to find a method to understand fullness?

2. Why do you think Rachael finds it difficult to understand her own hunger and fullness signals? Do you think it's a lack of trust in her body?

3. Rachael feels that this other teammate is "invading her privacy." Do you think the guy noticed she felt uncomfortable? What is this "invasion of privacy" surrounding food a signal of?

Mile Markers: Trust

1. For a few days, write all the thoughts you have before, during, and after you eat.

2. Look at this list. Is it extensive? Is it full of worry, anxiety, fear, or somewhat obsessive? Or is it calm, short, maybe joyful?

3. How well do you trust your own body? Do you eat when you want to?

Chapter 7

The Parental Dilemma

119 POUNDS

COACH WOJ STILL HADN'T heard the story of my conversion to the raw food diet, but by this point, nearing the end of the track season and school year, I felt it was time to tell him. As I wrapped up the essential raw food research and decided raw food would become my *lifestyle,* I could explain it to him with confidence.

Woj had never controlled or advocated certain ways of eating for the team. Judging by the way he filled the cabin at cross country camp each year with Rice Krispies treats, pretzels, animal crackers, peanut butter, and oatmeal, it was easy to think he didn't give too much thought to what we ate, as long as we replenished ourselves with enough calories after workouts.

"Remember to eat a good dinner and get in those calories," he always said after each afternoon run.

I remembered how strange it felt to hear him say such a thing, when all that ran through my mind was how to eat "dinner like a pauper" and "go to bed a little hungry" as the health magazines advised. But "a little hungry" meant famished for me, because

I thought true hunger was signaled only by the angry growls of the stomach. When it did reach that point many times, I made myself sleep through it because by 8 or 9 p.m., I told myself it was too late to eat. To eat after that time would store the fat, I was sure, and ruin my discipline.

One slip meant many future slips.

I was the first person Woj saw each morning at cross country camp that first year, curled up on the overstuffed armchair in the living room. I awoke early, thanks to that desperate growl of my stomach, and I ate my banana, peanut butter, and oatmeal in peace and solitude. Afterward I devoured the nutritional wisdom of *Nancy Clark's Sports Nutrition Guidebook* that Woj had available at camp.

"Are you learning anything new from that?" he had asked, walking into the living room from the kitchen.

"Sort of," I said. "I guess I haven't been eating enough protein."

That was about the extent of my conversations with Woj about nutrition. He did ask the team at the beginning of camp if any of us were considering becoming vegetarians.

"I've been thinking about it," Alina had said, shrugging. But no one else mentioned changing their usual eating habits, including me. At that time I thought vegetarianism was a stupid idea for runners.

How would you get enough protein? You need all the essential amino acids only found in meat.

Of course, everything had changed with my new raw food knowledge. Instead of explaining a vegetarian diet to Woj, let alone veganism, I had to explain *raw*.

Woj agreed to meet in his office one afternoon the following spring, a week after my race under the lights. I brought my binder full of the raw food notes, confident in the research I had done. After explaining what I had learned, I said, "I wouldn't put myself in a situation that would be detrimental to running. I feel raw food will help me."

Woj nodded. "Well, yeah, whether it's actually physically helping you or just a mental advantage, if you think this works, then I trust you."

Woj was the person I feared telling the most, but he seemed to accept it more readily than anyone.

My parents, on the other hand, acted uneasy about raw food when I first announced it.

"What about going out to eat at restaurants?" my mom asked quietly.

Going out to eat has always been an important event in our family. Even on vacations we spent most of our time anticipating when and where our next meal would be.

On top of the unanswered restaurant situation, pickiness was frowned upon in our family. "How can you say you don't like a new food if you've never tried it?" my dad would ask if my sister and I ever refused to try a bite of something new.

Now that I had embarked on this journey to raw food, would I suddenly become that picky eater? Would our family restaurant experience be ruined?

Eventually, armed with the results of my research, I drowned my parents in enough great information to convince my mom that this way of eating wasn't bad. The green smoothies I began making for her, sans Jill's precious calorie-laden agave nectar, made the case for both the tastiness and the nutrition of such a seemingly bizarre diet.

It was my dad I couldn't seem to convert.

"I like cafeteria-style," he said. "Take a little bit of this and a little bit of that."

My dad preached moderation, repeating the balance mantra each time I mentioned how excited I felt about starting the raw food diet.

"What I'm worried is that you'll lose weight," he said one night when I sat near him while he watched a football game in the living room. "You are already very thin."

I tried to reassure my dad that if I did lose weight, I would know how to put on weight again. "I can eat high-calorie foods like dried fruit, nuts and seeds," I explained, which were easily a few hundred calories in just a handful or two.

But I knew deep down that I would never allow myself to eat those calorie-dense foods abundantly. I knew the calorie count might still matter, no matter how raw they were.

Once I drop ten more pounds, I can eat them more often.

"I just don't want to see you wasting away," my dad repeated.

I smirked. And then anger coursed through me. *Wasting*

away? Did he think I couldn't handle this nutrition information? I had become the expert in the family! Who had been giving him health advice for the past year, controlling the meals he made, suggesting substitutions, and avoiding any ounce of extra fat in the recipes?

But my dad's response lingered in my mind as if I had just received a medal of victory around my neck.

"I just don't want to see you wasting away."

Food for Thought

1. Were you surprised by Woj's response?

2. What are some positive ways coaches can handle athletes preoccupied with or showing obsession with food? What do you think would be some of the best ways to promote healthy fueling of the athletes' bodies?

3. Why did Rachael feel that she "had just received a medal of victory" because of her father's concern that she might be "wasting away"? Consider several possible explanations for this odd response.

Mile Markers: Decisions and Skepticism

1. If you've ever made a new diet decision, write down all the reasons you gave to people who were skeptical about your plan.

2. Think about their reactions and thoughts. Or, if you've been on the other side of this situation, what are the reasons others have given you about their new food choices?

3. Write down a list of ways coaches can watch for disordered eating or eating disorders on their athletic teams.

Chapter 8

Potluck Gone Raw

120 POUNDS

I WANTED TO STOP thinking so much about food, but the new rules and all the information involved in eating raw were making me think about it more. The fear of not consuming enough calcium took hold next, so I started adding sesame seeds, a raw food high in calcium, to my green smoothies.

The possibility of breaking a bone scared me. I had a stress fracture during my freshman year of high school as the result of more vigorous training and unsupportive shoes, and I didn't want to relive that devastation. No, not now that I was one of the best runners in the NAIA.

So I learned more about calcium and how to get enough of it on the raw food diet. And come to find out, the ratio of calcium to phosphorus was more important than the intake of calcium itself.

But I still had my doubts. After having the concept of calcium and its relation to milk ingrained in my mind for so long with the "Got Milk" advertisements, I constantly had to remind myself that dairy products wouldn't help my situation and that *removing* them from my diet would actually help my bones.

» » »

Jill had told me about the Grand Rapids "Rawluck" group a week after introducing me to her raw mango pie, and I felt excited to join. It surprised me to learn how many people actually did eat raw food and gather together like this, even just within Grand Rapids.

Apparently the Rawluck group members took turns offering their houses. The first Rawluck I attended was held in an old Victorian tucked between two other homes in a quiet, tree-filled neighborhood a few blocks from Aquinas. Jill got me in contact with the new leader, Margaux Drake, so that I could join. But I remembered Jill didn't like to go to the events herself.

Thus I ventured out on my own that night. I was uneasy because I didn't know a single person there, but I was also eager to try the gourmet raw foods I had only salivated over in "uncook" books.

Everyone looked just as nervous as I felt that evening when I walked into the house, which was already packed with people. Many of the members kept to themselves and stood awkwardly in the living room waiting for dinner to begin. It seemed no one really knew each other, and not many people made an effort to introduce themselves. The most enthusiastic of the bunch happened to be a man in his sixties who shuffled around the cramped house, offering up what he promoted as "lettuce cabbage."

"Lettuce cabbage! Who wants to try my lettuce cabbage? It tastes delicious just as it is!"

Famished, I nodded when the man offered me a small leaf. And it *was* good; it had a stronger, sweeter flavor than any leafy green I had ever tried. I wanted another, but the man had already moved on to the other guests, some of whom looked quizzically at him while one snarky older woman said, "We aren't supposed to start eating yet."

"So are you all raw?" an older woman asked as she peered up at me moments later. Being 5'9" put me high above most people, but this woman was *short*.

"Umm . . . I'm attempting to be," I answered, curious. Wasn't *she* completely raw? I thought everyone there was a raw foodist. I didn't dare ask now, though.

"I hear that any time you eliminate a food from your diet," she began, "it is difficult for your body to process it should you start eating it again. Like yogurt, for instance. Those who claim they cannot digest it properly only have that problem because they think it's unhealthy and take it out of their diet. Years later they try to eat it again, and their bodies can't digest it because their stomach doesn't have the proper enzymes anymore."

I stared at her. What was the point of telling me that? I understood what she wanted to say; many raw foodists did claim that when they tried to eat cooked food again after going raw for so long, they got sick. But wasn't that because their bodies became purer and just couldn't handle the toxins in cooked food anymore?

This woman's suggestion made me feel uneasy about the raw food diet, but I just shrugged, unsure of how to respond.

"So what did *you* make?"

The next voice came from my left a few minutes later from a young woman with long, brown hair.

I hesitated. I explained how I had found a raw avocado pudding recipe online and that I had just started to learn how to prepare raw food.

Indeed, after a failed attempt at raw soup earlier that afternoon (I had mistakenly tried to just blend up beets and raw sweet potato together), I decided to stick with the simplest raw food recipe I could find online for the Rawluck. This avocado recipe was still appetizing and didn't require any oils, which eased my internal calorie counter.

All the pudding consisted of was blended avocado and banana. I added in a few sliced bananas to spruce it up, but it didn't improve the appearance like I hoped it would. It still looked more like a brown goopy mess with brownish-yellow chunks. I had also read somewhere that leaving the avocado pits in the pudding would keep the recipe a vibrant green longer, as if a bowl of green cream looked much better than a bowl of brown mush.

I hoped the Rawluckians would think my dish tasty enough and accept me into their posse, but the moment I set my bowl of green-brown "dessert" next to all the other extravagant, dehydrated, and hours-in-preparation raw dishes, I knew mine looked and tasted sub-par at best.

The leader of the Rawluck group, Margaux, finally got everybody's attention before we started the meal. She wore a large summer hat and an orange and red maxi dress. Her eyes blazed, wide with excitement as she introduced herself and looked around the room. I liked her from the start not only because she seemed like the most approachable person there, but also because I had heard from Jill that she was a runner and triathlete.

However, Margaux did not look like the elite triathlete I had hoped to see. She had a curvier body, much too curvy for a raw foodist, I thought. Other people in the Rawluck group came in a variety of "sizes," but I figured the thinnest had been on the diet for a while, and the heavier ones were just beginning the diet and wanted to lose weight.

In a small house packed with over thirty people, not everyone could fit into one room, but we managed to squeeze in as best we could while some members opted for the porch outside. After someone said a quick prayer to bless the living food we were about to eat, the buffet began.

I waited quietly in line, my stomach groaning for food and my mind wondering how to start conversation with those around me. We all seemed to be out of our element even though we were all here for the same thing: raw food.

Once I made it into the kitchen, I grabbed a plate and packed it in with samples of raw food, everything from dehydrated seed crackers with nut "cheese" to kale chips, dark-green leafy salads, fruit salads with nuts, and a thick raw chocolate cheesecake. I even added a little of my own avocado pudding to the side of my plate. My recipe, I realized, had a bland flavor against the date-and agave syrup-infused desserts, but I couldn't complain. My recipe was still appetizing to me, and I knew it was probably lower in calories than many of the others. I noted the way the kale leaves glistened with oil in the salads. Even though I knew I shouldn't or supposedly didn't need to count calories, I constantly wondered about how much oil and extra calorific sweetener had been added to the other dishes.

I can eat the blandest of foods because I am stronger.

As I moved out of the kitchen, I tried to find a place to sit. I ended up on the floor next to a girl in glasses who had previously been standing in the corner. I took a stab at conversation, hoping to make a friend my age who also had an interest in raw food.

"Have you just started eating raw?" I asked.

"Yeah."

"What did you bring?"

"The fruit-n-nut salad."

I couldn't think of what else to ask as she kept her head down in her plate, poking at large kale leaves and placing them delicately on her tongue. Looking at my own plate, I stabbed at the spiralized zucchini "pasta" with thick pulverized pecan sauce. From there I moved on to the fruit drenched in oils and the thick, nut-based raw chocolate pie.

The desserts were my favorite. They had a flavor similar to processed dessert, but these raw food desserts felt filling, very filling. So filling, in fact, that when I left the Rawluck without having made a single friend, I felt like my stomach was bursting at the seams.

Too much food.

My appetite, something I had pushed down for so long, crept in heavily. I wasn't supposed to feel satisfied. I wasn't supposed to enjoy fullness. It was wrong, my downfall, my disorder, the broken part of me I had vowed to conquer.

I feared my own body because I knew it could take over if I didn't gain control again, if I let myself "go" like this too often.

Food for Thought

1. Already in this chapter we see Rachael again gripped by fears: that she isn't getting enough calcium; that she doesn't know anyone at the Rawluck; that her dessert isn't good enough; that she's eaten too much; that her appetite will take over again. Think back to the previous chapters. What else is she afraid of?

2. Do you think there is a positive impact in Rachael's life for trying this raw food diet? Where might you see improvements despite the fear?

Mile Markers: Facing Fears

1. Write a list of your worst fears. It might feel scary to write them down, but this is good practice in helping you to see your fears, somewhat face them, and eventually speak up about them.

2. How often do those fears crop up in your life? Where or when do they show up?

3. Where might these fears stem from?

Chapter 9

Never Enough

121 POUNDS

THE SUCCESS I HAD with running and the admiration of my peers felt intoxicating that freshman year. I had always loved to run, had always been the girl who actually looked forward to workouts. Becoming a national runner doubled the high. This time, I could really *enjoy* the races, because I won with such ease. I could enjoy the races, because who could be disappointed with you when you won all the time? Who would question a school record-breaking time?

But when I ran my last track workout before the national 5k race that spring, the euphoria I had in running faster slid to a halt.

"Come on, Rach, you have to kick it in now!"

Woj's words weren't harsh, but the perfectionist, the people-pleaser, the one whose expectations are higher than anyone's, suddenly felt that she wasn't enough. She wasn't doing enough.

She *still* wasn't running fast enough.

I wasn't meeting the times Woj asked of me for the workout (which I reasonably attributed to wearing my heavy trainers instead of lighter, faster spikes), but Woj's bold encouragement shocked me. Didn't Woj realize I had a "magic" power now? Didn't he realize that I had all the confidence in the world, that this workout would not determine how I placed in the national meet? That my low body weight and raw food diet was the secret to success and joy?

But that extra push, that expectation, shook me. It made me question if I was actually good enough to feel happy. It demanded more when I already expected so much out of myself, when a coach I admired and worked to please asked even more of me.

You aren't doing enough.

The national 5k meet a week later was the first race that year where I could barely sleep at night due to nerves. I had never wished for a race to be over like I did this one—no, not since high school when the weight of expectation often overwhelmed me.

At this race, I worried that I wouldn't even make it in the finals (since we had a semi-final). I did make it, but not without berating myself over eating "too many" dates (high calories) the night before.

I walked away from the final national 5k race happy with my performance (a seventh place finish), but I thought about how I could never settle, that this was all just the beginning. That if I could hone everything, if I could make my eating and running more perfect, then I could live happily for the rest of my life. I would no longer have to deal with worry or anxiety about weight or running fast, and I wouldn't have to worry about injury because it would all be solved with food, and raw food, at that. I thought that if I hit the right times and pleased my coach, that I would no longer have to worry about meeting the expectations of others.

I would no longer have to please them because they would forever be happy and proud of me.

Food for Thought

1. Rachael walks away from a successful race "happy," but at the same time she realizes she can "never settle." What do you think she means by settling? Is she just referring to her eating and her running?

2. What similarities do you see between eating disorders and the drive to run "perfectly"?

3. Rachael believes that if those two areas of her life are just right, then she will be happy and free from worry. Do you agree with her?

Mile Markers: Finding Balance

1. In what parts of your life are you unwilling to "settle"? Write these down.

2. Do you have goals or wants that you believe will make you happy? Do you believe you can be happy before you reach them?

3. Write down three areas in your life where, if you put more focus, you can be happy *while* you strive for your other goals.

Chapter 10

Rawcipes

122 POUNDS

I DID REALIZE THAT raw food had its pros and cons. When school ended for the year, I returned home and felt a new freedom in obtaining and eating as many vegetables as possible. But I didn't have the vast array of vegetables to choose from like I did regularly at the cafeteria. Now I had to worry about getting enough variety of vegetables from the store and eating them before they went bad so that I didn't waste money.

Obtaining a blender saved my raw food life. Green smoothies were not only appetizing, but they provided an easy way to get many greens in and not spend all day chewing. However, after making so many green smoothies, I felt I needed some variety.

Enter Elizabeth, my cross country teammate, who to my surprise was the one who wanted to try these raw food recipes.

Elizabeth was staying with me at my parents' house that summer since she wanted to be in Grand Rapids to train with the cross country team. Having her there pleased both of us, since I wanted to get closer to the older girls on the team and she was quickly becoming a good friend. But I was afraid for Elizabeth to see how much I ate, and I didn't know what she would think about my raw food diet.

How often should I mention raw food?

Will she think I'm obsessed with it?

I began to notice Elizabeth's curiosity about my new diet when I walked into the living room one day and saw her flipping through some of the raw food books I had ordered from the library, specifically *The Sunfood Diet Success System* by David "Avocado" Wolfe.

Elizabeth and I came to find out that Wolfe was the ultimate raw-food guru. He even encouraged his readers to choose a raw food for a new middle name to redefine the new people we would become (hence David "Avocado" Wolfe). He seemed so much like a caricature from the raw-food world that I had trouble believing the man actually existed.

Nevertheless, Elizabeth and I drove to Harvest Health to buy some of the ingredients for the rawcipes found at the back of his book. As I read off strange ingredients like "Udo's oil" and "apple cider vinegar," my dad jokingly called our new ingredients "unicorn hooves" and "elf blood."

At Harvest Health, we walked past shelves stuffed with vitamins, supplements, weight loss tonics, and energy-boosting powders. We approached a rack of various nuts, seeds, and chocolate beans, passed aisles of gluten-free crackers and pasta, and peered into a cooler of organic meats, cheeses, and vegetables.

It took about ten minutes to find exactly what we needed in the small, cramped store, but eventually we bought apple cider vinegar (which Elizabeth found out also helps to get rid of seasonal allergies), lemons (for salad dressing), spirulina (a great algae protein power punch), Udo's oil, miso, and young coconut water (which came in little juice pouches).

When Elizabeth and I returned home with our new goodies, the two of us began "uncooking" for the first time.

"We could do the zucchini pasta al Pesto," she said, flipping through *Raw Food Made Easy* by Jennifer Cornbleet. "Or a walnut pate sandwich."

We decided to start with what seemed the easiest recipe, almond butter. It took over a day to make just because we had to wait for the almonds to soak and sprout to "awaken" the life in them, but other than that we just had to blend them with the other ingredients.

So when day two arrived, Elizabeth and I poured out the almonds from the jar of water and peeled off the brown, bark-like skins to reveal their smooth, white interiors.

I looked down at the next set of instructions.

"Shoot, we need a food processor!" I said. I hadn't realized until then how many other contraptions were required for the raw diet. But Elizabeth and I figured a blender would work the same way as a food processor for this recipe, so we just poured the raw almonds into the Blendtec and pressed start.

The reason for the food processor became apparent, however, the moment we tried blending. The blender barely made a dent in the almonds, as many of them lay out of harm's way beneath the blades. The blender whirred threateningly, but it only tore through the top layer of almonds.

"I think we are going to have to add water," I said, sighing. Almond butter did not ask to be watered down just so that it could be blended, but this became the only choice we had.

What resulted was almond soup, a milky drainage of almond residue that we decided only worked well for eating if you poured it over bread, which soaked up the flavor. So while the recipe was indeed raw, in the end the food that carried it definitely wasn't.

The next raw meal improved drastically when Elizabeth and I made a zucchini pesto "pasta." We chopped zucchini into long, thin slices, and the pesto sauce was made up of parsley, olive oil, heirloom tomatoes, and two garlic cloves blended in the Blendtec.

"It says two tablespoons of olive oil," Elizabeth said, looking at the ingredients as we stood in front of the blender.

I cringed. I hated using so much oil—or any oil, for that matter. This was one of the reasons why I was reluctant to try many raw food recipes in the first place.

Oils.

Nuts.

Fat.

But I felt I would look paranoid if I said anything.

» » »

The summer days continued with a variety of raw food recipes, and we were certainly getting more confident with our newfound "uncooking" skills. One night included a fresh, lemon-infused alfalfa sprout salad and a raw chocolate mousse for dessert.

I couldn't wait to show my dad my chocolate creation later that night. The moment he came home from work, I scooped out a cup of the chocolate mousse for him.

"This is actually really good!" he said, surprised. "What did you say was in it?"

"Just avocado, four dates, cacao beans, and water," I said, smiling. "Isn't it amazing?"

I couldn't believe I could eat dessert and not feel guilty about consuming it—or at least not to the extent that the processed desserts always made me feel. And I felt like I could win my dad's approval at last for raw food. I loved how shocked he looked, how he asked for another bite, the way he asked me how I had done it.

» » »

As I read through more raw food books, I came across a book that advocated *against* eating a fully raw diet, called *Catching Fire* by Richard Wrangham. I felt uneasy reading the book after I felt I could finally trust everything about raw food, because what Wrangham wrote made sense, too.

I knew from previous research that many raw foodists encouraged others to look at the life of primates and use that as an example as to how humans should eat. However, according to Wrangham, primates chewed food all day just to get in the sufficient nutrients, which meant that if we indeed want to "eat as primates do," it requires chewing on food all day as well (2009, 71-72). Then my dad had given me an article he found online about how primates were not completely vegetarian because they ate insects.

According to Wrangham, by consuming cooked food, humans had actually grown stronger and more intelligent because it helped the brain to grow. The body adapted to eating smaller amounts of food denser in calories (2009, 11-14). The evidence of consuming a cooked food diet is clear through our small mouths, digestive systems, and stomachs, which contrasts sharply against the considerably larger organs of the primate (2009, 40-44).

However, Wrangham did still have a few choice words to say about the drawbacks of cooked food. Cooking goes too far in society, to the point where it contributes to the obesity epidemic. Cooking makes foods calorically dense—the softer the food made by cooking, the more calories absorbed by the body (2009, 80-81).

As I read this, I felt raw food justified itself again.

But Wrangham was definitely right about the chewing. My jaw ached, exhausted from munching through pounds of leafy greens in an effort to avoid eating too much fruit (calories, calories!). After one afternoon of trying to just eat raw vegetables and salsa for over an hour (*Why can't I feel satisfied?*), I caved into a slice of leftover pizza and various fruits.

However, with that small chewing problem, I couldn't just throw the whole raw food experiment away. I had learned about the benefits of dark, leafy greens, how eating organic is healthier, how we didn't need as much protein as we thought we needed, and that we didn't *have* to consume dairy products to build strong bones. Thus I decided, after reading Wrangham's book, that some cooked food was acceptable. It was then that I planned to eat a "70 percent raw diet." To me, that meant I could continue to allow myself to eat salsa (which had cooked tomatoes) and hummus (cooked chickpeas and tahini) instead of slowly moving away from consuming those as I had planned. After two months on mostly raw food, I didn't feel any benefit anyway. I had no major revelation or increase in energy to record in my daily food journal.

But I wanted reassurance that I could keep my weight low, and raw seemed like the best way to do it.

» » »

The summer months continued in a flurry of raw food recipes with Elizabeth. But they also included nights where I began to secretly take fruit, avocadoes, hummus, or bread from the kitchen to eat in hiding so that my family, and especially Elizabeth, could not see how much I was consuming.

I hated sneaking food like this, did not want to go to bed on a stomach so full, but the hunger had intensified and the raw food diet—or what I thought at the time was just my sudden lack of discipline and control, perhaps emotional eating—made me want to eat like never before. Little did I know that these first secret snacks would lead me to that terrible moment on the kitchen floor with the frozen cake.

And then Elizabeth's body rebelled.

It was the "rawsagna" that did it, she said, zucchini cut into thin, flat "pasta" strips with almond-nut "cheese," tomato sauce, and olive oil. It was a recipe we had made together (as I would have avoided the olive oil if I had done it on my own), but after only a few bites she could not stomach any more. We blamed the dense nuts permeating the rawcipe for her discomfort.

Elizabeth lay queasy on the couch, refusing to eat any more of our lasagna while I happily treated myself to the rest of the dish. When my sister Angela came home that evening, she joined Elizabeth in devising a plan to buy ice cream and cereal for an upcoming splurge night.

"We'll leave you to your raw food," they laughed.

I smiled.

Food for Thought

1. Rachael seems to be worried what Elizabeth will think about the raw food diet experiment, but is there something more that Rachael fears Elizabeth will uncover?

2. Elizabeth and Angela are preparing for a "splurge" night. How might that be different from what Rachael views as a binge?

Mile Markers: Defining a Disorder

1. Write down how an eating disorder or addiction may be conflicting with other aspects of your life.

2. In what ways might your addiction consume your day? Write down how often you think about or engage in your addiction.

3. How often do you try to hide your addiction? Why do you want to hide it?

Chapter 11

Stretched Too Thin

124 POUNDS

WHEN THE NUMBER ON the scale had slipped from the three to the four, I panicked.

One hundred twenty-four felt unacceptable, and going to bed after another binge, I could no longer deny that something was off that summer, that this overabundance of food caused me to become that one-twenty-*four*.

Last summer you were one pound lighter.

You're supposed to do better this summer, not worse.

And as I pulled on my two-piece athletic swimsuit one morning before a triathlon race that summer, I caught sight of the marks, the *stretch* marks.

I thought I had seen the stretch marks before when I squatted down a few days prior, but seeing them again as I pulled on the suit was the final wake-up call. They were the same stretch marks I had seen in the mirror two years before, the first time I really cracked down on what I ate.

I can't come into my sophomore year heavier; people will see!

I will run slower, and they will blame it on the diet.
If not the diet, then the weight gain.

It was during a thirteen-mile run days later when the fear of extra weight hit me hard.

I had planned out this long run for myself months prior, a sunrise run where I set an alarm for five o'clock and drove out to a bike path that would allow me to have a full view of the morning sky. Indeed, the purple and orange hues shone magnificently over the grassy landscape, but that particular morning it felt distant, and the path felt long and tiring. I wore my GPS watch, and every time I fell over an eight-minute pace, I felt like I could see the pounds on my watch, could see them slowing me down with every step.

I forced myself to pick up the pace, but I could not escape the shadow that chased me. I wanted so desperately to run with nature again, to run *with* my body, not against it. I thought about how I didn't want to lose the success I had dreamt of for so long, didn't want it to slip out of my fingers during these next three years in college. I had already achieved this success so late, had wasted all that time in high school when I could have lost weight earlier, could have been the top runner in the state in *high school.*

I didn't want to grow up because I still wanted to make up for what I felt to be a failure in my past.

That night, I dreamed that I stood before the mirror, stretch marks trailing from my hips. They ran up the length of my arms, wrapped around my torso, hips, slithered down my butt. I looked at my reflection and saw a white-striped tiger standing upright before me, as if the claws themselves that itched and burned in hunger had crawled from my stomach and scratched my skin raw, scratched my body raw for filling my stomach.

I awoke and traced my fingers down my legs, feeling the small ripple of stretched flesh on my hips.

Food for Thought

1. Rachael loves to run, but now she is running against her body: "I wanted so desperately to run with nature again, to run with my body, not against it." In what way has the eating disorder already begun to destroy the things she loves? How is she losing herself?

2. The raw food diet was an increase in control over Rachael's food. What does this increase in control do? How does it backfire?

Mile Markers: Comparison and Control

1. Do you often compare yourself to others? Or do you compare yourself to your more "successful" self of the past?

2. Why do you think comparison can be so destructive? In what way does it increase our need for control?

3. The goal is to strengthen the healthy part of yourself so that it looks more appealing than the destructive behaviors of the eating disorder. When you are able to find and see your worth, it will aid the recover process. Write down the qualities you value in yourself and why these make you special. If you are stumped at all, ask others what they value in you.

Chapter 12

Stomaching the Realization

AS A CHILD, MY arms and legs looked like thin poles, making my round tummy look even bigger. My stomach begged to be poked, to be prodded by friends and adults alike. And because of this, I assumed they were mocking how fat I looked.

I first acknowledged my potential for fatness in kindergarten when I said my daily "Hello" to a chubby girl walking down the hallway. We were nothing more than friendly acquaintances at the time, and I felt especially fascinated by her body, because there was something about it that I felt resembled mine: a large stomach. But she had more, too—a round, heavy face and thick, sausage arms. If, like her, I had a large stomach, didn't that mean everything else had to be large, too?

It was inevitable, I thought. I would grow up to look fat, and it was something out of my control.

I would have to live with it.

My babysitter, a high-school student, prodded my stomach the most. "Lift up your shirt!" she said, laughing.

I knew how this went, knew I was about to endure the torment about my stomach.

"Come on, lift it up!" she said.

I wanted to be cool. I wanted her to like me as much as she liked my sister, who was the younger, cuter one.

I reluctantly pulled up my shirt.

"Ha!" she cried, poking at it with her finger, her other hand covering her mouth in a fit of giggles.

"Look at how big her tummy is," my babysitter would tell her friends at other times. "Look at her tummy!"

Once I mistakenly tried to suck in my stomach when I lifted my shirt before she poked it. It only made her laugh harder to see me try to fake thinness.

A few years later, I went shopping for clothes with my sister as a gift from my grandpa for my eighth birthday. My sister and I tried on a pair of black and white plaid dresses and walked out of the dressing rooms together to show Grandpa and his girlfriend, Sherry.

"Oh, you both look beautiful!" Sherry said.

My sister pranced back into the changing room, twirling as she went. I was about to follow her when my Grandpa guffawed and patted his large stomach.

"Got a stomach like your grandpa, dontcha?" he said with a grin.

It wasn't a question. He knew. He saw, they saw, *everyone* saw.

I didn't know what to say. I gave him a puzzled look and quickly turned away, my face hot. I wanted to rip off the dress. Fear had invaded my body, a fear *of* my own body.

I had learned from a young age that it was shameful to allow the stomach to relax. And I learned from a young age that sucking it in, faking it, even, could not hide how fat I really looked.

Running released me from the fear of food. I knew even as a child that I had to eat in order to run well, and I learned quickly from my mom that "runners can eat as much as they want!"

It was the "marathon" race for Field Day in kindergarten when I found my love of running, when I sprinted around that fence and heard my mom yell out, "Go, Cheetah!" With the wind in my hair and the burn in my legs, I felt a power and love so pure, so intense, that I wanted to experience it again and again. I loved the strength I felt in beating every girl in my class, all except one, that day of that race around the baseball field. And if it hadn't been for that one girl who finished ahead of me, the hunger to run more might not have taken hold. I needed someone ahead to always challenge me, to keep me yearning for more, to keep me wondering how to catch her.

I looked forward to every cross country or track practice, every meet and running event. My mom always encouraged me to have fun and that running was all *about* having fun. But she was also very competitive, and I felt that her lack of excitement after races where I didn't run my fastest meant disappointment. I began to feed off her ecstatic praise when I did well, and I wanted more of it.

I never saw weight in connection to how fast I could run and never knew it to be a factor unless someone were overweight. I allowed myself the occasional treats, but never dessert before a meal, even in childhood. My grandma always reminds me of what I said as a kid when she offered me cake at a birthday party.

"But, Grandma, we haven't had dinner yet!"

And even though Nutri-Grain bars were not the epitome of health, they sure didn't look like the Zebra Cakes or Honeybuns my disappointed classmates were hoping to eat when my birthday came around. By second grade I began to feel self-conscious when I noticed most of the Nutri-Grain bars I brought were only half-eaten and in the trash.

I grew up watching Disney movies, and the character I envied most was Megara from *Hercules*. I watched the svelte cartoon character in awe as she sashayed around Greece, her stomach the circumference of her neck. I couldn't believe women could have a figure like this, and dressing up as her for Halloween only made me realize how thick *my* stomach was.

» » »

It was the summer before my senior year of high school when I first saw the stretch marks.

I caught sight the white tiger stripes on my hips before jumping into the shower after a run. Were these stretch marks really there? On *me?* But I was a runner! I didn't care that I was growing. Puberty stretch marks were for inactive girls, just like periods were for "normal" girls. I got my period late in adolescence because I was a runner, I reasoned. I felt the power and superiority when my fifteen-month-younger sister got her period a year before me.

And then my sister, my inactive sister, had lost weight. It was a side effect of an ADHD medication that suppressed her appetite. She started to look thinner than me, and she barely even exercised. The injustice of it all, I thought!

"Look how flat my stomach is now!" Angela boasted in the kitchen one summer day. She was sixteen. "I've lost so much weight!" Angela glowed triumphantly as she lifted her shirt to show our mom.

I stood a few feet away as I watched the scene unfold. It felt like mockery.

Look at how skinny I am!

Yes, look at how skinny she is, Rachael.

What's wrong with you, Rachael? Why aren't you like this?

For the longest time, I thought the body "thickness" our family had was unbeatable. I thought I was destined for a large stomach because of our genes. I thought we had to always stay this size.

"We are just 'big,'" my mom always said. She meant broad, tall, and strong. But I didn't see it this way, and my sister's recent weight loss changed the way I viewed our bodies entirely.

Something clicked the moment my mom stood by as Angela announced to the world her newfound weight loss; my mom approved of it like it was a measure of success.

"Yeah, that's awesome, Angela!" she said. And I heard those words as a hint that I must achieve this, too. We could be skinny. We could control it.

That's when I realized *I* could make it happen. I had the power, and it all came through food, not exercise!

I didn't say anything as I watched my mom and sister. I couldn't. I was now the fat kid, the fat daughter in the family, the fat runner.

I climbed up the stairs to my room, quiet with humiliation. I pulled off my clothes and looked in the mirror.

My stomach hung out. The fat had to be located there.

Food for Thought

1. Rachael's perception of her body is distorted from a young age. What do you think is the biggest factor in this?

2. Rachael's sister Angela is striving for thinness as well. How do you think this ADHD medication may be affecting *her* in relation to food and weight? How do you think it might affect Angela later?

3. It's common for many girls and women to worry about their stomach looking "fat." Why do you think this is? What influences these thoughts if the stomach is designed to grow large when we put food in it and reduce in size as it empties?

Mile Markers: Back to the Past

1. Did you make any assumptions about yourself, positive or negative, based on things you heard when you were a child? Do you still have those assumptions?

2. Eating disorders often arise out of family or personal relationships, a history of physical or sexual abuse, difficulty expressing emotions and feelings, or a history of being teased (*Factors That May Contribute to Eating Disorders*). What situations might Rachael have experienced that contribute to her preoccupation with her weight? What is something you or someone you know has experienced that might have caused your/their eating disorder later?

3. When you were a kid, when did you start worrying about what other people thought of you? What marked this change? Do you think it affects you today?

Chapter 13

Colorawdo

I COULD BARELY CONTAIN my excitement during that summer of raw food when my mom first told me I was invited to visit her friend John and his wife Connie in Loveland, Colorado. The couple worked and lived at Eden Valley ranch, a clinic that treated patients with a raw food diet to cure cancer and other diseases. This was the perfect opportunity for me, as Elizabeth had just left for a month in Spain.

"Mom, they could teach me more about raw food. Maybe this could be like an internship. Heck, I could get a job there someday!"

My mom had met John at the senior Olympic games (since my mom ran, too) about a month before, where somehow the topic of raw food came up. I jumped at the opportunity the moment my mom called to say that John invited me to come visit and thought it even better that he was a runner himself.

When I entered the baggage claim of the Denver airport, I knew who John was despite never having met him before. I had imagined him as a short, lean-muscled man with a calm, relaxed demeanor. He would be like a gentle grandpa, a soft face, wrinkles, a tender smile.

And in spite of the fact that the man I actually saw reminded me of a cross between a hawk and giraffe, I still realized it had to be him. He stood tall over the crowd, scouting the airport with beady eyes above a nose hooked like a beak. He looked thin to the bone but solid with lengthy, lean muscle. Dark, coarse veins ran like vines down Colorado-tan arms, which at the moment held a rectangular package.

"RACHAEL!" he cried. Actually, it sounded more like "Rach-oh!" with his high-pitched, nasally voice, but the enthusiasm he put into it nearly toppled me over.

Dear God.

I could see the energy in his bulging eyes, in his hands that gripped the package tightly, and in the spring in his step as he bounded over to greet me. I wasn't sure I was ready for *this* much excitement.

"Hi!" I replied breathlessly.

"I knew it was you the instant I saw you! I thought to myself, now I'm not going to call Rachael's number because I want to pick her out. I want to pick out the runner in the crowd, and, oh boy, did I! You look exactly like a runner!"

"Thanks, you do, too!" I said.

After chatting for a few moments about my plane ride, John showed me the way out of the airport by jogging away from me. Confused, I struggled to keep up as I rolled my zebra-print suitcase behind me. I wondered if he thought I'd be bounding right behind him, a happy-go-lucky girl swinging my heavy bag to and fro.

I followed John onto a descending escalator, standing on one stair with my suitcase while he tore ahead down the steps. When he reached the bottom, he stopped to set the package on the ground and put his hands on his hips, waiting.

The moment I reached the bottom, John nodded toward the escalator with a mysterious grin. He asked, "What kind of training could you see happening here?"

I looked at the escalator. *God, no.* He was talking about running up the descending stairs. He was *really* talking about running up the stairs! This seemed too childish, and at a big airport like this, just plain stupid.

I couldn't believe what I was about to witness.

"You just have to wait until there aren't many people coming down. Of course, it's quite busy right now." In spite of that, he bounded toward the descending steps and hurled himself up the stairway just as two young women stepped on at the top.

John pumped his arms back as he tried to avoid the approaching collision. And just as he reached the women, he used his long, lanky legs to sidestep them. One of the women nearly jumped over the railing with fright, but John didn't pay them any mind as he made it to the top on the second floor and raised his hands up in victory, his eyes wide with childish joy. I gave him a thumbs-up but felt like making a face-palm as the ladies looked up in bewilderment and laughed.

We arrived at Eden Valley hours after leaving the airport, because of course we had to not only deliver the package John had been holding, but also go for a playful sprint across a soccer field, take a dip in the lake at a community beach, and catch a glimpse of the giant fish (a metal sculpture in the shape of a large fin) protruding from a nearby pond. The most puzzling stop was the one at a wildlife paintings store.

"Now I want you to figure out this puzzle!" John said, entering the small shop. I sat down on a shiny, white love seat across from him, a glass table between us. John pushed a white 3D puzzle toward me and looked on hungrily, his eyes wide and a large smile stretched across his face.

I smiled weakly, sorting out the chunky, plastic pieces.

I don't want to do this.

Why is he making me do this?

I began to fit a few pieces together, checking the figure on the front of the box for guidance. I looked up every once in a while when I felt stuck, only to realize John was *timing* me.

"Everyone who comes to visit does this," he said. "I want to see how fast you can complete it!"

» » »

John drove us into Eden Valley at last, entering through a sliver of an opening in a wall of mountains. The blue sky seemed endless above us without a cloud in sight as the sun penetrated the valley through the high-altitude air.

We had just entered a land of our own, a vast expanse of dry grass and buildings encased by the Rocky Mountains. Large gardens stretched behind tan buildings, the only green spots of land in a sea of grainy yellow.

I felt an eerie aura in the dry wind that whistled through the open windows of the car. There were many long white buildings, but not a person in sight. It was a place not only to relax, replenish, and heal, but also to meet something deep and dark within myself.

When we arrived at their small Ranch-style home, John's wife Connie greeted me with a hug. "Hello, hello!" she said in a delicate voice that matched her petite, fragile frame. I liked her instantly since her gentleness gave me some relief from John's wildness.

The three of us whipped up a late lunch (or according to my time zone, dinner) with the fresh food John and I brought from the supermarket. At the store he told me I could buy all the food I wanted for the next few days, so I picked up a large bag of spinach, mangoes, apricots, bananas, apples, spinach, and kale, nervous about how much it would all cost and if he thought I ate too much food.

Connie added mock-chicken salad to our meal, along with avocado, pumpkin seeds, homegrown tomatoes, and homemade, preservative-free wheat bread. I used the mock-chicken salad as my "dressing" on the greens and took handful after handful of fresh spinach. I felt famished, and there wasn't much other raw food on the table besides fruit and seeds, which I reminded myself not to over-consume.

I thought these people only ate raw food.

"So, do you run much with your mom?" Connie asked as John shoveled in a slice of bread covered with mock-chicken salad. Connie tilted her head, resting her fork on her plate as she chewed her food in circles like a cow chewing its cud. I tried to answer between mouthfuls, nervous about making a good impression while my body pleaded to shovel in the food like John.

Every question I answered was met with, "Ahh, ahh!" from Connie. She hung on to every word, and her small eyes widened in wonderment behind her wiry glasses.

After the meal, Connie showed me around the valley while John retreated to his room for a power nap.

"You know, I just get to a point where I crash," John explained. "I don't know where it comes from or why, but it is necessary that

I get my naps in."

Connie and I walked outside into the dry heat where grasshoppers bounced buoyantly around our feet. After showing me a few of the gardens, as well as the building where they prepare raw food, Connie dropped me off at another building where they used to house the patients. "We recently constructed a new building for them, so you can stay here with our other guest, Deb," she explained.

Deb, apparently, hadn't made it back from her mountain expedition yet.

Once I settled into my room, I stepped out into the first long, empty hallway of the building to explore. My ears met dead silence as I walked, my bare feet cool against the tile floor. Sunlight from outside seeped in through the windows of the doors located at both ends of the hallway as I approached the center of the building, where two long, large tables and a countertop stood.

A small side room next to this held a bare kitchen with a lone refrigerator.

» » »

About an hour later, John came by and suggested we go on a hike up what he called the "Red Rocks," a small plateau overlooking the valley. The plateau was only about two hundred meters away from the building I stayed in, so of course John proceeded to stride out towards it the moment we stepped outside. "You're going to love this!" he shouted.

The moment we reached the base, John dashed left and right over jagged rocks as I huffed behind. I didn't trip and fall like I thought I might, but I felt like a disgrace to runners as this man three times my age beat me to the top. Was I really this out of shape?

It only took about five minutes to make it to the summit, but the view made me feel like I had reached the top of the world. The sun set just beyond the mountains, giving the valley an orange-red glow.

On the way back down, John and I discussed nutrition. It surprised me to learn that he didn't know much about the raw food diet. John knew that raw food was important for the patients who came to Eden Valley, but it didn't sound like he actually tried to apply the health principles to his own life. After seeing me eat so many leafy greens at our meal together, John inquired about where I got my carbs.

"Well, fruits and vegetables *are* carbs," I said. I tried to hold back my frustration; it seemed no one associated fruits and vegetables with carbs anymore. Bread became the only carb that came to mind for most people.

John seemed genuinely interested in what I had to say, and I assured him that it would help him to have more success in running. I was honored that he respected what I'd learned. Our short, random dash across the field at the park before we made it to Eden Valley that afternoon gave me a sense that we were equal running partners. I was eager to talk to John about raw food and to learn how they practiced it at Eden Valley. I didn't care about whether or not John ran faster than I did.

"I'd like to try to eat more leafy greens," John said after I explained their importance.

John made me feel special as I talked to him about the raw food diet and practiced sharing the raw food information I had learned thus far. I was surprised that the people in Eden Valley didn't seem to be pure raw foodists as I had expected. It was like the Rawluck all over again.

After a few moments of silence, John looked back at me with a mysterious smile and dashed back to the building. "Race ya!" he cried. The sun had set behind the mountains, so the sky turned a deep purple-blue as he took off ahead of me.

I shook my head with a smile and followed.

Food for Thought

1. "It was a place not only to relax, replenish, and heal, but also to meet something deep and dark within myself." What might this phrase in this chapter foreshadow? What deeper meaning does it have for Rachael's experience?

2. Think about Rachael's main intention for visiting Eden Valley. Why might this not coincide with what John wants to show Rachael on this trip?

3. Think of the contrast between John and Rachael. Why might Rachael be uncomfortable with all of John's energy and games? What could she learn from John?

Mile Markers: New Influences

1. Have you ever gotten excited over a diet that you wanted to advocate? How did you feel if you met others who knew just as much about it as you did?

2. Have you met a stranger who was very much unlike yourself? Did their differences influence you in any way?

3. Write down what we can learn from people who come into our lives and offer a new perspective on life, even if (or because) they make us uncomfortable.

Chapter 14

Mountain Mayhem

A DIM, MISTY LIGHT shone through my window when I woke up at six o'clock the next morning. John and I had agreed to meet at the crack of dawn to head to Horsetooth Mountain, where ultra-marathoners would be running up and down a peak for twenty-four hours. John and I were just going to run the route once, but we figured it would be fun and good training.

I started up the mountain path slowly that morning, as I knew that running four and a half miles up would require patience and discipline. I never stopped to walk, but I did make sure to slow down occasionally to soak in the view. Of course, the view at the top looked better than any point I saw on the way up.

On my descent, I zigzagged down the rocky dirt path, putting on the brakes at treacherous moments, at others allowing my body to fly. I could feel the pounding in my knees, the slight twist of the ankle over rocks, and the uncontrollable speed that forced me to hold back so I didn't career off a cliff. Occasionally, I walked to recover and to take in the view of the mountains that jutted into the sky, clouds hanging like crowns over their peaks.

When John and I had both made it back to the bottom over an hour later, he offered me a drink from the gallon of fresh spring water he kept in the car. I lifted the heavy jug to my lips, slurping eagerly.

Even when my body had had enough, I pushed down more, just in case, just so I wouldn't mix up hunger with thirst, just so I could be sure I wouldn't take in even ten extra calories from food.

I drank until I felt sick.

» » »

After breakfast that morning I galloped through the tall dry grass back to my room, grasshoppers leaping into the air in front of me and the breeze whistling gently.

Until I felt it.

What began as an ache in those first few strides slowly increased to something deeper. I felt it at first in my right knee, a pain too foggy to pinpoint. I felt the ache increase with each step until, like a crack of lightning the ache turned into a sharp jolt of pain and stopped me in my tracks.

The day shone bright and sunny, the heat rising as I halted in the middle of the crackling grass. Crickets chirped in the wind as I looked down and rubbed the inside of my knee. I lifted my leg and swung it forward, and back, and forward again. Something felt loose, unhinged, uncertain. What could be wrong? My knee hadn't bothered me on the run that morning.

I tried walking. The pain pricked painfully through the soft tissue.

I tried to stay calm as I walked the rest of the way back to the building and grabbed the roller from my room. I massaged the outside of my knee, since I figured that might be the cause of the pain. I tried walking again.

Still painful.

It's just a small ache. It will loosen up and dissipate.

» » »

A few hours later, John gathered two of his friends to hike with us up Twin Sisters Peak in the Rocky Mountains. Mike joined first, a man in his fifties who worked at Eden Valley in ministry. Deb was a visitor to the ranch just as I was. But she wasn't there for the nutrition; she was an avid hiker. In fact, she had hiked a mountain the day before I arrived and had been lost for nearly twenty-four hours. I remembered seeing her after I had climbed down the Red Rocks with John. She had looked exhausted and disheveled as she muttered a weak "hello" in her southern accent before retreating to her room, her hair matted and frayed. It had been a scary experience for her, as she was quick to inform me, but apparently she already felt prepared to take on another adventure in the mountains; this time with company.

Indeed, Deb looked like a new woman that day, eyes bright and her brown, gray-streaked hair pulled back in a bushy ponytail. "Sorry I didn't say much to you last night," she said with an apologetic smile. She had a squint to her eyes and a motherly affection that drew me in.

We carried small backpacks, water, and plenty of sunscreen to protect against the more intense sunrays at higher altitudes. I cracked jokes about how, as the youngest one, I could barely catch my breath. Even though this trio was ages older than I was, they were well acclimated to the thinner air. And running nine miles up and down a mountain that morning didn't help my case.

About twenty minutes into the hike, my enthusiasm dwindled to silence as exhaustion and boredom hit. The rows and rows of pine trees and the constant back and forth climb up the trail felt monotonous. Not only that, but my right knee ached.

There's nothing you can do about it now.

About halfway up we passed a young boy, probably around seven years old, climbing down the mountain with his family.

"He made it all the way to the top?" Deb asked the family in awe.

"Yup!" the mother said, smiling.

It made me feel better to hear that; after all, if the boy could do it, then how bad could this expedition be? The summit couldn't be *that* much further ahead. John had said it would be a three-and-a-half-mile hike, but his timing didn't compute. "It will probably take about three or four hours," he had said. I figured he probably overestimated. Even if we *were* hiking up and down a mountain for a total of nearly four miles, how could it possibly take that long?

It wasn't until a teenager passed us about twenty minutes later and said, "You're halfway there!" that I realized I had misunderstood John.

This guy wasn't kidding. We wouldn't be hiking three-and-a-half-miles.

We were hiking seven.

The dense forest gradually became scattered pine trees, and finally an expanse of large, gray boulders where I could see other mountain peaks in the distance. Had we made it?

The sun shone bright and strong. I couldn't see a single tree for miles, and we even spotted a mountain goat about fifty yards away. I smiled in awe. Maybe this had been worth it.

The four of us took a few pictures and sat down to drink water before our descent, that is, until Deb began walking further among the rocks ahead of us. Apparently there was a very hard-to-see path that continued on. I pretended to know exactly what we were doing as I gathered myself again, but inside I was screaming to turn the other way and go home.

Thirty minutes later I found out exactly what "the top" of a mountain actually looked like. Turns out, it is the actual pinnacle of the mountain, not just the mound of rocks we had found ourselves at earlier. You really can climb to the tip of the mountain, spread your arms at the edge of a cliff, and raise your head to the sky.

That is, if you are Deb.

I never had the chance to feel that exhilaration of victory. No, the moment we reached the tippy-top, I buried myself in the deepest rocky crevice I could find and watched John and Deb in stunned silence.

How will I ever get down?

What if they have to get a helicopter to save me?

Can they do that?

I nestled further into my rocky crevice until Deb saw the distressed look on my face and came to my aid. "You afraid of heights, Rach?" she asked, opening her water bottle.

I nodded, laughing maniacally through the tears as she poured a few splashes of cool water down my neck to calm me down. I had an irrational fear that this dizzying sensation I felt in that moment would send me spiraling off the mountain.

John dashed over the rocks to help me out, but not before he took a few candid shots of my comical distress. I forced a smile that couldn't cover the fear evident in my eyes as I gripped the rocks around me, as if they were the only things keeping me from flying into the rocky abyss.

As I tried to take a few deep breaths to calm down, John sang to me. It seemed hokey at first, but as he continued, his melodic voice carried eerily in the wind and soothed me. When he ended his song, I realized how silent, how peaceful the mountains felt, so silent that I swear I could hear the sun shine down on us, its rays penetrating our warm, tired bodies.

"You ready to head down?" Deb asked quietly when my tears ceased. I nodded, breathed deeply, and reached toward John's outstretched hand. As incredible as it felt to be at the top of this mountain, I wanted to find safe ground again, and it would take that first step down to get there.

» » »

It took another two hours to make it back to John's car, but we had survived. The euphoria of hitting level ground was overwhelming as I nearly wept with happiness and began to laugh and crack jokes.

"I am starving!" Deb said.

"Yeah, I have to keep pulling my shorts back up!" I said, giggling.

Deb laughed in bewilderment. "You think you've already lost that much weight through this journey?"

Meanwhile poor John, missing his power nap, trudged down to the car in silence to drive us back home. Deb and I sighed deeply as we sat in the back seats, our sore feet stripped of our dusty shoes, our heads lolling out the open windows for fresh, closer-to-sea-level air.

We came home famished. The sun had nearly set behind the mountains by the time we marched into the house to whip up a feast of vegan food. Connie pulled out leftover homemade pizza that consisted of flatbread, dehydrated vegetables, and fresh tomato sauce. I didn't realize until later that it didn't have cheese on it, of course. Deb and I made a kale salad with chopped avocado, fresh baby tomatoes, and strawberries, no dressing. I loved that these people never added dressing to their salads.

I couldn't believe how close I felt to everyone at Eden Valley just because we all enjoyed the same food. Not all of it was raw, but at that point fresh, vegan food felt good enough to me.

"Would you all like some dessert?" Connie asked as we began clearing the table afterward. I cringed. Even healthy dessert wouldn't sit well with me since I felt I had eaten too much anyway.

But how could I refuse? Deb perked up instantly at the idea, so I joined in the fun as we pushed frozen bananas and berries through a juicer for raw "ice cream." We ate the refreshing concoction outside as we gazed up into the clear night sky, where I had never seen stars so bright.

Food for Thought

1. Write about why you think Rachael has named this chapter "Mountain Mayhem." Look up *mayhem* in the dictionary and notice all the possible meanings. Which ones fit this chapter best?

2. "I drank until I felt sick." Rachael says she does this to try to keep herself from eating too many calories, but is there a punishment she brings upon herself when she strives for the "sick" sensation? Why do you think she wants to punish her body?

Mile Markers: Blinded by the Disorder

1. John is exposing Rachael to a great sense of adventure, and she isn't taking it so well. When has someone pushed you to explore more in life? Did you trust them and encourage yourself to take that leap?

2. Write down ways in which you can take on more adventures. This may mean finding ways to develop relationships with friends and family, or finding new people in your life to hang out with.

3. Why might trying new things help you to grow? Could it bring happiness or hope into your life? Do you think Rachael is taking advantage of that? Do you think she can even see it?

Chapter 15

Colorawdo Cake

I THOUGHT ABOUT THE ache in my knee—my knee, which hurt more than the day before. I knew climbing the mountain probably didn't help matters, not to mention the small mountain we climbed the next morning as a warm-up to the day. Granted, that climb took two hours instead of four, but it still wore me out.

And the knee throbbed, irritated.

I ate. I ate out of fear for my knee pain, out of the desperate hunger that surged within. I ate even after I had breakfast with John and Connie, where we consumed a feast and I gave into the cooked quinoa.

Mind the calories, my dear.

I added almond butter.

Just this once.

Be careful.

I finished off with a few mango slices and a banana, but the moment John and Connie left, the voice called me to their freezer because that was where I knew the leftover vegan pizza sat, taunting, from the night before.

I ate the pizza. And I only ate it because I had let myself "go" at breakfast when I had eaten the quinoa and almond butter.

Those small mistakes had allowed the floodgates to fly open, and here I was, the shadow crowing while the small voice of Rachael screamed beneath.

And that small Rachael tried to wait, tried to hold onto the last shreds of dignity and control. She tried to reassure me that I should just stop for a moment and relax, that I hadn't ruined the whole day, that I could get back on track and avoid the calorific, cooked foods. But the shadow voice was stronger, and it called again. It convinced me to return to the freezer to eat frozen fruit, the chilly blackberries crackling like gravel against my teeth. And then I opened the refrigerator door to eat the quinoa, still warm from our breakfast. I shoveled in the grainy, nutty texture and savored this feast that no one else could witness.

» » »

I ate more throughout the day, with the patients who ate a variety of cooked and raw vegan food and on my own with the fruit I had stashed away in my suitcase. And later that night, when John showed me around the greenhouse and storage units on campus, all I could think about was food and how I could get more of it.

The wind picked up speed, and the sky had darkened as we left the last building. When John and I parted ways, I gave up all rules, all discipline, all effort to turn away from food. I had no energy to fight back.

Sweet.

I needed something sweet, and fruit didn't cut it.

Kitchen.

I remembered the kitchen in the building where I was staying, and desperation took over as I crept to the small room where the refrigerator sat, the refrigerator that I had noticed on that first day, the refrigerator that had been waiting for me. I crept as if someone would catch me, as if getting away with this would take away how much weight I would gain.

I knew exactly what I was doing, I knew I was the one in control, I knew no one forced me to do this, and all I could hear was the small Rachael screaming in protest, begging, *Rachael, stop, please stop.*

Perfectionist Rachael, raw food Rachael, Rawchael gone.

Outside a storm was brewing, and I could feel the heaviness in the air. I wanted so badly to run that night, to just try running again, but the knee, the damn knee!

I saw the crack of lightning in the distance, counted down, and heard the rumble of thunder that always follows, felt the old urgency to run, longing to wash away everything in the rain. I wanted to start over. But I hid in the cold, lonely building, because my knee stopped me, my body held me captive. I felt trapped, alone in my thoughts, and there was no one to ask for help, to pull me out of the madness of my own mind.

I will be fat.

That meant running slower. That meant a return to the old Rachael, the mediocre Rachael, a Rachael Coach Woj had not known and, I thought, wouldn't care to know—a Rachael my team would not praise. I could already imagine how difficult a nineteen-minute 5k would feel, how others would look on and think I just wasn't trying hard enough, and say, *What happened to the 17-minute 5k runner?* I remembered how tough it had felt when Emily, a freshman during my senior year of high school, often pulled ahead of me. And now I would have to endure all that again if someone else threatened to take my crown, if by my own gluttony I packed on the pounds and ran slower.

And if I stayed injured, if I couldn't run, how would I keep the weight off? I felt that the call for food would get louder than ever because without running, I couldn't eat right, and without running, I couldn't stop the hunger, the thought of food, from invading my mind all day.

Without running, who *was* Rachael?

I opened cupboards in the kitchen—empty. I needed sugar. I checked in the large freezer—nothing. I knelt to the refrigerator and found the god I worshipped, the god I bowed down to, beckoning me to its frosty lair. I felt that cold air hit me again, because of course I had felt this before. Late at night, alone, scared, dark voice screaming, head pounding, body growing larger with every bite. Hadn't this need for more food erupted all summer, hadn't I lost all control? I had the butter knife I salvaged in one hand, the tool I used to unsuccessfully cut through the frozen bits. I clawed for the sugar like a raging monster, tried not to breathe, feared someone would catch me in the act, tried to slice through the cold chunk of frosting, the chocolate crumbs peppering my fingers like fresh blood, my suicide, my skinny-no-longer demise.

    I ate cake.

Food for Thought

1. Rachael seems to be doing some emotional bingeing, meaning she is eating more food than her body needs in reaction to a life situation. Other than her injury, what might be triggering this compulsive eating? What is she feeling?

2. Rachael's bingeing probably also stems from not eating enough for the past few years or simply restricting entire food groups. What do you think is contributing most to the bingeing?

3. Why do you think Rachael feels so much pressure on herself? She shows little indication of any parental or coaching figure asking a lot from her. Is this internal pressure a result of nature or nurture, or both?

Mile Markers: Battling the Binge

1. If you think you have or have had binge eating disorder, write down some of the reasons for your binges. Recognize that they can be emotional *and* physiological.

2. When you feel a binge coming on, give yourself permission to eat, but figure out what may have triggered the binge so as to prevent it from happening or being as intense next time. Was it emotional? Have you been eating enough?

3. Write down what you learn from each binge. Don't think of them as failures, but as steps in better understanding your body and moving forward.

Chapter 16

Escaping Colorawdo

I NEEDED TO RUN.

Start over.

Burn calories.

Try again.

I wanted to test my knee that next morning when I awoke to a calm, bright sun shining through the window. I hoped the pain had just been a nightmare, a bad dream, a storm that had passed. If it was, I could eat right again. I knew it.

As I stepped outside, I felt hope rekindle. A run was worth a try. Maybe the knee pain was only temporary. Maybe it had resolved itself in my sleep.

Three minutes into the run, I passed the vast green gardens and made a right turn towards the crevice in the mountains, my exit.

And there was no pain.

With each minute my excitement mounted.

I can run.

I am fine.

I can run!

I felt boundless energy despite the higher elevation. I began to plan how I'd make up the miles I had missed. I exited the Valley on the other side of the wall of mountains, and I felt it.

The pain crept back in like an annoying sibling, taunting and aggravating. With each step the sharp jolt pierced the inside of my knee. I stopped, breathing deeply, and gazed at the vast green valleys before me. With my hands on my hips, I looked down at my knee.

This isn't good.

I felt an ache in my chest. I knew the pain would only intensify if I tried to run further, so I turned back towards Eden Valley and slowed down to a walk on the way to the building.

Don't cry. You will fix this when you get back home.

» » »

Before I sat in on an informational session about raw food later that afternoon, John came by my room to ask if I wanted to climb yet another mountain with him and Deb.

"Well, I went for a run this morning," I began.

"YOU DID? Oh, good!" John smiled. I had told him the other day that my knee had been bothering me.

"But it didn't go well," I said.

"Oh, I'm so sorry," he said. "Would you still want to hike?"

Did he not understand what I had just said? I was in pain. I had a cross country season ahead of me. My knee was *injured.*

"No, John, I don't think that would be good for it," I said. My frustration had mounted, what with the binge eating, the knee injury, and what I perceived at the time as John's unnecessary playfulness despite what I now saw as dire circumstances. I just wanted to learn more about raw food (hadn't that been the main reason for visiting Eden Valley?) and go home to start physical therapy on my knee. I didn't need to climb another damn mountain.

I took a breath. John was a sweet man, and I could only imagine how much more interesting it would have been to hang out with him if I had been in a different frame of mind. At this point nothing seemed to matter except my running and nutrition, which had suddenly gone abruptly downhill on a trip I thought would enhance it.

» » »

I left for home later that evening, but not before Connie offered me a large green smoothie for the ride. Stuffed to the brim from bingeing again that afternoon, I took the smoothie with a smile but wanted desperately to dump it out, to smash the glass, to get it as far away from my body as I could. But I had to drink it before we arrived at the airport, before I left John.

The smoothie was thick, sweet, and cool in my throat.

I cannot have this.

My body should not take this.

I slurped it down, hating myself.

» » »

"Now before you leave, we have to stop at the shop for you to try that elephant puzzle again," John said, driving through the vast, dry lands of Colorado toward the Denver airport. I looked at my watch nervously. I just wanted to get home, to get on that plane and get out of Colorado. What if, somehow, I missed my flight? "You can see how much faster you put the puzzle together!" John said with a smile.

I don't know exactly how I got out of doing the puzzle game again, but I found myself muttering something about how my flight would take off sooner than I had originally thought.

I escaped the elephant, but I couldn't escape something else, something I seemed to carry in me no matter where I went.

I just didn't know what to call it.

» » »

At home I felt pounds heavier. Alone in my room, I clicked through the pictures on my camera from the trip, searching, fearing someone had caught the exact moment the weight started piling on. But I came across one picture, one digital slide of me on top of the mountain. I had been squatting, low to the ground with my spindly hands gripping the rocks. My arms looked like thin poles. I marveled at the way my knees jutted upward, the deep angles of my bent legs; and suddenly I could see the thinness.

But why did I feel so big?

An eerie feeling crept over me as I looked at that digital photo. It was as if I were looking at someone else. In fact, it was the same feeling I had my freshman year of college, when I had seen myself in a picture for what seemed like the first time ever. It had been a picture from my first college cross country race.

I knew something felt different at that meet. Even as I dashed effortlessly to the front of the pack, pulling ahead of all the competition, and even as I looked around to see where everyone had gone, it did not sink in what had happened or how I had gotten there. I had gone from a middle-of-the-pack runner in the state to the leader against women who had crushed me in the past.

I crossed the line that day in second place and in a twenty-second personal best time. I pretended to slump over with exhaustion, but I knew I had not really given it my all. I knew, and almost hated the realization, that this did not feel difficult, and it was because of something beyond just training hard.

That's when the key had turned in the lock, and I opened a door into something I could not pinpoint. It used to make incoherent phrases, mutterings, whispers, as I researched food, as I typed out hundreds of pages of food notes and curled up at the library shivering in my sweatshirt and sweatpants, eager to get any tips I could from the health magazine articles.

And that day, as a college freshman, I crossed the line in shock. I heard the voice loud and clear at last, screaming bloody murder, a voice from the depths of my own body, in fact, my own voice.

This is mine.

It was not my intention in the first place to lose this weight for speed. I had no idea it even worked that way.

I tell you, I did not know this would happen!

Days later, I found photographs online of me from the race. My cheeks were shallow, my arms lithe, my left leg the circumference of a pole, pushing up into the air. I couldn't help staring at it—that leg, that leg! It became a measurement, a mile marker against which to compare pictures of myself in my future races. I would now check my legs. I never saw them before like this, and now? Now I saw them so clearly.

Shock. Confusion.

No, it's power.

I didn't see this girl in the mirror, yet the pictures became evidence that something had changed.

I just never thought weight loss could actually happen to *me*.

But running had lost its spark. As wonderful as it was to suddenly win races without even breathing hard, running became lackluster. I had searched for the "secret" to success for so long, and it came down to this? *Food?*

If food was the secret, I knew I had to continue controlling it in silence. I had to act like I always ate a ton, and I just happened to be a skinny girl. Because if I admitted the discipline, the calculation of calories, and the obsession with weight, then I would have to admit that something was wrong, that I didn't run this fast out of pure will and determination.

I would have to admit that my success was a fraud.

And that freshman year, as I looked into the mirror, as I stepped onto that scale every morning, as I crawled into bed every night, stomach growling, mind racing, heart anxious, I laughed and I cried. I soothed the aching, empty belly, and I whispered, *She is mine.*

Food for Thought

1. Rachael is trying to "start over" to help her feel better about the binge from the night before. But when this "starting over" plan doesn't go the way she had hoped, she goes back to bingeing. Where does this all-or-nothing mentality get her? What is she depending on to get her out of the bingeing, and why doesn't this work well?

2. Rachael writes, "I could only imagine how much more interesting it would have been to hang out with [John] if I had been in a different frame of mind." Think back to the question about what John has to offer Rachael. Why do you think she cannot see beyond her life of running and food? What keeps her stuck?

3. "And that freshman year, as I looked into the mirror, as I stepped onto that scale every morning, as I crawled into bed every night, stomach growling, mind racing, heart anxious, I laughed and I cried." Why do you think Rachael feels this mix of emotions? Do you think there is some confusion and disappointment here with this new "power"?

Mile Markers: Beyond Running and Food

1. As she sees her thinness in the photographs and asks herself the question, "Why did I feel so big?" Rachael seems almost about to recognize there's something wrong. But she doesn't. Instead, she connects the dots, weight loss and faster running, and avoids anything other than pushing further into the problem. Write about a time in your life when you have almost "gotten it" and avoided a bad decision. What kept you from seeing the situation clearly?

2. Did you ever have a time where you depended on something destructive to "fix" a situation? Did it help you to cope? What are some coping strategies that might be more consistently available and effective? Write these down to refer to them later.

3. Do you have a main focus in your life that you think might be an obsession? Write down other areas in your life that make you happy. Do you think you could depend on these if your main focus crashes? What could you do to strike a balance between what might "define" you in life right now and other parts of your life that may need more attention?

Chapter 17

Silence

124 POUNDS

THE MOMENT I RETURNED from Colorado, I set up and attended multiple physical therapy appointments. Pinpointing the knee pain as a strength issue, my physical therapist gave me exercises to build up the gluteus maximus and cleared me to run here and there if I didn't have too much pain.

I was on a time schedule. With the fear that my food intake would fly out of control, I felt I had to run to save my weight, to keep everything aligned, and not because exercise burned calories, but because I knew that if I were running, I'd be motivated to keep losing weight.

One evening I tested the knee before heading to a low-key road race downtown. My knee didn't hurt on this mile warm-up run, but a familiar feeling of instability crept over me with each questionable step. I thought the knee felt less painful near the end of the run, so I went to the race thinking it would improve.

However, not even a mile into the race that night, Coach Woj, who came to this road race each year, jogged by me effortlessly while he pushed his daughter Cecelia in a baby jogger. My pace slowed further due to the pain now radiating like daggers in my inner knee.

Should I stop?

Luckily, Woj's wife Amorena stood to cheer at the two-mile mark, the spot where I decided to stop. I explained to Amorena what had happened with the knee, trying to hold back tears. She suggested we walk to their home, which was only a block away, and drive back to the start of the race.

"So are you still doing raw food?" she asked as we walked together. Woj must have brought it up to her at some point.

"Yeah, definitely!" I said with a weak smile.

» » »

The moment I returned home, I opened a can of salmon.

Should I be eating this?

I wondered if I needed more protein.

But it's not raw.

I told myself it was fine to eat some cooked food; canned fish had fallen into the "acceptable" category, right?

What if I get fat from cooked food? Don't I want to at least try to eat all raw?

But it had protein to keep me full, right?

What if this is emotional eating?

I ate the salmon with chopped raw carrots and celery. My jaw ached as I shoveled the food in, chewing, chewing, faster and faster. The house darkened as the evening closed in on me. I sat there, alone in the silence save for the *clink-clink-clink* of the fork hitting the glass bowl over and over again. I hadn't even bothered turning on the lights as I filled my body with guilt.

» » »

I left the house soon afterward to meet my friends at a house party near Aquinas. Warm tears ran down my face as I wondered what the hell I was supposed to do about food, about running, when my control over both seemed to be escaping me. Friends were just a side note for me at this point. I enjoyed spending time with them, but even more so if my running was a success, because didn't that mean I didn't have to do much work to be *me*? Didn't that mean others would respect me more, that I would get all the attention and admiration if I had my life together with a great body and running accolades?

Wouldn't running and a thin body speak *for* me?

If I'm just thin, if I'm just fast, I don't have to say anything. Everyone will love and appreciate me, and I won't have to show off anything.

But what do you do when that's not working?

When I parked the car a block away from the party house, I couldn't stop thinking about how my legs must have swelled up with this accumulated fat, my shorts growing tighter around my waist, the stretch marks reaching upward into my stomach like roots, expanding my body, giving room to more skin and girth and pain.

I looked down at my phone, not quite ready to get out of the car.

What am I supposed to be feeling?

This was no raging anorexia, and I was not vomiting into toilets. "Eating disorder" never even crossed my mind. There had to be something else wrong with me, because I felt most people would say I was just overthinking things, just not thinking positively, just too worried, and *should just stop thinking about it.*

But I didn't know how.

In my desperation to find solace, to have someone understand, I tried to think of anyone who could somewhat hear me out.

Who can I turn to?

And then I remembered.

I texted my friend Ariel in the darkness of my car. Ariel was a good friend I had run against years prior and even more recently gone on a run with despite the pain in my knee. I typed out the message, all the while thinking, *This is ridiculous.* But when I had visited Ariel the day before, she had asked me if there was anything I needed prayers for. I couldn't think of anything then, but tonight it came to me easily.

I typed out my humble plea and hit "send."

Sitting in the car for another moment, I rested the back of my head against the seat. My phone lit up with a new text message almost immediately.

"What would you like me to pray for you, Rachael?"
I stared at Ariel's reply, shame curling in my stomach.
The scale.
The food.
The fear.
I wanted her to pray that I would stop gaining weight, that I would eat less, that I would get rid of these binges. I wanted her to pray that I could find balance and security, to *live* each day instead of living in fear of weight and food.

My throat tightened. I couldn't stop the tears from falling.
"I'm sorry, I can't tell you," I texted her.
I couldn't tell anyone.

Food for Thought

1. Rachael sends a text to her friend Ariel, but then doesn't explain why she needs help. Why do you think she does this?

2. "I felt most people would say I was just overthinking things, just not thinking positively, just too worried, and *should just stop thinking about it.*" How might these thoughts about what Rachael is dealing with be a reflection of our society's attitudes toward weight and, more generally, toward any kind of mental illness?

3. Think about our opinions about someone who is overweight and about someone who is thin. Do we feel that weight gain is a sign of emotional instability and lack of self-control while thinness suggests an ordered life? Is this a logical conclusion?

Mile Markers: A Positive Response

1. How do you feel when something threatens an activity or hobby you love? What is your response?

2. If you react badly to that kind of situation, how might your response be more positive?

3. Many of us experience frustration, shame, fear, and grief over losing an activity we love, even if it's just for a short time. Write down your feelings and think about sharing these with someone to vent to instead of coping in a destructive manner and keeping your emotions bottled up.

Chapter 18

We Need You

"There's a loneliness that only exists in one's mind. The loneliest moment in someone's life is when they are watching their whole world fall apart, and all they can do is stare blankly."

~F. Scott Fitzgerald

120 POUNDS

SCHOOL BEGAN, AND EVEN though I had planned a year of eating more raw salads, I found myself bingeing a few nights each week. I craved heavy, dense foods, and I crept into the campus café to buy yogurt parfait and granola bars. Sometimes I caved in to the cafeteria's pasta, pizza, and cookies even after eating large salads and fruit with my teammates.

And just as I had vowed to myself in Colorado that I would never binge again, I made the same broken promises each night as I hobbled with a swollen stomach back to my dorm, now knowing, deep down, that it was never truly the end. I was weakened by the pain in my knee and a slave to my craving for rich, dense food.

At that point my life seemed empty and pointless with neither the satisfaction of controlling my food nor the joy of running. I ran a workout with the team once, pushing through the discomfort in my knee, but that put me out for good. Thanks to my foolishness and my desperation to feel better about myself, the knee pain was so severe that I couldn't run at all. I ran when I shouldn't; I ate when I didn't want to. I had lost all vestiges of a disciplined life, and I had no idea what to do now.

I continued to send email updates to my family and friends just like I had when I began the raw food diet. In the updates for this new school year, I described my success in school and reflected on the good times I was having with my friends, but I also mentioned my downfall in my eating habits once in a while so that when they saw me again, it might not be a surprise to see I had gained weight. In the email updates I acted like food was a small matter.

Meanwhile, the worsening food antics played out even when I was with my friends.

Abigail, who owned an apartment on campus, often invited all of us for dinner. We would collaborate on large veggie-filled meals because my friends were passionate about whole foods and Abigail was a vegetarian. Only the vegetables were cooked in more oil than I was comfortable with, and most of it wasn't raw, of course. What's worse, this meal was often a second dinner for me, and I stuffed myself to the brim. I ate even when I knew I was not hungry, and when they noticed I seemed sad immediately after eating with them, I told them it was because I was frustrated with my knee, which was partly true.

I continued to show up for cross country practices, only to run less than a mile before the knee pain stopped me. I felt too defeated even to cross-train on the elliptical or bike to maintain fitness. I figured that if I couldn't run, I might as well not exercise at all. Nutrition and weight loss had warped my mind so much that I also felt as if training itself was *nothing* compared to controlling my body through food.

Only now, I couldn't even control food.

» » »

At the first cross country meet of the season I woke up with a cold, a rare occurrence for me. Despite wanting to lie in bed all morning with the sore throat and stuffy nose, I grabbed my Aquinas cross country warm-ups and headed out the door to drive to the meet and cheer.

I found Coach Woj the moment I walked onto the course. While he and I waited for the team to race into the final stretch, we talked about my knee.

I felt disgusting, ragged, and exposed as I stood there, failing before Woj's eyes.

"We need you to get better, Rachael."

I know. I'm trying.

"We really need you out there."

I nodded as I looked down at my feet. The words cut deep, even though I knew it wasn't Woj's intention to hurt me. He wanted me to race as badly as I did.

The lead woman of the race suddenly rounded the corner near us, about a quarter mile away from the finish, and Woj and I separated from there to cheer for the Aquinas ladies coming in a minute later.

"Brittany! Go now! Come on, Britt!"

"Go, Samantha! You can do this! Now! Now!"

"Let's go, Jamie!"

I yelled for my teammates, made my already sore throat rip from the effort because it felt like the only way for me to scream for release, to scream out my anger and frustration. And I yelled with tears in my eyes, wishing more than anything to be out there with them, wishing I had not lost that edge so quickly when I thought it all could have easily been avoided.

I should never have gone to Colorado.

After I watched the last woman on our team run by, I walked to the finish where I found maroon jerseys among reds, yellows, and blacks as all the runners exited the chute. I hugged my teammates and felt genuinely excited for their performances, which had been strong for just the first race of the season. But when I pulled back and they took off for their cool down, it hit me again that I was just a spectator now. I stood there amongst the excited parents, coaches, and opposing teams, unsure of what to do with myself, unsure of where to go.

A year ago here, everyone was praising you.

I walked towards the woods to find shelter, and I called my mom on the phone.

The moment I heard my mom's voice, I couldn't hold back the tears any longer. Snot dribbled down my face, my sore throat constricted, and I knelt down on the ground, the phone held close to my ear. I wanted to feel a sense of security, to feel someone close to me in a moment when I felt so alone. My throat ached and burned as I finished telling my mom how much I missed running, how tough this was; but deep down I missed the controlled, successful Rachael the most.

I am a mess, a downfall to the team.

After five minutes I finally calmed down enough to breathe evenly and bid my mom a tearful goodbye. Walking back to the team with a forced smile, I eyed the brownies one of the parents had brought, a tray of brownies on a taco station with beef, chicken, salsa, chips, vegetables, and fruit.

But the brownies, the brownies! I couldn't hear the voice that tried to convince me I shouldn't eat one.

I grabbed a brownie.

Talking with my teammates, I pretended to be engaged in conversation, to act like it was fine that I was not running, that a brownie was just a treat away from my raw food diet.

That I could be flexible and happy. And see, everything is okay!

Everything is okay.

Everything is okay.

Everything is definitely not okay.

All my mind and body wanted at this point was to be tucked away somewhere with the entire tray of brownies and to eat them as fast as possible. It was as if eating them faster would make the whole thing feel less real, that eating them faster wouldn't give me time to *stop* eating them. For this moment, they were the bits of euphoria that, paradoxically, kept me rooted in this world.

I grabbed another brownie.

Woj saw me grab my third.

Food for Thought

1. Why might Coach Woj telling Rachael that she "needs to get better" make her feel like more of a failure?

2. "But when I pulled back and they took off for their cool-down, it hit me again that I was just a spectator now. I stood there amongst the excited parents, coaches, and opposing teams, unsure of what to do with myself, unsure of where to go." What does this image suggest about Rachael's relationship with running?

Mile Markers: All-or-Nothing

1. In your journal write about a situation in which you thought in extremes, black or white, all or nothing, like Rachael: if I can't run, I might as well give up training completely. What were the results of thinking that way in your case? What do you think the consequences are likely to be for Rachael?

2. Why do you think many perfectionists are stuck in that all-or-nothing mentality? Why might it feel like "failure" or less of a "high" to just take the middle route?

3. Draw a horizontal line and write bingeing on the far left and restricting on the far right. Where do you think you are along this spectrum? How close are you to the middle (eating in a balanced way)? Write below this line the ways you might be able to work towards that happy medium.

Chapter 19

Boarding the Banana Bandwagon

129 POUNDS

IT WASN'T UNTIL LATE November, soon after the cross country season I had not competed in had ended, that I could run without pain again. And it was then, as my problems with food continued, that I came upon a supposed "cure" for my bingeing.

30 Bananas a Day, it was called. The vibrant website explained why I was bingeing, why I kept slipping. I had come across this saving grace one day after track practice, found myself scanning through everything for the next few hours in my hooded sweatshirt and black stretchy pants in the Aquinas library. Nothing could tear me away from the screen as I consumed the website with my eyes, eager to learn more.

Eat all the fruit you want.

Never get fat.

Raw. Food. Diet.

Only, it was a new way to approach the raw food diet, perfected raw food within raw food.

A banner blazed at the top of the webpage. Hanging beneath

a rainbow and a bright blue sky, it read "Woodstock Fruit Festival." A smiling sun with drooping rays danced below the colorful arch. And under this banner, the icon: "30 Bananas a Day: The High Carb Raw Vegan Lifestyle" with a rack of three bananas pictured next to it.

I scrolled through the website and read the questions posted on the forum. Remembering what a failure my mono-meal of eight bananas had been in the beginning of trying a raw food diet, I figured that I could try the mono-meals again or simply mix fruit in each meal. Plus the prospect of losing weight yet again blinded me to all the little things that could go wrong. Because with every comment on the forums, one thing ran through my mind. *I can gain control of the bingeing.*

Durianrider, named after a tropical spiky fruit called the durian, was the leader on 30 Bananas a Day (or as the members wrote it, 30BAD). Freelee, another young Australian who was known as either "Raw Fit Bitch" or the "Banana Girl," was Durianrider's partner in crime. He promoted her like a goddess, proof positive that "fruit doesn't make you fat."

Freelee was the envy of 30BAD and perhaps of all YouTube vegan enthusiasts. She was a star, of course, because she was Durianrider's woman, but it was her body that did it—her svelte figure that looked as if someone had laid her on a table and rolled out her stomach like dough to bake her into a wide, blue-eyed, California-tanned Barbie. And she was not skeletal thin, either. In fact, she looked curvy but without an ounce of fat. She was the thinnest you could look without appearing too thin and sickly, I thought.

How does she do that?

The couple were acquaintances of author and raw-food guru Dr. Douglas Graham, who wrote *The 80/10/10 Diet* book I had read earlier that summer. I had decided not to follow its suggestions for fear of the calories from too much fruit, but 30BAD changed everything.

As I read the 30BAD website further, I saw that it made a promise: if I ate almost *only* fruit (plus leafy greens), I would lose weight. It was as simple as that.

I was mesmerized; I watched nearly a dozen YouTube videos of Freelee promoting a life of satiety and freedom, freedom from weight gain, freedom from bingeing, freedom from worry. In each video, Freelee stood before the camera in a cut-off T-shirt touting "30 Bananas A Day," her midriff in clear view of the camera.

"Everyone, I want to talk today about how to get a flat belly," she said, spinning around with her hands reaching toward the sky. I got a 360-degree view of her rail-thin stomach. "I just want to let you know," she said with her arms open in a welcoming gesture, "that this" (she turned to the side to show off her flat stomach) "is after two fruit meals."

I sat there, appalled. How could I get that?

Maybe that is what is wrong with me, I thought. *Maybe the way I eat now is why I have a large stomach.*

Maybe I was meant for a fruit-only diet.

"The number one tip is to eat fast-digesting foods," Freelee said. That meant fruit and nothing else. Simple meals.

Ease.

No calorie counting.

I clicked on another video.

"So when it comes to cravings, I have ten tips for you," she said. "Number one is, go fruit yourself! Always eat sufficient calories from fruit." My eyes wandered over her shrunken body, her thin arms. Her body was the epitome of everything I wanted.

"If you think you're full after one banana, you are seriously mistaken. You are not in tune with your body." (Freelee, the Banana Girl, 2012)

Eat as much as I want? I could even force fruit in and lose weight?

"Sometimes you have to eat when you don't want to eat."

Would I finally get to that point?

"Aim for over 1000 calories at each meal."

1000 calories? I could eat all the fruit I desired.

"If you're not getting enough glucose to your brain, then you will be craving things."

It makes so much sense now.

"If we don't have large quantities of fruit, then we're going to go to fat. And then we're gonna wonder why we binge out on fatty, raw cakes." (Freelee, the Banana Girl, 2011)

The 30BAD diet seemed logical enough after what I'd learned about raw food in general. I already knew it was more difficult for raw food to break down and be absorbed by the body, so it made even more sense that only eating fruit might work that way. And according to the 30BADers, if you only ate raw carbs, your body didn't store any of it as fat.

"You cannot get fat just eating fruit and vegetables, no matter how much you eat."

Macronutrients suddenly became more important than ever. I had lived by the rule of a low-fat diet since I started restricting food, but to find out it was good to have a *"no-fat"* diet? It seemed so simple, so perfect, and like something only I could do as (previously) the most disciplined, healthy-eating college athlete I knew. As long as I ate fruit and only fruit, I would be lean, fit, and strong.

I signed up for an account as Rawchael.

» » »

These people are just like me: they care about weight; they care about health.

Just like me!

This was all I could think about as I interacted with the members on the 30BAD forum. I loved that they didn't seem as strange as many of the modern-day raw foodies I had met at the Rawlucks. No, this clan was different. These 30BADers went back to the simplest principles of raw food: don't buy the expensive so-called "superfoods;" avoid colon cleanses; stay away from fat-heavy raw food dishes (like the raw food pies, dehydrated "pizzas," and seed crackers I had come across at the Rawlucks and in raw food recipe books).

According to 30BAD, these were the mistaken approaches of the "inferior," *high-fat* (a detested phrase on the 30BAD forum) raw foodists. Cacao, maca powder, and spirulina weren't "superfoods." All you needed was fruit!

One 30BAD member called these crazed raw foodies "orthorexics." I had never heard the term before, but with the ring of "anorexia" in the word, I felt curious to research further.

Orthorexia, although not an official eating disorder, identifies those who become obsessed with eating healthy, so much so that their lives are ruled by eating only the "purest" food. As I researched more, I found a documentary online called

"Health Food Junkies."

"So this is . . . fresh pee," said a woman with a diamond-shaped face and wide, blue eyes. She held a glass of yellow liquid to her pursed lips.

"And this is a daily thing?"

The woman took a sip and swished the urine around in her mouth. "Yes, daily urine therapy."

I watched, revolted. It only made sense that the same woman worked at a natural health center where she extracted fecal matter with colon cleanses.

But drinking urine and washing out intestines were just two of her many purity rituals. She also ate only organic raw food, jumped on a trampoline to flush out the toxins from her lymphatic system, and wore a device on her hip to attract and "zap" parasites in the body.

The same documentary also followed a raw food couple who invited their friends to their home for a dinner party.

"Yes, I think it would be a really good idea to bring everyone into the idea of raw food," the husband said to the camera as his guests arrived. He proceeded to show off his sprouted pumpkin seeds and nut-laden lasagna ("No cheese. That's animal, and we don't eat animal").

"Do you think what we do is extreme?" the man asked his guests after they finished the meal.

A friend spoke up.

"I just think it becomes . . . kind of . . . you become fixated with it. Because I think it takes over" (healthfoodjunkies, 2008).

These raw foodists, according to the 30BADers, provided only a glimpse into the orthorexic world. But when did a simple desire to be healthy become a full-blown mental disorder? Where was the line?

Will I know if it's happened to me?

The diagnosis of orthorexia tickled something inside me, that every thought, decision, and action became dictated by food, and now, by the purity of it. I didn't worry as much about aging or developing a disease as I felt concerned about gaining weight and getting injured. I believed that if I could control all the aspects, if I could understand every possible thing about nutrition, then I wouldn't have to worry about anything anymore.

Food for Thought

1. Previously Rachael told her friends and family that she was working towards a raw food diet for her health. With this in mind, do you think she is developing orthorexia (the preoccupation with "clean" eating)? Why or why not?

2. "If I could understand every possible thing about nutrition, then I wouldn't have to worry about anything anymore." What does this phrase indicate about Rachael?

3. Rachael is grasping onto another "diet." Why isn't she able to see these diets as "diets," besides the obvious pitch from their advocates claiming they are more of a "lifestyle"?

Mile Markers: The Bingeing Cure

1. Have you ever tried to find a "cure" for bingeing? How well has this worked out for you? Make a list of everything you've tried. Underline the things that have not worked in red, and things that seem to be getting you somewhere in yellow. Underline what has worked (if anything has) in green.

2. How often have you been able to follow through with the approaches underlined in yellow and green? Rate their difficulty.

3. Do you think the green or yellow lines are something you can keep up in your daily life? When you did try them, what obstacles brought the bingeing back with the same frequency and intensity? Write down the steps you can take to work toward using the yellow and green strategies more effectively.

Chapter 20

Truth Unveiled

128 POUNDS

I WENT TO DINNER in the cafeteria one night expecting it to be like any other raw dinner I created for myself: a simple salad with fruit. Little did I know that I would have to put the 30BAD program to the test.

I walked around the cafeteria with a large salad plate, spooning raw broccoli and cauliflower into the dish. But I felt less than thrilled about the vegetables in that moment, and I couldn't pinpoint why. After a few lackluster bites at a table by myself, I got up and grabbed a small plate of pineapple. I chewed the sweet, acidic slices, unable to shake the feeling of needing something . . . something *more*.

Thick, steamy pizza taunted me from the counter. And that's when it hit me: What if the 30BADers were right about how much fruit you had to eat to stay raw? "You're not eating enough fruit," the members said when anyone craved cooked food. "You have to eat more fruit."

The website wasn't called *30 Bananas a Day* for nothing; 30 bananas equaled 3,000 calories, a third more calories than the average person requires in a day. Apparently that was enough to get rid of the cooked food cravings. And of course, a vegan can't touch the cooked flesh of an animal. Eggs are chicken ovaries. Milk is cow pus. So, even though you're consuming 3000 calories from the fruit, they are basically the only calories you get. According to the 30BADers, it all added up to weight loss.

"Eat as much fruit as possible," they told me. "You *still* won't get fat, as long as it is all fruit."

So that night in the cafeteria, I ate more fruit.

I grabbed another plate of pineapple. The urge to eat cooked food still lingered as I finished off the last few bites, but I refused to give in. Instead, I grabbed an orange, melon, grapes, and canned pears. Peeling the orange, I tried to convince myself it would be tasty.

Something like relief slowly washed over me as I finished the final few bites of the canned pears. Something settled within and curled up to sleep as my body relaxed and the cravings diminished.

It *worked*. It actually worked.

The cravings had disappeared.

It was the most satisfying feeling in the world, eating the right food and feeling full without guilt. I had read countless times in my 30BAD studies that this was what I had to do to get rid of the cravings, but to actually live it felt like a revelation.

» » »

That night and into the next morning I felt as if I had found the secret to life, and I couldn't wait to put it into practice again and again. Sitting at a table with the cross country guys for breakfast, I unashamedly placed eight small bananas before me, a mono-meal again at last, and felt happy to find that my appetite for fruit had returned.

The guys at the table stared at the bananas, exchanged glances, and exchanged their usual sneers. One of them looked up at me and offered his one and only banana.

"Do you need one?" he asked.

I laughed.

» » »

As excited as I felt about this new method of raw, there was still the old doubt, the familiar fear that it wouldn't work, that I didn't quite have all the facts, that I would make a mistake, that this time, as always, the hope was false.

You will still gain weight.

Calories are calories.

But I reasoned that eating too much fruit was better than trying to limit portions or count calories, because that felt like deprivation and only led to bingeing on high-calorie food like sugary yogurt and granola, pizza, and pasta. Plus, Freelee ate as much as she wanted, didn't she? And she had the body I desired.

I still decided to voice my fears to my fellow raw vegans. After much internal debate, I figured it couldn't hurt to put myself out there, specifically, online, to people who didn't know me personally anyway.

One night, Rawchael started a new post on 30BAD:

> *I am a runner who started raw food eight months ago then got injured. I have been bingeing on and off ever since and have gained ten pounds. So I just started this method of raw food with some worries; will I be able to lose weight on this diet to get to my racing weight again? Can I even lose weight by eating 3,000 calories a day from fruit? How does one lose the weight eating 3,000 calories a day, even if it's just from fruit? Does your body naturally lose what it needs to lose?*

The replies came an hour after I posted my questions. Durianrider, the leader, was the first to step in:

> *It's simple. You're just out of shape compared to where you want to be IF you're really fat, but I'd put money on it that you were already underweight to start with and now ten pounds is "overweight?" lol! 99 percent of runners starve themselves anyway, and you're probably the first time in your life at a body weight your hormones can work properly. Something to consider. People say "Oh, no, if I drop weight, then I can run faster!" but the reality is that doing the training and racing makes us faster combined with sufficient early nights and glycogen.*

Other members filtered in with their thoughts.

Member #1:

I've seen Freelee's website and videos where she says she was eating raw, trying to get in shape, and it wasn't until she stepped up her calories that weight started to come off. And there are dozens of personal stories all over this website where you'll see people saying it wasn't until I finally understood Durianrider's message of "EAT MORE FRUIT" that I saw the results I wanted. So it's just a matter of either trusting in what they're saying or falling back on your own instincts that you know aren't trustworthy.

Member #2:

It seems your body needs the 2,500 calories to thrive. Keep in mind that when eating food, you are not just eating calories for energy, but eating vitamins and minerals, which build up tissues and organs. So please do not reduce your calories to lose weight. That is why we say eat more to live more. I expect after a few months that you will have a "Whoosh"!

Durianrider:

Post a photo of you today, Rawchael. Show us how much a chubber you are now you weigh an extra five pounds. Heck, I'm gonna eat at least eighteen pounds of fruit today, not including skins.

I would never even have considered posting a picture of my body online like this, but I had learned a lot about myself since starting raw food; I was gutsy. I tried things that scared me.

I was willing to do whatever it took to get everything I wanted.

So that night, I shed light on the body I felt didn't match the right runner's body standards. When no one was in the dorm bathroom shared by eight girls, I brought my camera and stood before the mirror with nothing on but a sports bra and underwear.

As I stood before the mirror, bloated from a dinner of fruit and salad, I turned to my right side. There I saw, with disappointment, the round, protruding stomach.

"Got a stomach like your grandpa, dontcha?"

I hated staring at my body like this, but I had to; I had to remember exactly how I looked so that if anything changed, I would be able to catch it and turn it around before it was too late. Holding up the camera, I knew I had to show the world—or at least the 30BAD members—what had happened to me.

Help.

Wary that someone might barge into the bathroom, I took the picture quickly and looked down at the screen shot to make sure it was good enough to post. And even though I had taken the picture, I still had doubts about posting it online.

What if someone I know finds it?

Durianrider responded the moment I posted it:

> *Yeah, looking heaps fat! NOT. You even have ab definition, and you're totally relaxing your stomach. I'd say you could put on a few pounds if anything. Reality is, Rawchael, that you're making up excuses why you can't run better. You want to blame 'I'm not lean enough,' which is ABSOLUTE rubbish based.*
>
> *Let me go drink a gallon of water and let my stomach hang out and ask people if they think I'm fat lol! Stomach is DESIGNED to extend by the end of the day.*
>
> *Go to bed like Buddha, wake up like Ghandi. "Hey, Rawchael, I've started running, but my hair gets messy and I get sweaty and my heart races up the hills . . . is that normal?"*

He had a good point.

"Thank you for taking time to respond and help me out," I typed. "I'm wondering if I have a skewed image of myself or something."

Durianrider:

> *It's just in your head, Rawchael.*
>
> *Who is the fastest chick in the US? Goucher? She is trim, but not ripped. Ripped means you start to overtrain and focus on being ripped versus focus on getting faster.*
>
> *Somewhere, sometime you got it in your head that you need to be shredded in order to set personal bests.*

Nothing could be further from the truth. You have to be trim, NOT shredded lol!

I sat there in the darkness of my dorm room, having finished reading Durianrider's comment. My roommates lay fast asleep, and only the glow of the computer kept me awake as I typed out a quick thank you, shut my laptop, and crawled into bed in the dark.

Food for Thought

1. Rachael is beginning to expose herself more physically (with photos online) and emotionally (telling the 30BAD members her thoughts about her weight and food). Do you think that even though it's sharing online, this is a good direction Rachael is headed in? Why do you think she's crying for help so desperately now?

2. Rachael has discovered yet another solution to her problems with food and weight, this time in an online group that advocates getting nearly all your calories from fruit and claims that even if you consume more calories, you will lose weight. She has some doubts, but she quiets them and takes the leap into this new diet. Do you think that 30BAD might really be her answer? Write about your opinion and specifically why you have it. What has convinced you one way or another?

3. Do you think there are positives to this 30BAD diet? Where might they have good points or suggestions?

Mile Markers: Battling the Binge

1. If you find yourself bingeing often, write a list of the foods you binge on. If they are high-calorie, processed, low-nutrient food, you might consider following a principle similar to 30BAD's to see how it works for you, eating more whole food carbs before you eat foods that are low-nutrient/highly processed. Write a list of whole foods you enjoy that you could try to eat before you get to the low-nutrient/highly processed foods.

2. If you are already bingeing even on whole foods, consider the fact that your body *is* hungry and needs that nourishment. Make it a goal to give yourself "permission" to eat these foods. Write down why you may be hard on yourself even though these are foods your body is asking for.

3. If you wrote a list of whole foods to eat, make it a goal to eat at least a few of these whole foods first and gradually increase the amount each time. How does this work for you?

Chapter 21

Rawchael the Fruitarian

130 POUNDS

I CARRIED BOXES AND boxes of bananas, watermelon, and melons into my room each week. My roommates never said anything about it, but once when two of Anna's friends came into the room while I sat, unseen, on the other side of my desk, they saw the five melons I had on the floor and shrieked with laughter.

"Holy *shit*, how many melons do you need?! It reeks in here!"

I heard murmuring a moment later. "Is anyone here?" the friend asked, her voice suddenly uneasy.

"Yes," I replied from behind my desk.

The girl fell silent, and I felt embarrassed.

» » »

I started to feel as if my clothes were suffocating me as my once loose T-shirts hugged my growing waist and stomach. My pants clung to my legs, the space growing smaller between my thighs. My belt sat unused in the corner of my drawer.

"When you crave cooked food, eat more fruit!" Freelee urged in her sweet Australian accent via her YouTube videos.

I began to accept the diet and everything it promised, that time would give me my life back, that as concerned as I felt about my increasing weight, the weight would decrease eventually. I just had to relax and allow my body to adjust. After all, why not enjoy the ride? I realized how little I would have to worry about food now, when in the past, just the thoughts for one meal felt exhausting:

Too much or too little? Will I be hungry later? What if I'm actually thirsty, not hungry? Does this bread have added sugar? Is it really whole wheat, or are the advertisers deceiving me? Did I have my three servings of dairy today to avoid stress fractures? How is my stomach going to feel on this run? How is my stomach going to look on this run?

Check the mirror, check the mirror, check your weight.

Did this person add butter and salt to the dish? What if the salt makes me too thirsty, I mistake thirst for hunger, and I eat too much? Should I wipe off the sauce, or would that look too obsessive? Do the other people see how much I think about all the food I eat? Why can't I be as relaxed around the dinner table as everyone else? Is this piece of chicken the right portion size?

Am I eating too much? How do I tell when I'm full? Should I have eaten a banana instead of that slice of cake? Did I eat too much fruit today? Why do I feel so tired just walking around? What if I'm not hungry enough for dinner and end up eating too much for the day because my parents are eating dinner and I can't refuse?

I have to go to bed hungry. I must go to bed hungry.

The fruit "lifestyle" made food easy. Hungry? Eat fruit. Still hungry? Eat more fruit. Cravings? Just eat fruit. Not super hungry? Fruit.

"WTF? Where's the fruit? Eat the fruit, fruit bats!" Freelee smiled, taunting me with her body, twirling around.

I want it, I want it.

I want that body.

Food for Thought

1. In writing about her desire to have the kind of body Freelee has, Rachael uses the same language she often applies to "forbidden" food: "I want it. I want it." What do you think Rachael really "wants"?

2. Do you think how Rachael thinks about raw food is a sign of an eating disorder? In what way may it or may it not match up with what you've learned about eating disorders?

Mile Markers: Want

1. Is there something you want in the same way Rachael wants a body like Freelee's? Is there anything bad about this kind of wanting?

2. What might your "wants" say about you? What deeper understanding of yourself can you see in examining your wants?

Chapter 22

Spiky Surprises

129 POUNDS

I CAME HOME FOR Christmas break to a refrigerator reeking of stale food, or at least I thought. My dad asked me if I had left anything bad in there a while back, but we could find nothing. The only difference was the large spiky tropical fruit the size of a basketball resting on the left side of the middle counter.

My mom had bought it: the *durian*.

"I had to go to an Asian market on the other side of town," she said when I ran into her bedroom to thank her. "Eighteen dollars."

I had learned about the durian through 30BAD and learned that was how Durianrider had come up with his 30BAD name. In fact, he had chosen this fruit to be a part of his name because he enjoyed the durian so much.

Supposedly the biggest and baddest of the 30BADers loved durian. Thus, I held the fruit in high regard before even trying it, hoping I would somehow be initiated into this "club" of Durian-eaters. But there was one thing that might stop me: the smell.

Yes, the Durian was one of the smelliest fruits known to mankind. There are even laws in many places where it grows that forbid it in public because of the stench.

But if Durianrider and Freelee could overcome the smell for the divine flavor, I had to try it. They made the durian look creamy and sweet in their YouTube videos as they dug into its white, frothy "meat." And although many members warned that it might look like meringue but it tasted more like garlic or onions, I couldn't shake the idea of dessert from my mind. I figured it would be a memorable experience, whether I liked the flavor or not.

My enthusiasm died down quickly the moment my mom and I wrestled the barbed lump onto the counter, while my dad watched warily from the corner of the room as he sorted through his mail. The stench of the durian was strong enough to send anyone reeling out of the kitchen.

"Well, here goes nothing," I said, grabbing a knife. How *did* you open this thing?

Luckily the spikes around the fruit felt soft enough to penetrate effortlessly, and, sure enough, the knife slid into the flesh between them as I cracked it open on the counter.

I peeked inside.

The durian looked and felt as soft as I had seen it in the YouTube videos. The enticing cream-colored flesh filled the shell, but the odor was overwhelming. Eying it uncertainly, I scooped up a spoonful, and placed it into my mouth.

Garlic and onion was the perfect way to describe it. What's worse, the smooth, creamy texture made it feel like it should be sweet.

I hated it.

"Mom, Dad, I can't do this!" I said, holding the spoon away from my mouth and scrunching up my nose. They both took a small bite while I began desperately peeling and biting into a stash of bananas. My parents liked the durian enough to eat a few more bites, but it took eight bananas to get the pungent flavor out of my mouth.

» » »

My dad still wasn't enthusiastic about my fruit diet, and the smelly durian probably didn't help matters. But I was determined for him to understand how this way of eating was important for the health of our nation.

"Dad, this fruit diet can cure people of cancer," I told him one evening as we sat together on the couch.

My dad looked off to his right. I knew I had hit a nerve. His brother had died of cancer four years earlier, and here I was telling him that the answer was in the food we ate.

"But why would doctors be hiding this from everyone if it was true?" he asked. "No one would be out to sabotage sick people just for money."

"Dad, our nation runs on money. It's how businesses keep their business running," I said. "And the medical business makes its profits from illness." *He should know this stuff,* I thought. *He owns a business.* "And many people just don't have the information; that's why I want to teach everyone about 30 Bananas a Day."

"But these people telling you these things about fruit, they are not licensed doctors or anything," he said.

"Actually, Douglas Graham is a doctor," I said, referring to his book, *The 80/10/10 Diet.* "And if so many people thrive on this fruit diet, how can you ignore it? The best results come not from a nation dying of diseases while trying to follow the government 'food pyramid,' but from the people thriving from eating the simplest, purest food that we were *meant* to eat!"

I then tried to explain to him how fruit was alkaline in the body compared to food like meat and dairy, which was acidic, and that I had read how cancer grows abundantly in an acidic environment (Russo 2008, 116).

"It's not the cure for cancer though," my dad said, dismissing or merely refusing to comprehend what I had just said. "Why would they have so many people going through chemo if it was as simple as just eating only fruit?"

I wanted to tell him cancer was a moneymaker, as I had learned from many raw food videos and forums. I wanted to tell him that medicine was a business; but that seemed absurd, if not scary.

I felt afraid to say it.

Since the whole disease and cancer idea wasn't getting through to my dad, I had to at least tell him about the women of 30BAD, many of whom were finally conquering eating disorders. "The website is helping them, Dad," I said. "They no longer have to think about food, or battle with food, or limit their food." I had tears in my eyes as I said this. "They can eat until they are full. Anyone can."

I can.

I didn't know if my dad acknowledged or even understood what I had just said.

I can't remember if he asked me a question about something else or if he went on rambling about his blessed Detroit Tigers. All I could hear were my own words repeating over and over in my mind: *Women with eating disorders. This is helping women with their eating disorders.*

And as I thought back to my obsession with food, the wall of denial began to crack. Maybe my attempt to go raw really *had* been a result of a fixation; maybe all along I had tried to convince others, and myself, that I was striving for health and vitality when really I came to the raw food diet in the first place for the same reason these women did.

Food for Thought

1. What do you think of Rachael's conversation with her dad? Do you agree with Rachael or her dad on this one? Do you think they both make important points?

2. Do you think Rachael's dad suspects an eating disorder at all?

3. How is Rachael's mom's view of the situation different from her dad's?

Mile Markers: Cracking the Wall

1. Sit down now with your journal and just start writing about this moment when, for Rachael, "the wall of denial began to crack." What do you think she was feeling when she heard her own words, "This is helping women with eating disorders"?

2. Write about a time like this in your own life when something suddenly became clear, when you broke through your own denial or blindness about a difficult or painful problem.

3. Take a walk and breathe in the fresh air. If the day is cold or rainy, take a long steamy shower or soak in a hot tub. Relax. Enjoy this time fully.

Chapter 23

Racing Weight

*"Someday, sometime, you will be sitting somewhere.
A berm overlooking a pond in Vermont. The lip of the
Grand Canyon at sunset. A seat on the subway.
And something bad will have happened: You will have
lost someone you loved or failed at something at which
you badly wanted to succeed. And sitting there, you
will fall into the center of yourself. You will look for some
core to sustain you. And if you have been perfect all
your life and have managed to meet all the expectations
of your family, your friends, your community,
your society, chances are excellent that there will
be a black hole where that core ought to be."*

~Anna Quindlen, Being Perfect

132 POUNDS

I STAYED GLUED TO the computer for much of the Christmas break, researching raw food and scrolling through the posts on the 30BAD website. I found a post by a young woman who felt upset after four months of sticking to the 30BAD diet with little to no overt fats. Her weight had stayed the same with a small increase in body fat.

My stomach lurched. I couldn't let this happen. No, I could *not* gain more weight.

But I could already see how much weight I had put on. Later that same week, I wore a blue spandex tank top that I had used for track my senior year of high school. The material used to hang off my body, but today it hugged me, held tight to my sides as if to point out the pounds, as if to grab each cell of fat and scream, *Look at what you've done.* My thighs met for the first time in my life, and as I lay in bed, feeling the warm skin touch, I felt trapped in this unyielding skin of fat.

I felt claustrophobic in my own body.

I wondered if I could continue to handle this. Over and over the 30BAD members told me the weight gain could be muscle or water weight. But I could see the fat accumulating.

I could *feel* it.

» » »

January arrived and with it, my first race back.

As my teammates and I ran warm-ups outside in the winter chill before the indoor 3k, I could feel my sweat pants rub against my legs.

This is not a good sign.

At least my uniform still fit, or so I thought. It wasn't until I ran my strides back inside the building, in the middle of the track with my warm-ups still on, that my uniform top curled up over my belly.

My *belly.* Not my stomach anymore, but a belly with a layer, a layer of fat creeping over my tight bun-huggers. And I hated that even though I hadn't eaten for at least eight hours, my stomach still stretched out the uniform top.

The starter called us over to the line for the women's 3k. And I knew I had to take off my warm-ups. I had to expose myself, reveal the food-gorging monster beneath.

What if my uniform top rides up during the race? What if my new layer of fat jiggles? What if my bun-huggers reveal an even bigger butt?

But the damage had been done, and I had to face everyone like *this*.

"Runners, it's time to strip down," the starter announced.

I took a deep breath.

Have fun.

You are racing again.

You should appreciate this.

I pretended that everything was fine, that nothing was different as I first pulled off my Aquinas warm-up jacket. But that was the easiest part. I still had to remove the T-shirt and expose my body to the world.

I felt my parents' eyes from the stands the moment I did it. I could almost hear the gasps, could feel their penetrating stares as I threw the clothes to the side and stepped to the line. I wasn't sure how big a difference there was since the last time I had stripped down like this, but no one had seen my body exposed in a uniform since my national 5k track race seven months earlier.

Fruitarianism will make everything better.

Standing at the line, I pulled down my Aquinas spandex uniform top, thinking about how useless this was because I knew it would just ride up once I started running anyway.

And then the gun exploded.

I dashed to the lead and thundered around the first curve of the indoor track, but another of our best distance runners, Carly, scooted around me moments later. This did not surprise me, as I knew she was in far better shape than I was now, and she liked to go out hard. But I also I knew that I was supposed to be there with her; that is, if I were not packing all this extra weight and if I had not been injured.

I felt as if the 200m oval took the full impact of my sudden weight gain, shuddering under my monstrosity. It took time for the extra weight in my thighs to exert its pressure downward as my feet hit the surface of the track. It took extra effort to lift my knees, to pull the weight back up again and power my body around the turns. Everything happened in slow motion.

Two seconds slower per mile for every pound gained.

You would be so much faster if you only had more control.

Why the hell did you do this to yourself?

It was as if God mocked me as I circled around and around,

constantly passing my friends and family who looked on. It felt like torture, feeling their stares and surprise again and again, lap after tedious lap.

Fifteen laps felt like one hundred.

Teammates yelled out to those of us racing, but hearing their encouragement for me felt different this time. My mind spat out what they must have been thinking:

This girl can't control herself.

She must eat so much.

How can she get fat on fruit?

I had never wanted so badly to stop, never wanted so badly to crawl back into a cave until the weight came off again. Alina usually finished races about a minute behind me, but I found myself racing next to her now. As we ran side by side, I could see how far I had fallen back from where I had been before.

"But it's not the fruit's fault."

They told me this—the 30BAD members.

"The weight gain is not from the fruit. It is from any bite, any mistake you make throughout the diet."

I passed the finish line in just over eleven minutes. And to my surprise, Woj high-fived me with a huge grin on his face. But I wanted nothing more than to pull my warm-ups back on as fast as I could.

My parents didn't say much when I stopped to talk with them after the race, and I could feel their uneasiness. Minutes later I saw Woj talk to them as I ran a cooldown around the track with Emily, Alina, and Brittany, and I wondered if Woj and my parents were talking about my weight gain.

And what about the track team? They seemed happy to have me back out there, and no one said anything to me about the weight. But I could tell something had changed, could feel that people looked at me differently now.

I figured that just like at the Olive Garden, they knew something had gone awry.

Food for Thought

1. Why do you think Rachael is still so determined to make the fruit diet work?

2. Rachael doesn't even consider that she has not exercised/trained much through her injury; her sole focus is on food. What does this say about where Rachael is in her life?

Mile Markers: Loss

1. Reread the quote at the beginning of this chapter. How might this apply to you or someone else in your life? Have you developed a "core" for yourself? Do you feel you've given enough to yourself to rely on later when "you [...] have lost someone you loved or failed at something at which you badly wanted to succeed"?

2. Have you experienced a situation like Rachael, where you feel you have lost what you worked so hard for? Write down your feelings from this experience.

Chapter 24

Two Toasts to Twenty Bananas

*"Heroics are important and we certainly need heroes,
but I think we've lost touch with the idea that speaking
honestly and openly about who we are, about what
we're feeling, and about our experiences (good and
bad) is the definition of courage."*

~Brene Brown

I DECIDED TO SAY something.

It was through an email, an email to my mom confessing that I had a problem with food, that maybe it was an eating disorder, that I wasn't sure what to do or feel. That yes, I had gained weight, and I was scared, and I was constantly thinking about food.

That it was taking over my life.

In the email I told my mom that raw food was supposed to help me. It was still going to help me. I just needed her to know about everything, to support, to understand, to be there for me. I didn't want to feel alone any longer.

The email was not sent without much contemplation and fear. But I knew that, just like posting the picture of myself on 30BAD to get some answers about calories and weight, making any sort of progress anywhere required openness.

My mom received the email hours after I sent it, and she responded that we could talk at a restaurant, of all places.

» » »

"When did you start counting calories?" my mom asked softly. We had sat down to eat, me with my salad, her with lasagna. And even though my mom's words sounded gentle, hearing the forbidden "calories" dug into me like a knife. The word was enunciated so carelessly, so seemingly without effort when I had done everything to hide it deep down, never to be said out loud. Even though it was a word I said over and over in my mind, day in and day out, it never felt so real and hurtful until she said it then.

To her, it was a word without power. It meant nothing.

To me, it meant everything.

It should only be whispered in my head.

I looked down and poked at my salad. I would have to go into detail, would have to start from the beginning . . .

Doctor's office. Summer's end.

I was going to be a high school senior.

I stepped up to the scale next. My sister, a year younger than I am, had just walked off, having seen "132" smile up at her. She had lost weight over the summer thanks to the new ADHD medication that had a side effect of suppressing appetite.

Black dashes flashed across the gray screen as it calculated my weight. Angela peered over my shoulder. It took all my willpower not to shove her away.

"145 pounds," the nurse said, recording it on her clipboard.

145? What did this number mean? Was it big? I wasn't used to being weighed. We didn't even own a scale at home. But suddenly the number carried meaning, a personality, because I could compare it to my sister's number.

I never felt so big in my life.

"Whoa, I weigh less than you, Rachael!" Angela said once

we settled into the doctor's office. I looked down at my hands. Angela was happily surprised, and I felt shocked into silence. My yellow T-shirt with "ROXY" written in large letters across the front suddenly felt too small, and I became aware of how tight it felt against my stomach.

I tried to suck in again.

I felt tired of doing this.

About a week after that doctor's visit, I participated in a triathlon with my mom, and afterward we stopped for breakfast at a local diner. During the entire drive there, I felt like I needed to ask her about my weight. I felt scared to talk about my body, to draw attention to something I had felt self-conscious about. Besides, we were the family who collected *Nutri-Grain* bars and ate pasta, vegetables, and meat each night for dinner, drank milk and said "no" to Honeybuns and Zebra Cakes. In fact, nearly all of us ran, my grandma included. How could anyone in our family, let alone a runner, be concerned about weight?

But I am broken.

There is something wrong with me.

I have to ask. I have to know.

Before we got out of the car, I looked down into my lap. I had to do it; the more I contemplated asking, the harder it felt to form my thoughts into words. I forced the question out of my mouth before I could avoid it any longer.

"Mom, do you think I've gained weight?"

There. It was out, but hearing the words come from my own mouth made me cringe.

My mom turned to look at me. I continued to stare into my lap, trying to act like this was no big deal.

"Well," she said, "if you feel that way, then you could change a few things. Like just eat two pieces of toast instead of five."

Anger boiled in my veins. For years my parents had praised how I could eat stacks of pancakes, bragged to their friends about how I could wolf down two burgers, how I could lick a plate of spaghetti clean, and now she was suggesting I eat less?

"Okay," I replied. I wished I hadn't said anything. My question had only further exposed what I now saw as my big body.

But what kind of answer did I want anyway? If I wanted the truth, I had to be strong enough to take it. And it wasn't like she had said it in a mean way. What else did I expect? People who wanted to lose weight had to eat less.

Calories in, calories out, my mom had always said. *Just eat less and exercise more.*

Maybe I *did* eat too much food. Maybe there *was* something wrong with me.

My mom and I didn't say anything more as we got out of the car and walked into the restaurant. I hoped the question would be forgotten, that we could go on with our day. But I knew I would never see food the same way again.

I ordered scrambled eggs and two small pancakes that morning. Famished from the triathlon race, still I forced myself to eat slowly. But now I had to lose weight. Clearly my mom saw the weight gain. Compared to my sister, I weighed too much. The only way to lose weight was to eat less, like my mom had said.

It started now.

"You aren't going to finish your pancakes?" my mom asked, raising her eyebrows when I set down the fork at the end of our meal. Anger surged through my body again. Hadn't we just discussed this? Maybe she *had* forgotten my question already.

"No, I'm full," I lied.

She finished the pancakes for me.

And now here we were, more than two years later, discussing weight again. It felt more embarrassing than ever, thanks to how I felt I had ballooned. Perhaps it felt more embarrassing because numbers meant more to me now, had so much more significance.

I finally let my mom in on what I had been going through that past year with calorie restriction and fear of the weight gain. I told her about the doctor's office, about the triathlon breakfast, everything.

"Well, if you're uncomfortable with the weight, you still have time to lose it again!" she said. "Now you know you just need to eat twenty bananas a day instead of thirty." She smiled, as if it were easy to just stop eating so much and everything would be fine.

My heart sank. My mom knew I was trying to do the 30BAD diet. She knew we were instructed to eat 2500-3000 calories a day from fruit or more if we could stuff it in. If I didn't eat enough calories from fruit, I would binge on cooked food. I knew this because I had experienced it time and time again.

"Just eat two pieces of toast instead of five" kept ringing in my ears. Only now it was "eat twenty bananas instead of thirty." Had she understood a word of what I had just said?

I felt at loss. I tried to explain that sticking to the fruitarian diet would help me to get back on track again, but only if I followed the principles to eat a lot of calories from fruit. Without those calories, I would binge on cooked food, on the forbidden, and I would *become* the forbidden: fat.

Nothing seemed to click for her.

» » »

The moment we came home after dinner, my mom dug the knife in deeper.

"Alright, how about you get on the scale?" she asked, pointing to the bathroom.

I looked at her, horrified.

Get on the scale? What the hell?

"I . . . I can't," I replied, feeling my eyes well up with tears. I felt pathetic and exposed. That was *my* secret, *my* ritual. She had no right to check my weight. She had no right to look over my shoulder and see the numbers I held in secret and shame every day. There was no way I would let that slip through my fingers. Besides, we had just eaten supper so the numbers would be unkind.

I was full of *food.*

"Well, you want to see your starting point, right?" she said, curious.

Did nothing sink in that night at dinner? Weight scared the hell out of me. What was she doing?

"I can't. I can't!" I said.

I began to cry.

"Rachael!" My mom looked shocked and confused by my sudden outburst. It must have looked ridiculous; after all, it was only a number to her.

Only a number.

A number with a voice. A number that spoke to me. A number that knew me.

Look at what you've done. Look at how out of control you've been. You are so stupid, so fat and greedy.

I will make your life a living hell.

I wanted to erase everything I had said.

I should have followed my instincts, should never have said a word.

This was just like two years ago, only worse.

I never should have asked her if I was fat. I should have kept my silence.

» » »

I lay in bed that night, tossing and turning as I tried to swallow everything that had just happened.

"Would you like to get some professional help?" my mom had asked at dinner. "What can I do for you?"

But I had refused her offer. This didn't feel like it should be such a big deal, and that's what made it feel so shameful. I didn't feel as if I were in the depths of despair, not on the edge of death or starvation.

I just feel insecure about my weight, like any girl might be, I thought. *I just counted calories and ended up getting fat.*

Maybe I just wanted sympathy. Maybe I just didn't want to feel so alone.

You are not really sick.

As I lay in bed, I felt more alone than ever.

Food for Thought

1. Rachael first tries to cry for help through a text to her friend Ariel at the end of the summer (chapter 17) and now through an email to her mom. Why do you think she doesn't come forward in person? Do you think writing instead of speaking out loud eases the fear at all?

2. This is a book about Rachael's relationships: with food, with her teammates and friends, with her mother, her sister, her father, with Coach Woj, with herself. Choose one of these relationships and write about why you think it's troubled.

3. From what you've read so far, do you think Rachael is "sick"? Why might it be difficult for her mom to see this? Where do you think the confusion lies?

Mile Markers: Recognizing the Relationship

1. Consider a relationship in your life that has problems and write about why you think those problems exist.

2. Would you be able to talk directly to the other person? Describe this person and what you might say.

3. What would your method be of confronting this person? Think about how you might go about this.

Chapter 25

A Moment More with Mom

"Very rarely can you see an eating disorder."
~Marya Hornbacher

THE NEXT DAY, I could not bring myself to come downstairs from my room. I couldn't face my mom again, no, not after she had seen the real me the night before. I wanted to erase everything that had happened, wanted her to forget and for me to have lost the weight again.

Later that afternoon, I heard the slow thuds of my mom's footsteps walk up the stairs. She found me at my desk on the other side of the room, my back to her so that she could not see my face, which was now burning with humiliation and fear.

"Can we talk?" she asked. Her words were gentle.

I nodded, and she sat on the edge of my bed as I turned in my seat to face her. As uncomfortable as I felt, part of me wanted to thank her for coming to try again.

"I've been thinking everything through," my mom said. "I guess I just don't understand; I always thought you ate so much!"

That was it, the slice, the cut, the burn in my chest that had hurt for so long.

Am I just making all of this up, just looking for sympathy? What do I call these feelings, this obsession?

But her unconscious cruelty was my permission to lash out at her, to finally spill out what I had been holding back for so long, how she had been wrong about food, how I had been right, how I had restricted food and cut calories right under her nose. But the familiar feelings were no longer as invigorating or empowering because now I was no longer thin enough.

As I looked inside myself at that moment, as I observed the Rachael from the past, I could see her so clearly, the skinny Rachael screaming, laughing at other people for their ignorance about food. I had wanted to point in their faces, push those I loved in the chest and say, *Ha, if only you could see my weight now. If only you could see the changes I've made, how I can control my body.*

Something had clicked into place when I saw, really *saw* a box of cereal for the first time. It was Raisin Bran that spoke to me, the food that laughed and mocked me when I found out it had *sugar* in it, that dried fruit like raisins sprinkled throughout such a cereal were a calorie bomb in just one measly handful.

And I had been eating it. I had really been eating it.

How many other foods are lying to me?

Growing up, I had learned that calories existed, but to actually look long and hard at a label, to piece things together, made me realize there was a chance to perfect food. I grew more excited as the foods revealed their secrets to me, as every bite of anything spoke to me, told me whether I should eat it or not. I could see everything so *clearly* now.

To label a food gave it meaning and purpose. Special K cereal no longer stuck out to me as breakfast, but as dessert. Eggs became egg whites. "Whole" had to stand before "wheat" in the ingredients. Olive oil and butter were to be shunned, and I learned how to find their sneaky presence in food by looking for the way the oil clumped in soft ovals in any bit of the sauce or liquid drizzled over food.

One hundred, two hundred, three. Four hundred, plus six hundred, so one thousand. Roughly one thousand for the day.

Minus three hundred for the run.

They wouldn't go away, these thoughts. They dominated my mind. I tried to release them by gradually talking more and more about food in front of my parents. And the more I revealed to them what I was discovering, the easier it became.

But "calories" were a frightening word to say out loud—my swearword. It would reveal my secret, my knowledge of counting, measuring, tracking. When someone mentioned that word, I perked up. They could say it? Out loud?

You don't count calories. You're not that kind of person. That's someone else.

Denial.

So I won't tell them. I will act like I'm fascinated with nutrition, that I just love health.

My parents fell for it. They believed I was innocently looking for a healthier way to eat. They didn't notice the measuring cups. How could they? When my parents were gone, I measured out the proper portion of cereal. I rinsed the cups, wiped them dry, and put them back in the drawer. I learned to eyeball a cup of cereal; it was the only way I could be sure I had poured correctly without measuring in front of my parents.

We'd go out to restaurants as a family and I'd calculate the calories, mine and theirs, in my head.

"Rachael ate all of hers!" my mom would say as the waitress took my plate away.

She is saying that you eat too much.

My mom often left half of her one-thousand-calorie lasagna for leftovers. To me, this was a sign that she didn't have to eat all of her food like I did, a sign that she could stop halfway and box it up, as if she were being modest and petite, as if she barely ate a thing.

You know what she is doing. You know what she is getting at.

But the knowledgeable Rachael, oh, that knowledgeable Rachael knew how ignorant she was. And as I sat in silence and heard my parents laugh at "how much Rachael eats!" I seethed knowing their calories for that night were so much higher than *mine.*

Non-buttered vegetables: forty calories.

Five-ounce fish: two-fifty.

Sure, my mom only ate half of her lasagna (five-hundred), but she also dunked half a loaf of bread in 120-calorie-per-tablespoon-oil before the meal even arrived. Meanwhile I sat there, smiling sweetly as I refused the *white* bread, as I refused the *calorific* oil. I knew, in the end, that my mom consumed more calories than me at every meal, and I secretly celebrated it and despised her for "mocking" how much I ate when it was nothing like that.

Ignorance. Stupidity.

They know nothing.

And how stupid were they, when we took a trip to California, that by offering me orange juice ("freshly squeezed, Rachael!"), they thought that they were doing me a favor, that it was *healthy*.

"But California is known for its orange juice!" my mom said when I shook my head. "Are you sure you don't want just a sip?"

My mom offered the glass to me, and it took everything in my willpower to keep from shoving the orange juice back in her face. It took everything in my willpower to push down the Rachael who wanted to tell them I was right and they were wrong, that this was my body and I was skinnier and if only they knew what I knew, if only they could see that the orange juice they were offering to me like some sort of health drink was nearly two hundred calories of empty sugar.

You must not drink your calories.

I wanted to make the same disgusted face my mom had made when we grew up scoffing at those who ate "junk food," at those who were "fat and lazy," and just "didn't take care of their bodies."

Little did my family know what junk *they* were eating and drinking. But now I knew the secrets of food at last.

I wanted so desperately somehow to show my mom what the scale had shown me when 123 flashed before my eyes half a year after the doctor's visit at 145 pounds. I wanted to dance in victory, to hold that damn scale in her face and taunt and laugh that I had done it. I would scream that they were wrong about everything.

I fought a battle within, a side of me that wanted to tell my parents and a side that couldn't. How would telling them line up with the Rachael they had known in the past?

I had learned and practiced lying to earn the greatest praise and amazement from my parents.

"I love school!"

No, I don't love it, but I want you to love me because you think I love it.

"I always want to practice piano for hours every day!"

I feel pressure to please my piano teacher each week, even if it's more work than she expects out of me.

"Of course I'll run with you!"

When all I really want to do tonight is draw and read.

I loved being a good student, I enjoyed piano, and I had a passion for running, but I felt I had to say "yes" every time I had an offer to run, that I had to practice piano and grin as I did my homework, that every day was filled with opportunities to show what a good, disciplined girl I was without anyone having to tell me anything.

But food? Food, I could pretend to say "yes" and pretend to eat enough, when inside I knew the truth: I could deceive them, and they wouldn't know, and I could lose weight. I could do something for *me* now. With food they could see me as the normal Rachael they thought they knew, but I could treat the real Rachael inside.

Until my self-righteousness began to seep out.

"Orange juice really isn't that healthy," I pointed out to my mom months after the California trip.

"See, we need the 'whole' before 'wheat' for it to be healthier," I told my dad when I began to monitor cooked dinners.

Each comment was a silent jab at them, *Look at how ignorant you were, look at how much you don't know and I do.*

Look at how thin I am now.

My parents, my mom especially, began to adopt my tips, which I both wanted and wished wouldn't happen. Because now she could lose weight too, and somehow she was able to eat less than I could.

"I feel so full!" she said after a small bowl of vegetables or one-banana lunch.

Translation: You should feel full, too. This, this right here is what would keep a *normal* person full, is what got *me* full, and this is how much *you* should eat, Rachael.

They mock you, those good eaters. They never had to cut

back on their food. They never had to worry about food. They never had to deal with this.

"Just one or two itty bitty bites of dessert is perfect," she said when we went to restaurants or holiday parties together.

Translation: you should feel perfectly satisfied after "two itty bitty bites" also.

Something is wrong with me.

I knew I lost weight doing what I did, but her words angered me more, reminded me how gluttonous I was even when I did eat "better."

If your body were normal, you wouldn't have had to cut back in the first place.

I tried to explain to my mom that afternoon in my room how the words hurt over the years, how even now they felt like a slap in the face. Every comment about my food, no matter how innocent they sounded to someone without this dis-ease about food, turned the voice inside me from mutterings into a scream.

See? They are proving you are a glutton, a pig!

But my mom did not understand. And perhaps neither did I. We sat there that afternoon, the radiant sun shining through the window, both of us lost and confused as we tried to communicate truly for the first time in my life.

I felt dirty, contaminated for my mom to know this much about me now. I felt uneasy exposing a part of myself that seemed so *unlike* the Rachael everyone knew.

"Were you throwing up the food?" my mom asked near the end of our conversation.

I felt my face grow hot.

I am wrong. I must not have an eating disorder, and this proves it.

I shook my head. No, I never threw up.

Then what the hell is wrong with me?

I felt guilty, wondering if I had made a big fuss over nothing. Even more, I hated that my mom thought I ate so much still and that I couldn't have an eating disorder unless I purged it all.

Food for Thought

1. What does Rachael mean when she thinks, "You don't count calories. You're not that kind of person"?

2. "I couldn't face my mom again, no, not after she had seen the real me the night before." Who do you think is the "real" Rachael? Why is identity so important in dealing with this eating disorder?

3. Rachael exposes a side of herself she hasn't even shown her parents before. Why might this be scary for her?

Mile Markers: Hidden

1. The chapter begins with, "Very rarely can you see an eating disorder" by Marya Hornbacher. In what ways might your addiction or eating disorder be difficult to see? Or why might someone you know be able to hide his or her addiction so well?

2. Who would be the first person you could tell about your eating disorder? How do you think they would react? Does this worry you? What could be the worst possible outcome? What could be the best?

3. What do you think about telling someone that instead of simply having an eating disorder, your eating disorder is just part of a deeper issue? That the eating disorder is simply a coping mechanism of that issue? Rachael turned to her eating disorder in order to feel successful, worthy, and valued (because she thought it made her a better runner). This was a sign that Rachael didn't feel

worthy in other areas in her life and that she lacked balance. What do you think is the deeper meaning behind your eating disorder?

4. To prepare further for this step in recovery, refer to the **SUPPORT: Laying a foundation** in Appendix B.

Chapter 26

Unexpected Approval

JUST AS I HAD found the pictures of me from my first college race, I found the race pictures of my body *now*.

Who is *this runner?*

Round hips, full legs, chubby face, and all I could feel was horror.

But Woj thought differently.

"It looked like you had more 'meat' on your legs at the race," he said at practice that Sunday. "I think this is going to benefit you a lot in the future."

I stared at him, mid-bite into a banana.

You mean the fat I've gained? That meat?

"I can definitely see you running in the sixteens now for the 5k," Woj said.

I smiled back and nodded. I acted like I felt fine with the weight gain, that I had been ignorant to the changes in my body. *Yes,* I pretended to say to him, *it is most definitely muscle on me now, not fat! And look, this banana I am eating? It has helped me to become stronger and more muscular.*

See, this raw food diet is helping me.

But I knew the truth; I had gained fat. I wanted to laugh at his ignorance, to shake him, to show him how much I was dying inside.

But Woj stirred something in me. I had not expected him to feel happy about this, especially since my mom had said it would be helpful to drop the ten pounds again. Woj made the extra weight a positive thing.

How can he possibly think this will help?

» » »

I was on my laptop again in my room that night when my friend Elizabeth messaged me on Facebook. Somehow, the topic of the race—and my weight—came up.

"I noticed the weight gain (I hope you don't mind me mentioning it), but you look good! It seems like a healthy weight gain."

I thanked God this message took place on Facebook instead of in person. I didn't want her to see how mortified I felt in that moment as I shifted in my seat.

"I figured most people did," I replied. "It feels embarrassing to me though."

"Naw, don't feel that way. Some people did comment, but it was all good stuff."

I felt a heavy weight sink into my chest.

I was right. Everyone is looking at my body.

I felt exposed and dirty, as if the fat had contaminated me. I wanted to pull it out of my legs, my hips, my stomach. I wanted to burn it, to destroy this weight and never let it come back.

"You (no offense) look healthier," Elizabeth typed. "A bit more womanly,"

The weight in my chest sank lower. *Womanly?* The last time I had heard "womanly," it had been just before high school when my mom mentioned how girls who developed large hips and bigger boobs ran slower ("But we're not those kind of people," she had said).

I did not want to look *womanly*. I did not want to grow up at all, at least not yet. I had not had enough time with the most successful Rachael I had ever known; *that* was who I had wanted to be, and to lose her so soon? I had tasks to complete, goals to reach, so much still to accomplish.

I told Elizabeth I felt scared about what people thought about my weight gain.

"They're all very skeptical of the raw food thing, but to see you gain weight shows that you are getting enough calories and nutrients."

To my surprise, I felt a small sense of relief.

Maybe this is a good thing. Maybe it would allow me to keep up with this whole raw food ordeal with less skepticism from others.

Maybe I could convince everyone that I tried *to gain weight with raw food.*

» » »

I was happy to be running again that winter; I was enjoying my dinners at the cafeteria because I was burning all the calories; and I felt proud to show off my fruit eating skills. While the other runners grabbed macaroni and cheese, burgers, and salads slathered with ranch dressing, I grabbed dry lettuce leaves and eight oranges.

Digging into the thick peels, I plowed through the oranges while everyone watched in what I thought to be a mix of horror and surprise.

"How many oranges is that now?" Carly asked, astonished. Some of the other girls laughed, staring.

"Hmm . . ." I said, looking down at my peels and laughing. "Eight?"

"Holy shit!"

Eddie walked by our table on the way out of the cafeteria, staring at all the orange peels overflowing my plate.

"Yeah, she ate all those!" Elizabeth said, giggling.

I grinned.

Food for Thought

1. When she talks to Elizabeth online, Rachael seems to have returned to talking more about weight and food through written words than face to face. Do you see any improvements in her methods?

2. Rachael seems more confident eating a lot of food in front of her peers. Why do you think this is? Is Rachael on the upswing?

3. Do you think the fruitarian "lifestyle" could be the cure for Rachael? In what ways could it be helpful or detrimental? Do you think it has helped her at all so far?

Mile Markers: Fear of Growing Up

1. If you are female, have you ever felt the need to look less "womanly"? Why might this be? Write down what you feel are the drawbacks of becoming a woman or having a woman's body.

2. Why might having an eating disorder be a way to "pause" life and relive the past? How would it be a way to "stop growing up"?

3. Write about what you may fear or look forward to in growing up. Could this be a part of your eating disorder or addiction? Could it be a factor for anyone else you know who struggles?

Chapter 27

Just Eat More Fruit

I LOST MY MOMENTUM with fruit.

It came unexpectedly, seemingly out of nowhere, and it had nothing to do with my attitude. I was all for eating more fruit, but my body had had enough.

By the end of January, after two months strong with fruit and raw vegetables, I wanted a baked potato.

The baked potato came to mind the moment I woke up one morning that winter. I told myself that I just needed to eat more fruit, that eating fruit would take away this intense cooked food craving. Only I couldn't stand thinking about another bite of anything sweet. On the fourth banana of my breakfast mono-meal, I gagged.

When all else failed, dates usually fixed things, so those were next. I choked down twenty-seven moist medjools, but I still had the damn baked potato floating in my mind's eye.

30BAD was my final hope. What answers would this group have for me? What could I do when I felt like I was going to vomit if I ate another bite of fruit?

The members suggested I eat more variety—of fruit.

So I drove to the big supermarket in town.

I figured that perhaps just seeing what was available would spark my interest in fruit again. And that's when it happened; the tomatoes spoke to me. The celery screamed, "I'm crisp and crunchy!" from the shelf, and the pineapple radiated like gold.

I had found what my body needed; it *was* variety.

I bought anything that looked even remotely appetizing and jogged to my car as the snow swirled in the wind. The moment I slammed the door shut, I knew I couldn't wait. I opened the package of pineapple in the front seat and dug in with my bare hands.

Cold, sticky pineapple juice ran down my wrists. My fingers grew numb as I grabbed more and more, too desperate to even turn on the car and warm up.

Food.

Now.

I had never eaten with such ferocity in my life, had never cherished pineapple so much. I felt like a Burger King drive-through binger.

» » »

Early the next morning, I woke up feeling nauseous, and with my tongue burning from the acidic pineapple binge. On top of that, the cravings were back for anything cooked. Anything but *fruit* remained at the forefront of my mind.

Oatmeal.

Baked potato.

Pasta.

I went for an eight-mile run with my team on an empty stomach, much too sick to eat. The thought of anything *raw* made me want to vomit. I felt sure that the Rachael from a year before would have eaten oatmeal without a question, but I knew better now.

I have learned so much.

After the run, my stomach screamed even louder for cooked food.

It must mean I'm not truly hungry. If an apple doesn't even sound good, how could that be hunger?

Detox. This has to be the detox.

I was able to force down banana smoothies that afternoon for lunch. And for dinner that night I ate salad with a few cups of strawberries and three ears of corn. But I kept wondering, as I cut the tops off my strawberries, why I was doing this, why I kept going with it.

Rachael, do you really want to live like this?

I stopped slicing and looked at the strawberries.

How much do you want this?

I knew there were 30BADers who said eating cooked food was acceptable as long as it was high carb vegan food. But at the time, many said that it stalled weight loss, that the best way to go was raw food.

I have to lose this weight.

But that night, this dinner of strawberries and salad was my breaking point. I had tried, God, I had tried to eat the fruit. But I couldn't do this any longer.

I jumped into my car and drove into the night toward my parents' house twenty minutes away where there was a kitchen, where I could cook, where I could eat alone to my heart's content because I knew my parents were gone and they wouldn't see me in such a state.

And when I arrived at the house and ran into the kitchen, I fired up the stove. Scrambling through the pantry, I found brown rice and poured it by the handful into a pot of water.

It wouldn't cook fast enough.

Is this all that's left?

Me wolfing down food like a beast.

Me thinking about food constantly?

The minute the rice even looked close to being done, I poured a bowl full of it and used the biggest spoon I could find. I was on autopilot, shoveling the rice in faster and faster, pouring bowl after bowl. I didn't care that it burned my tongue, didn't care that I nearly choked on it as it made its way down my throat. I needed it, this, wanted it forever. I felt possessed as my body finally devoured what it had wanted for so long.

The meal felt so satisfying, had released so much, allowed me to think so much more clearly, that I didn't feel an ounce of guilt as I climbed into my car and drove back to campus.

Food for Thought

1. Today, years after Rachael's experience, the 30BAD members mostly promote a vegan lifestyle of eating only fruit until 4 p.m. and then cooked food into the evening. Based on Rachael's experience, do you think this is a good adjustment? Do you think this might have helped Rachael in her quest at all? In what ways might this be a healthier way to approach 30BAD?

2. There is a moment when Rachael asks herself if she "really want[s] to live like this." What is she realizing?

3. Do you think Rachael recognizes how much her life would change if she wasn't so deep in the obsession? Does her leaving the house without guilt after the binge signal this change?

Mile Markers: Forbidden Food

1. Think about a specific food you were desperately craving but didn't allow yourself to eat. Do you think you ended up eating more of everything else than if you had just given into that food?

2. Consider an alternative to this all-or-nothing approach: You could have a small amount of the "forbidden" food when you crave it and see how you feel. If you often binge on this food, is it possible that you aren't eating enough food overall to feel satisfied after a small amount of this food?

3. Write down other alternatives that might work for you. As always, keep notes about your binges to better understand you and your body.

Chapter 28

More Raw Research

138 POUNDS

I PANICKED WHEN I stepped on the scale. I didn't think it was possible to gain six pounds within one week, especially from *vegan* food, but there it was, staring at me. Only, where could I go from there? I had fallen into the idea that veganism was the only way to keep me thin and immune to stress fractures or bone breaks. If I ate animal protein, the vegan advocates told me that my body would become "acidic" and break down with disease and injury. If I drank milk, it would do more damage to my bones than good. Cooked food and too many calories even from fruit would make me get fat, but just eating vegetables wasn't enough to keep me from bingeing.

I continued to feel sick when I tried to force down any fruit. Hopelessness replaced the guilt I usually felt, so I began eating more cooked potatoes and cooked vegetables.

I still tried to eat as much fruit as I could tolerate. And as I continued, I grew weary of the very act of eating. I felt like I could never feel satisfied, could never feel full.

» » »

Late one night, I ate grapes in bed as I searched through old forum posts on the 30BAD website. I wanted to find any cases where weight gain never reversed itself, where the 30BAD member never lost the weight.

A post like this was rare because 30BAD banned any member who disagreed with them about anything, especially if the member claimed too much fruit caused fat gain.

I did find one member who had not been banned, a high school kid, actually. He had gained the weight while playing basketball for his school. He even posted pictures showing his body before and during the diet. In the first he sported a defined, washboard-ab stomach. In the second, he was bloated, the lines of muscles nearly invisible.

The boy talked about how his dreams of doing well in basketball faded because he felt heavy and lethargic. But he also said that, with fruitarianism, there was light at the end of the tunnel if he just kept at it.

One member wrote a response:

> *Thank you for writing such an honest account of your journey thus far! I really feel what you're saying here, because I'm in the same boat. I'm experiencing benefits in terms of how I feel, but my athletic performance hasn't improved. I've gained a crazy amount of weight (30+ lbs) in about six months, and I'm the slowest I've been since I took up running years ago. You're right; it's tough! How do we reconcile a drop in performance when we're making lifestyle changes in the name of health?*

I pushed my bag of grapes away, horrified.

I don't want to wait that long and run slower!

Images began forming in my mind, images I had had for weeks at that point: gaining a ton of weight and running slower for the next two years, and finally dropping it with the "whoosh" members told me about, just in time for an outstanding senior year of college where I would prove to everyone what a great diet it was, what a great runner I could be by just eating fruit.

But this image faded fast. What if the weight *never* came off?

Food for Thought

1. Rachael originally went into this raw food diet to feel full on as few calories as possible and because she wanted to eat more. Do you think this diet is fulfilling her wishes at all?

2. Rachael has the hope that even if she does gain weight from this 30BAD diet, she will prove to everyone by her senior year that it was all worth it because it will "whoosh" off her body. What are your feelings on this promise by the 30BAD community?

3. The moment of realization in the previous chapter turns to "hopelessness" in this chapter. Why do you think Rachael may be feeling this?

Mile Markers: The Downfall of Extremes

1. "Just eating vegetables wasn't enough to keep me from bingeing," Rachael writes. When she started it, Rachael thought that the raw food diet gave her an excuse to eat mostly just raw vegetables, but she now comes to a point where she realizes it has just put her in a worse place than when she was also eating carbs, protein, and fat. Even though vegetables may be the lowest-calorie, highest-fiber food, eating nothing else has created cravings that lead to bingeing. Suddenly, eating at all has become a nightmare. Think about the consequences of extremes in any part of your life.

2. Write down an extreme decision you have made and how it might have negatively affected you when you originally thought it would increase your happiness or success.

3. Extremes can also lead us to succeeding magnificently, although with extreme discipline and sacrifices to get and stay there. Write down an extreme decision you have made that resulted in success. What discipline and sacrifices were required? Was it worth it?

Chapter 29

Rawchael Relinquishes

141 POUNDS

I FOUND THAT MORE and more women like me on the 30BAD website were confessing that they gained weight on the fruit diet and then apologizing for fear of being banned for speaking ill of 30BAD.

Sure enough, someone decided to take a stand against all the so-called complaining.

"Why are women always bleating about their weight?" a male member had asked. "Shouldn't health matter the most? You just need to accept your bodies the way they are. I'm tired of reading all the complaints."

I was furious at the scolding! He was right about one thing. The women were complaining a lot more about weight gain on the website recently, and with good reason. The more I searched 30BAD, the more stories I found of women asking some hard questions. They were plumping up and wanted to know why. Other members offered support and love in their comments below the posts and, of course, continued to encourage these "complainers" to pursue the diet.

"You just have to trust the lifestyle, and your time will come!" they'd say.

Of course, it was easier for those who succeeded on the diet to tell those suffering to accept the diet for all it was worth.

"My time never came," one member had privately messaged me. "I am a runner, too."

My heart dropped looking at her photos. Durianrider even had enough gall to comment below one photo, "Heaps of fat, you say? Far from it!"

She *was* fat though; Durianrider had to see that. He either refused to acknowledge it, or he just didn't want *her* to think she had gained weight. But this woman told me how she was running slower and had to buy bigger clothes.

In her photo, I could see her squat stature and her thick legs as she ran on a trail through the woods.

"I just don't know if I can trust the diet anymore," she had told me in our message exchanges. "I've been on it for a year, and the weight keeps climbing."

A year?

"When I cut my calories down, I lose a little weight, but I have never felt so ravenous in my life. And the cravings for cooked food come back. It's like there's no way out."

After reading this woman's story, I realized I had to speak up on the website. I didn't want to be banned since part of me still hoped the diet would work for me in the future, but my outrage had mounted to its breaking point with that post about complaining women.

"It's easy for you, as a male who is not gaining, but losing weight, to say this," I typed in response. "You have no idea what we've been through. We were told by Freelee and Durianrider that we would lose weight, and that is not happening, so we have every reason to feel dissatisfied with the body fat and skeptical about the diet."

Durianrider then claimed that any woman who complained about a few extra pounds had been anorexic. Of course, this wasn't true in clinical terms for everyone, but I believe his point was that we had too much focus on the size of our bodies due to past food restriction or purging. I was just insulted that he had somehow tricked us into fruitarianism by having Freelee promise we would lose weight, only to tell us not to be upset now if we didn't.

Fruitarianism wore me down emotionally. I didn't want to eat all day. I didn't want to gain weight. I didn't want to lug around fruit anymore, worried that I would crave cooked food if I didn't have any fruit with me. I didn't want any of it, and I realized it had taken over my life.

I cannot go on this way.

In fact, fears about fruitarianism had simply replaced fears about food.

How will I get enough fruit?

What if I binge without enough fruit?

The obsession with food did not go away with raw food. If anything, it intensified.

» » »

At the end of January, I went with my friend Sharon and her boyfriend to a dance hosted by their college. After twenty minutes of dancing, Sharon could tell something was wrong.

"Are you alright, Rach?" she asked, pulling me to the side when we went to grab some water.

I nodded, but I felt tears rush to my eyes. I had felt much better now that I was with friends, but I still could not silence those thoughts: *food, calories.* As people took pictures of us in our dresses, I was sure that the old friends who hadn't seen me in months would shake their heads. *Is Rachael a little chubby*? Would I hate to see these pictures later? Would they stand as an accusation next to those from a year before? Was everyone wondering what had happened to me, just like my teammates wondered when they saw me at that first indoor track meet?

But an hour into the night, after talking with Sharon and avoiding the topic altogether, something shifted. Whether it was the music or the dancing or the room full of carefree people, I suddenly realized the true Rachael could be in control. Not Rawchael, but *Rachael.*

It was simple, really. There was no one telling me I *had* to eat only fruit. If I felt deep down that I didn't want to keep on, that I would know how to lose the weight again my own way, then I could do it. I mean, hadn't I lost it all by myself with cooked food in the first place? I had a choice.

I had a choice.

I told Sharon that it had been a tough semester so far, especially with the knee injury that past fall. She gave me a hug. Even though I hadn't revealed much to her, it helped to have a friend notice that I just wasn't doing well.

When we headed back into the ballroom with Lady Gaga's "Bad Romance" blasting, we put our hands in the air, tilted our hips back and forth to the beat, and laughed together. As one song changed to the next, I realized the enormity of the change I was considering. I would no longer be a fruitarian. Heck, I would no longer be a raw foodist. By choosing to avoid 30BAD altogether, I would step away from all I had researched and come to know so well in the past few months. I would be unbuckling my safety belt.

I'm free now.

I tried to think it through as rationally as I could.

Fruit doesn't keep you full.

But what if it is the best option for your body like they say?

You keep bingeing, and these cravings feel awful.

But what if you just need a little more time to get past the cravings?

What if you risk the rest of your college running career?

I realized that I could allow myself to eat cooked food again, because I was the one in control of my life.

I had a choice.

Food for Thought

1. Things are moving fast now, and Rachael is thinking about a big change in her eating. What do you see happening next for her?

2. Rachael is leaving the raw food diet more for weight loss now rather than because she thinks it's healthiest. What does this signal to you in her journey?

3. A 30BAD member writes, "When I cut my calories down, I lose a little weight, but I have never felt so ravenous in my life. And the cravings for cooked food come back. It's like there's no way out." Why do you think she feels like there is "no way out" when she could just go back to cooked food? Why might this be so difficult to do? Do you think there is some brainwashing involved?

Mile Markers: Fear of Change

1. Rachael is going through a process that includes recognition and hopelessness, and now she is taking action to change things. Think about a time you may have experienced something similar to this after a diet or time of confusion and frustration.

2. Write about how change can be both invigorating and difficult.

3. Write about a time you felt that you had a choice at last. Did a specific event or person help you to believe you were the one in control of your life?

Chapter 30

Bananas and Banishment

*"Sometimes it's good to learn how to be a little bad.
It's called getting real."*

~Dr. Kelly Brownell

"YOU HAVE BEEN SUSPENDED from 30 Bananas a Day! Sorry, you cannot access 30 Bananas a Day! as you have been suspended. If you think you've been suspended in error, you can contact the administrator."

I stared at those words on the bright screen of my laptop and felt a jolt in the pit of my stomach.

Banned. I had been banned. I knew it shouldn't have mattered anymore since I had already decided to stop the fruity diet, but I at least wanted to stay connected to the community. Part of me wondered if I was really ready to leave it all. Banishment just seemed so harsh, so *final*. And me, of all people—health nut, Veggie Queen, wannabe nutritionist. *Banned?* I felt like I had broken some rule or failed a class. Did this make me a bad person?

Looking back, I believe Durianrider and the other male members were right on many counts, that health was supposed to be the ultimate goal and that our bodies had to adjust to allow us to eat so much again. But Durianrider always seemed to turn things around and trick us into sticking with the cultish banana group despite *any* reservations from the members.

And there *were* people who thrived on the diet. Why wouldn't Freelee promote something that helped her to drop forty pounds? Why wouldn't she shout to the rooftops about a plan that allowed her to eat as much as she desired and not get fat? It worked for her. And that was the thing; it worked very well for some of these people. Whether that will be true in five or ten years, I do not know, but if I learned anything from this group, it was to be aware of what you put into your body and to increase the intake of whole food carbs.

Maybe I *didn't* try the diet long enough. Maybe I had done parts of it "wrong." But I knew from that moment on that I couldn't live in the yo-yoing world, didn't want to deal with cravings and worrying about having the "right" food at all times.

I did find other raw vegan websites that were more open to outside opinions, which helped ease me out of the fruitarian diet because I didn't feel ready to just jump back into any and all cooked food. I still felt I needed to follow purist food thinking, and online groups like "80/10/10 Vegan" helped me do that.

On these sites, many people spoke out about 30BAD. Finally, they had free reign to do it.

"I began gaining too much weight and finally figured it out. I was simply eating too many calories."

"Durianrider offered a ten-thousand-dollar reward for a fat fruitarian, and he wouldn't hand it over. I was proof of it, but he kept accusing me of bingeing on burgers."

One woman I met on the site was named Heather.

Heather was an ex-member of the 30BAD website and had started a blog about going on a thirty-day Paleo diet trial (a diet of mostly meat, vegetables, and fats, based on what early humans supposedly ate) after eating vegan for a year and exploring raw veganism. She had gained weight on 80/10/10, but continued to pursue the diet with the encouragement of the 30BAD members. Heather wasn't obese, but she certainly had some padding, a padding that never came off on this diet, and her supposed "detox" symptoms never waned.

I had heard Durianrider mention the Paleo diet dozens of times in his YouTube videos, chastising such eaters as fat and ignorant.

"How could you call eating animal carcasses healthy with all that fat clogging your arteries?" he'd say.

Paleo was not as bad for Heather as she had thought it might be when she had been vegan. But while it did help her to feel better, it was not a lifesaver. Heather decided to return to drinking green smoothies, a staple from the raw food diet, while still eating a meat-heavy meal for dinner.

I read over Heather's online Paleo trial reports with a mixture of fascination and horror. After being bombarded by colorful pictures of bright fruit for so long, it was a shock to see a large chunk of brown meat and fatty mayo dominating a salad in nearly every photograph. In all honesty, the "purity" thinking of raw veganism made any type of meat look too gross to eat. However, the more I viewed the photographs, the less awful they looked. Heather had crossed the parameter I had set in my mind for so long now, the belief that there really might be a perfect way to eat. Her experiment started to convince me that whether you advocated low fat fruitarianism or high fat paleo, there were going to be success stories at either extreme. There were also going to be people for whom certain diets just weren't a fit. They weren't failures. Maybe, just maybe, some creative mix was best; maybe "pure" wasn't always necessary, maybe it was possible to loosen up and enjoy food and even life.

Heather wrote that fat would satisfy me. Was my lack of dietary fat why I felt hungry so often and why I had binged so much? Was dietary fat really as bad as many of the 80/10/10 members made it out to be?

"I may just add a little more fat to my diet in the form of nuts and seeds," I told the outside raw vegan website members. It would take some time to get rid of all the brainwashing I had been through.

As I walked to my Humanities class the next day thinking about my new "banned" status, my sadness suddenly turned to a feeling of empowerment. I had lost both the community and my faith in the diet, but I felt like a *maverick,* not just for deciding against this popular, controversial diet, but for standing up for myself and finding a way to break free on my own terms. As uneasy and foreign as it felt to suddenly be Rebellious Rachael, the spark ignited something special, and I loved myself for that.

Food for Thought

1. What does Rachael's banishment from the 30BAD community reveal about how Rachael has changed?

2. Based on Rachael's experience here, why might telling someone to "just recover," "just move on," or "just eat balanced" not help someone to recover? What must often happen for those with eating disorders to change their ways?

3. Why do you think it is so difficult for Rachael to accept banishment even though this change is probably good? How does it make her different from the Rachael who tries to please everyone?

Mile Markers: Empowerment

1. Rachael has decided to relax her strict, "purist" approach to food and try for something more balanced. This decision makes her feel like a rebel and a maverick. On the face of it, this really doesn't seem like such a radical move. Why do you think it's such a big deal for Rachael, and can you identify a situation in which a moderate change made you feel "empowered"?

2. Reread the quote at the beginning of the chapter by Dr. Kelly Brownell: "Sometimes it's good to learn how to be a little bad. It's called getting real." Why might this be especially important for a perfectionist? In what ways is perfectionism not "real," and why can "getting real" improve one's life?

3. Write down ways in which you can step outside your comfort zone and consider trying something new. Even if these aren't "crazy" moves based on other peoples' perceptions, congratulate yourself on these small courageous steps.

Chapter 31

Not-So-"Egg"-cellent Changes

139 POUNDS

"I DON'T KNOW HOW I'm going to do it," I said to my mom over the phone, my voice shaking. "I think I have to eat eggs again."

My mom, now that she had taken a step onto the vegan bandwagon herself (though not too strictly, as she loved going out to dinner with my dad and ordering whatever sounded good), seemed to find it strange that I had decided to start with eggs.

"Why do you feel like you have to do that?" she asked. "What about them being chicken ovaries?"

I remembered our past discussion about this, about how disgusting eggs were if you really thought about where they came from. But now I told her that if I was going to try to lose any weight again, I had to eat more protein to feel full (making it easier to eat less), and eggs seemed like one of the best options. Beans, I found out, were more carb than protein, so they didn't quite fit into the new equation.

"I just can't feel full on beans," I told her. "And I will *just* eat eggs for protein anyway. I can't imagine eating actual *meat.*"

I started going to the cafeteria again, now that I planned to try a wider variety of food. After a normal easy run at practice, I entered the cafeteria with Jessica and Catie, set down my belongings at the large round table with the familiar crew, and walked to the buffet.

You can take the eggs now.

I grabbed the same small black bowl I had used for legumes a few days before and poured in chopped hard-boiled eggs from the salad bar.

Chicken ovaries.

Next, I grabbed a large salad plate and poured beans and steamed vegetables over the lettuce. I sat down with my new dinner, looking around at other plates filled with roast beef, ranch-covered salad, and macaroni and cheese.

I stared at the eggs.

You have to do this for weight loss.

Even though the eggs made me uneasy, I was thankful for my knowledge of food. It would be a cinch to drop weight *now*.

But I felt self-conscious about the extremes of the past few months, and there was no way to explain what I had learned and been through.

In all honesty, I didn't think most of the team really cared anyway. It's not like I had built strong bonds with anyone; I had been too consumed with my search for nutritional "truth."

They must think I'm a glutton.

They must think I'm a weirdo with food.

I wanted so badly to explain that, when I ate bowl after bowl after bowl of salad, peas, corn, and lettuce and now eggs, I felt enormous. I felt ashamed when they looked at me, a freak, a girl who couldn't seem to control how much food she ate.

Because have you seen her lately? How big she is? She can't stop eating.

This is the monster she has been hiding all along.

Food for Thought

1. "My mom, now that she had taken a step onto the vegan bandwagon herself (though not too strictly, as she loved going out to dinner with my dad and ordering whatever sounded good), seemed to find it strange that I had decided to start with eggs." What does this say about Rachael's mom? Do you think she has an attitude that could lead to an eating disorder? Or is it a healthier way of thinking about food?

2. "I wanted so badly to explain that, when I ate bowl after bowl after bowl of salad, peas, corn, and lettuce and now eggs, I felt enormous. I felt ashamed when they looked at me, a freak, a girl who couldn't seem to control how much food she ate." Why do you think Rachael wants to explain her situation? What feelings may she have now that she is on the "other side"?

3. Rachael also writes how she felt "ashamed" that she looked like "a girl who couldn't seem to control how much food she ate." How do you think society influences this perception she has about her own appearance and food?

Mile Markers: Your Social Life

1. "I didn't think most of the team really cared anyway. It's not like I had built strong bonds with anyone; I had been too consumed with my search for nutritional 'truth.'" Where in your life might have an obsession or addiction taken away from your social life?

2. Brainstorm how you might move away from your obsession. Would this mean working on relationships with your friends and family? Might this mean reaching out for help?

3. What would your life look like without thinking about and obsessing over food, and instead using that time to spend with family and friends? To work towards dreams and goals that doesn't involve your weight or appearance? What do you want out of your life?

Chapter 32

Dog Breath

142 POUNDS

NOW THAT I WAS eating cooked food again, I bought bags and bags of microwavable broccoli from the store and cooked it in the dorm each day for breakfast, lunch, and dinner.

"Ewww, what is that awful smell!?" I would hear girls say from the hallway. "Is it from the trash?"

"It smells like barf," another girl would say.

I knew it was my broccoli. I knew, as Elizabeth even put it when she came over to watch *America's Next Top Model,* that it smelled like "dog breath." But I could not stop eating this broccoli, even at the expense of the dorm mates.

Broccoli would help keep my calories low.

I wonder even now how my roommates stood it. The only subtle hint I noticed was the way they increasingly began to prop the door open in order to get that "dog breath" smell out into the hallway as winter turned into spring.

» » »

I returned to school after spring break to discover I'd earned only an average grade on my mid-term exam in Nineteenth Century American Literature.

"I was surprised by your exam," Professor Dawson said when we met. "After all you've contributed in class, it didn't seem to capture the 'real' Rachael."

A "B" was not terrible, but I knew Dr. Dawson was right. I knew I had not put in my best effort the night of that exam.

Food had taken over again.

I had gone to the cafeteria and binged—carrots and peas and potatoes all over my salad. Just like before, I couldn't feel full.

A track friend sat down next to me, took one look at my plate, and said, "You sure eat healthy!"

I smiled and nodded. Healthy? Stuffing myself with food was not the epitome of health. I had eaten way beyond my calorie limit!

On the way out of the cafeteria, I emptied my water bottle and filled it with diet Pepsi from one of the machines. I never drank pop. But I hoped the artificial sweetener would stop the cravings without adding more calories, hoped the caffeine would help me focus and the carbonation would fill my stomach, because apparently food wouldn't.

I had to get through my three-hour exam that night without thinking about food.

And when I faced the questions, when I looked at the pile of books I had read stacked next to me in that exam room, my heart thumped madly in my chest, and I felt panic rise in my throat. My hand was shaking from caffeine and nerves, and I couldn't think clearly or write fast enough.

Why did you have to eat so much today?

Why can't you eat like normal people?

Meanwhile, Dr. Dawson set down Hershey Kisses next to everyone for what she called an "energy boost."

Dr. Dawson might have been disappointed with my performance, but I was grateful I had at least scraped through with a B.

"What happened?" she asked me.

The sun was shining through the large window behind her; her face was gentle, her eyes soft. There was no way I could explain. I had studied and loved the literature, had loved her class, and yet . . . and yet, my concentration blurred as I struggled to find myself through food.

"I guess I was just overwhelmed and unsure what to expect on that first exam." I willed myself to hold back tears. "I think I will do much better on the final."

» » »

I left Dr. Dawson's office wondering who I had become that year. Rachael the runner. Rachael the encourager. Rachael the All-American. Rachael the raw foodist. Rachael the injured. Rachael the fruitarian. Suddenly, instead of being defined by running, I was defined by food, by what and how I ate. And what and how I ate determined whether I was "good" or "bad."

I was always trying to become the ideal Rachael so that everything would fit into place, so that I could leave my mark on the world. I had wanted to make straight As. I had longed to be on top in the running world because that's what I had grown up knowing success to be, and no one could be as passionate and strong in running as *I* could.

And now, no one could be as disciplined and passionate about food.

And these two passions had complemented each other, at least for a year. Food and running, the perfect formula to make me the best athlete out there! It was meant to be, as if God had given me the ultimate gift. And I had thrown it away with a yearlong binge? Just as I believed that if I broke every record and earned every accolade, I could rest easy on my reputation as a runner, I was now convinced that exactly the right way of eating would guarantee peace of mind.

Running and food could speak *for* me.

I wanted to be remembered as stable, reliable, perfect Rachael who had done everything right. I didn't want a process. I just wanted to *be* the ultimate Rachael so that I could live the rest of my life as *that* Rachael and succeed in everything.

But as I searched for food perfection, and as I gained weight, I began to realize that the race for perfection in anything was the path to destruction.

Food for Thought

1. Rachael's eating disorder has not only affected her "perfect" running life, but now her "perfect" grades in school. How does this need for perfection create more chaos than if Rachael didn't try so hard to be "perfect"?

2. Rachael writes that "[r]unning and food could speak *for* me." In what ways has this voice broken her? In what ways has it allowed her to cope with life? What is her newer and probably better mode of "speaking"?

3. What do you think Rachael means when she says that the attempt to be perfect leads to "destruction"? Do you agree?

Mile Markers: Perfectionism

1. Write about your own experience of trying to be perfect in some area of your life.

2. Why might it be difficult to forge relationships with a perfectionist? Besides the work it takes to try to be perfect, what else might be a downfall to perfectionism?

3. Take the chance to try something you're not very good at. How do you feel making mistakes in this new activity? Encourage yourself to be satisfied with not achieving "perfection" in everything you do. Find success in trying and "failing" because of what it took to just try it.

Chapter 33

The Confession

I FINISHED THE SCHOOL year with *As* in all my classes, and I ran a decent track season as I worked myself back into shape. I was not as fast as the year before, which my peers and Woj attributed to the knee injury.

I knew it was the weight.

I had to lose it.

The Sunday after classes ended, I met up with Alina for a thirteen-mile run downtown. We started at the new house she shared with our friends Elizabeth and Jamie. I had dubbed the house the "Sherman Shire," after the street they lived on, Sherman, and because the cozy structure made it feel like a home from the Shire in *The Lord of the Rings*.

Alina and I wound through the neighborhoods toward downtown, chatting about Alina's 10k race from a few nights before. We finally reached the downtown streets, free of traffic on a Sunday morning, and crossed the bridge over the Grand River to run along the water on the other side.

When we arrived at the next bridge to work our way back towards the Sherman Shire, somehow the topic of my knee injury came up. I allowed this conversation to segue into my appearance, specifically, the weight gain.

"You look stronger," Alina said.

Stronger. It sounded like Woj when he referred to the "meat" on my legs that past winter.

I wanted to roll my eyes. But the ache, the yearning to speak prompted me to say more. Would this be the right time, the right place, the right person? Would it really even matter if Alina knew?

Do it.

We jogged further down the neighborhood street.

"I'm going to be honest . . . I'm very uncomfortable with the weight I've gained this year."

I held my breath, ashamed.

"What do you mean?" Alina asked.

I exhaled and breathed in.

"I mean, gaining this weight hurt; it was not intentional, not what I had wanted even though I acted like it was fine. I hated it, hated everything about it. I was out of control."

"Out of control?"

"I binged."

I described the conflict in high school when I had started counting calories, discovered "clean" food, and resolved to lose weight . . . and before I knew it, everything spilled out of my mouth: the obsession with the nutritional research, the need to feel normal about food. I told her how I hated the counting and obsessing and fear.

The great part about running is that you don't have to look at someone while you talk. They don't have to see that you are about to cry, at least not until they hear that your breathing is off, that you are gasping between sobs.

"The extra weight has been slowing me down, and I know it," I said. I couldn't stop; I was going tell her exactly how it was, how I felt about everything.

"But do you think raw food helped you?" she asked.

Did it help me?

Maybe it did.

I wasn't sure how to answer because I never went completely raw long enough, but the attempt led to the binges and thus the weight gain, weight, I now admit, I did need to gain. The raw food diet relieved me of all those attempts to restrict food. And heck, 30BAD delivered my wake-up call: I had a terrible relationship with food.

"I went into the raw food diet to lose more weight," I admitted. "Raw food did help me, but it also hurt me."

Alina glanced over at me. "I'm so sorry you went through this," she said. "And now *I'm* going to be honest; you do look bigger. But strong, Rachael. You look strong."

"I hate it."

"But most people were worried about you for a while."

"Worried? Why?"

"You were too thin."

In Alina's neighborhood the streets looked unfamiliar. I had become so engrossed in what I was saying that the trees had whizzed by, unnoticed. I was only thinking about what I needed to explain, what I wanted to tell her, because I didn't know if I could ever speak about it again.

We finished our run at the Sherman Shire and stretched on the porch. We talked more about food, but it felt awkward now that we were no longer running. Fat Rachael stood before Alina, visible and vulnerable, her thighs touching, extra skin creeping over her shorts line. I was looking at Alina, but all I could see was what *I* must have looked like to *her*.

» » »

My eating-disordered mind still needed work, but surely talking to Alina was a big step. I wondered, too, if this was the end of it, if I had finally been released from the longing for a perfect diet. I did believe that after all I had learned about the raw food diet, I could lose the weight again and make my way back.

And with Alina's encouragement, I convinced myself that it was fine to eat differently each day, that the caloric needs of my body would vary. If I felt hungrier one day than another, it was nothing to panic about. I also realized that daily fluctuations on the scale could reflect shifts in water, in muscle, and in the amount of food in the stomach.

However, as much as I believed I would listen to my body again, the rules were deeply ingrained. I couldn't allow myself to begin eating each day until I felt hungry enough to eat plain, raw vegetables like lettuce, cucumbers, tomatoes, and bell peppers. I chopped these up each evening before bed so that they would be available in the refrigerator for breakfast. That way, I wouldn't mess up anything by eating something as delicious and tantalizing as whole eggs on toast or pancakes and maple syrup.

Food for Thought

1. Rachael finds it easier to confess to Alina because they are running. How do you think this activity makes it an easier transition to speak?

2. Rachael doesn't like the word "stronger" for her heavier body. In what ways are eating disorders encouraging the "beauty" of weakness? In what ways does society control women's bodies through this ideal of thin bodies?

3. Why do you think it's so difficult for Rachael to just pull herself out of the eating disorder after talking with Alina? Why won't just talking about it fix Rachael's problems?

Mile Markers: Speaking Up

1. What are your fears about opening up? What are the benefits in doing so?

2. You've had some time now to consider who you might talk to about your eating disorder or addiction. Send your email, letter, or note to the person you're willing to confess to, or arrange a time to sit down with this person to talk.

3. Prepare yourself if this person doesn't react in the way you might have hoped. Know that there are other people you can choose. Consider looking for a support group in your area.

Chapter 34

The Paleo Plan

140 POUNDS

I BEGAN TO EAT meat.

It happened when I looked further into the Paleo diet. I had gradually worked canned fish into my list of foods to eat along with eggs, but the Paleo diet convinced me that any and all meat would be acceptable, too. In fact, I learned the health benefits of incorporating grass-fed, free-range meat, and the concepts of Paleo were closely tied to that of raw food in that it encouraged the removal of dairy and grains, as well as eating whole, unprocessed food.

But legumes were out, too, which I found surprising. And if you wanted extreme, tried-and-true weight loss, you took out fruit, potatoes, and rice.

Translation: you took out *carbs*.

Now there was more to learn again, more secrets about food, ways to lose weight, how to do Paleo *properly*. I started adding the occasional chicken and turkey to my weekly menu, and after re-reading the blog entries of Heather-the-vegan-gone-Paleo, I felt fully convinced that Paleo could work for me.

I just wouldn't eat all the fat that came with it.

The new diet made sense to me. I would be filling myself up with satiating protein and so was bound to lose weight. And just like 30BAD, Paleo wasn't about restricting calories.

"Eat an abundance of Paleo foods and still lose weight!"

And then I decided to tell my dad that I was eating meat again.

"Good for you!" he said, giving me a high-five. He broke out in a victorious smile, which sent a twinge of annoyance through me. I didn't want him to think I agreed with everything he seemed to think about with food, that moderation was the key, because I still had rules, still had "good" and "bad" foods. I did not suddenly believe I could eat anything and everything.

"Yeah," I said, determined to show my dad that I had learned a lot through the so-called raw food experiment.

"After researching everything with veganism and fruit, I've decided that it's good to have a little more protein here and there. I'm not going to eat any processed food, but I feel like, after learning that cooking essentially made us human, meat is what we were meant to consume. And anyway, the 30 Bananas a Day diet encouraged everyone to stuff in as much fruit as possible."

"Yeah, that's ridiculous," my dad said, shaking his head.

That word, *ridiculous*, made me swell with anger. Because, sure, it sounded ridiculous now, but if my dad had ever experienced the frame of mind of someone facing a problem with no apparent solution and had then seen exactly what the 30BAD members had said, that eating that much fruit was supposed to prevent a binge, he would get it! I didn't believe myself to be the fool he must have thought I was, that I just believed whatever diet offered a plan that allowed me to stuff myself silly and then wonder why I gained weight. Besides, piling in the fruit *did* help to prevent some cooked food binges.

"I know I've gained a little weight," I admitted to my dad at last as we stood there together in the kitchen. I felt as if I were balancing on a tightrope as I said this. My mom hadn't told my dad about my eating disorder, and I sure as hell wasn't about to say anything about it.

"How long do you think it'll take you to lose the weight?" my dad asked.

"Well, I'm hoping in about a month," I said.

"That's pretty fast . . ."

Was it? Hadn't I done it before, though?

I shrugged. We fell silent.

"Would you be able to help me cook chicken for dinner tonight?" I asked. "So that I can learn how?"

He was obviously relieved and delivered his "of course" with genuine enthusiasm. A few hours later, we took a trip to the grocery store so I could learn what to look for when I bought chicken. I hardly even knew how to find the meat department, let alone how many varieties there were or what part of the chicken to buy.

Unfortunately, I didn't see any chicken that would meet Paleo qualifications.

"We should buy free-range, cage-free chickens," I said, looking at the breasts, thighs, and legs of the slippery, tan lumps covered in Saran Wrap. I picked up a package of chicken breasts.

"Organic," I read. "Do you think we should get these?"

"But look at the price!"

I paused.

"But Dad, the health benefits are worth the price."

"Does it taste better?"

"I'd think so . . . but I don't know."

"Look, if we get three packages of the organic, then we're spending way more than the price of the regular chicken," he said.

This was going to be tougher than I had thought.

He gave me a quick look, then picked up the caged, farmed, corn-fed, sorry-sad chicken breasts from the fridge and laid them in the cart. It was clearly not my day to win the battle, and I decided I would have to go to the Farmer's Market to buy what I needed. Besides, it didn't look like Meijer, our local supermarket, had the quality meat I wanted anyway.

» » »

When we had unloaded the groceries at home, I pulled out a Paleo recipe that called for a marinade of lemon, orange juice, tarragon, and thyme. We unwrapped and soaked the chicken in it for an hour before starting the grill.

"Now we cook these on each side for ten minutes," my dad said, showing me how to turn on the gas. He had set the plate of raw chicken on the picnic table, the green tarragon sauce decorating the pink breasts. He grabbed the tongs to demonstrate how to place the chicken on the grill, but not before advising me to "put some oil" on the meat.

I shook my head.

No. Calories.

"Look, Rachael, if you don't add the oil, they're going to stick to the grill."

"No, they won't. They'll be fine," I said. I didn't feel very confident since I had never cooked chicken on the grill in my life, but I wanted to prove to my dad that it would still have plenty of flavor and fewer calories without the oil. It was the same routine we had gone through when I began to hover over him years earlier at my lowest weight. I had always watched to make sure we only used a tablespoon of oil and berated him when he added more salad dressing to the asparagus (I remember I started crying about the dressing).

This evening, when we took the chicken off the grill, one of the breasts did hang on. My dad struggled to pry it off in fuming silence while I stood next to him, heat rising to my face and the silent screams of *"it'll come off, it'll come off"* ringing through my head.

Knowing there were fewer calories made the awkward moment bearable.

My mom, dad, and I sat down at the table together for dinner that night, chewing through the tough protein.

"It's delicious!" my mom raved. It galled me that she enjoyed a healthy dinner this much. I wanted to like it more than she did, just so I could show how much more discipline and power I had. My dad, meanwhile, remained quiet for the most part as we cut through the bland meat. He did congratulate me on cooking meat for the first time, but he didn't seem impressed with what we had made, and looking back now, I wouldn't have felt too thrilled, either. The chicken wasn't very good.

But I fell in love with the Paleo recipes because of how little fat some of them had and how low-calorie they were. The monotony in such low-fat cuts of meat meant fewer calories and more discipline, and I reveled in the thought that I could keep eating this way without any cravings or problems. I thought I could go low-carb for maximum weight loss as well and thus *reduce* any sugar cravings.

I could stop the bingeing.

» » »

Eating wasn't the only way meat became the focus in my life. Like Woj's comment about the "meat" on my legs, Mrs. Wilson, a family friend, lovingly grabbed my arm one day that summer and said, "Good, you've got some meat on you now!" She said it with a smile, as if this were a good thing, as if I needed to gain the weight.

I felt heat rise in my face.

How fat do I look to people? What makes me skinny or fat? How am I supposed to know, how am I supposed to see the difference, when 124 pounds used to feel too heavy for me?

Was I failing if I allowed myself to appreciate these comments, if I tried to convince myself that this was "acceptable" when I felt deep down it wasn't? Mrs. Wilson's words were a kind gesture and eased the ache when I looked in the mirror. But I also heard, *She's saying you're fat now.*

» » »

I spent hours in my room researching Paleo that summer. I could barely sleep at night as I dove into this new realm of food, as I flipped through the various Paleo books from the library, searching for what I thought was the final answer to end my obsession with food.

Just a few more pages. Just hang in there a little longer.

I powered through book after book, taking notes, trying to absorb as much as possible. Even if my body felt tired enough to doze off, the thoughts would keep me awake, and I would have to turn the light back on to hit the books.

» » »

My next challenge, after cooking chicken and fish, was to cook a steak.

For this experiment, I kept to the confines of the kitchen

since the grill outside seemed too daunting on my own. I wanted to use YouTube as my guide, and it was easier to set my laptop on the kitchen counter for optimal viewing.

I began with a video called "How to Cook a Steak, With Jamie Oliver's Mate Pete" (Jamie Oliver, 2010). I watched as Pete, the main man of the video, held the soft, pink meat in his hands, placed it on a plate, and fluttered salt like snow over it. He made that raw hunk of meat look appetizing even before it was cooked, thanks to his fancy flourishing.

I finally mustered up enough guts to grab my own squishy steak from its container. It was not free-range or grass-fed. But I figured that lower-quality meat would work for a trial run.

I removed the steak from the Saran Wrap and slapped it on the plate before sprinkling a "generous amount of pepper" as Pete instructed. Turning on the stove, I set down the pan with a clang and waited for the coconut-oil spray to jump like dancing droplets on the surface.

The moment arrived to throw the steak on the stove. Steam rose from the hot pan. I stood back, wary of the sizzling oil.

And I tossed it; I tossed the hunk of meat and heard it hiss on the hot metal. I covered the pan and realized I didn't know how long it was supposed to cook. Three minutes? Four? What was it that Pete had advised?

I started the video again.

"An undercooked steak is better than an overcooked steak," I recalled my dad's words from years ago. After all, you could just put an undercooked steak back on the pan.

After three minutes I flipped the steak with the tongs. Three minutes later, I turned off the stove and lifted the lid.

It looked promising. Reaching for the tongs again, I grabbed the steak and set it on a small plate; the video said "ten minutes."

The "finger test" required grabbing the steak between two fingers to determine firmness.

Still a tad squishy.

But was it too squishy? Not squishy enough?

What if I end up eating raw steak?

I Googled images of steaks, medium, medium rare, overcooked. I finally sliced open my masterpiece and compared it to the Googled images. I looked at the screen, back at the steak, and back at the screen. Finally, I held up the dripping, oozing steak right next to the laptop for the final test.

Medium-rare. Definitely medium-rare.

Perfect.

Slicing into the steak that night felt like a celebration, as if I had created a work of art. I felt proud that I had not only accomplished such a foreign feat, but that I had done it alone.

And then, as I finished my meal and cleared the table, the voice kicked in:

How many calories?

It hissed, and I felt a lurch in my stomach.

It shouldn't matter; it's Paleo. It's protein. It's filling.

But it does *matter, and you know it.*

I looked up the calorie count for a large steak on cronometer.com and panicked.

1000 calories!

You're just testing this out, and you needed this experience.

But 1000 calories? I thought I was supposed to feel full sooner!

And then the 85 percent dark chocolate called to me.

You aren't supposed to want that. You should feel full now like a normal person!

Moments later, I bit into the bitter chocolate, my taste buds singing with relief. And before I knew it, I was halfway through the bar.

Put it back.

I did.

Have a little more.

I grabbed it again.

I raced through the rest of that chocolate so fast that I didn't notice the nausea until I had finished the entire bar. I sat with an empty wrapper in front of me and wondered how many more times I would have to endure this self-inflicted torment. I wanted so badly to look into my body, to pull apart these chinks and broken pieces, to ask it why it wanted the "wrong" food so badly, why it wouldn't cooperate with me.

Do you really want to run with all this extra weight, body?

I yearned to understand myself, to fix the shattered parts inside me.

How can we come to a truce, body? How can I get us out of this?

Why do I keep bingeing?

I thought that focusing on macronutrients would fix all my hunger and bingeing problems, but no matter what diet I tried, I was always bingeing on something and not feeling satisfied.

A disorder—did I feel qualified to call it this? I kept denying it, because didn't I just overthink things? After all, I was not hooked up to an IV, mere skin and bones. This obsession and worry were hidden deeper, which scared me even more. I was left to confront my own mind, to look Rachael in the face each time I sat down to eat. No one could see the thoughts when the body looked normal to them. The voice wanted it to just be the two of us. It wanted to hide. If no one saw it, then no one would believe me.

No one would ask.

Food for Thought

1. Mrs. Wilson's comment about the "meat" on Rachael's body now makes Rachael feel uneasy. Why might their perceptions of this comment differ? Think about ways in which others can trigger eating disorder behaviors with comments like this.

2. Rachael talks about the perception society has about eating disorders, that it's often "easy" to see through appearance (like a skeletal body). How does Rachael's eating disorder differ from this view? How might this complicate asking for help when someone is experiencing similar obsessive thoughts about food, but doesn't have the body to "show" for it?

3. Rachael writes, "No one would ask." Do you think she'd rather have people ask about how she's doing in her life than having her make the first step to explain it? Why might it be helpful for others to reach out to her? How would it make her feel?

Mile Markers: Triggers

1. When have peoples' seemingly "innocent" comments hurt you? Why do you think they bothered you more than they would bother most people?

2. Make a list of all the triggers of your eating disorder. Try to come up with 10-15 items that fall into this category.

3. Bring this list to someone close to you who is willing to support your efforts. Be ready to discuss the list with them, as they may not understand why you feel certain ways.

Chapter 35

The Group

"I found that every single successful person I've ever spoken to had a turning point, and the turning point was where they made a clear, specific, unequivocal decision that they were not going to live like this anymore. Some people make that decision at 15, and some people make it at 50, and most never make it at all."

~Brian Tracy

I HADN'T COMMUNICATED WITH my mom much since I had first told her about my problems with food, too ashamed of my bingeing. Why could I not harness the willpower I had exerted getting to my lowest weight? Didn't I want to lose weight just as badly now?

The further I worked through Paleo, the more I realized it would not cure my bingeing.

I needed more help.

I had talked with Alina about food a few other times after that first confessional run, but only when *she* brought it up. I am thankful to this day that she initiated those conversations, because I felt guilty asking for help, just as guilty as when I asked for food. I didn't want to show I wanted or needed *anything*.

I am not needy. I am not that kind of person.

I still had to learn there are some problems that require "needing" in order to be solved. As in, my body needed to regain its proper hormone function.

In the toilet at the end of July, I found:

Blood.

That's strange, I thought.

Wait . . . oh, no.

It had been almost three years since my last period, three long, blissful years because no period meant low body fat and no hassle, of course.

No *need*.

But it had returned. And that blood, more than anything, made the weight gain official, made me a failure. It also forced me to face the reality: I was supposed to be a grown woman. I was not supposed to live in the past, could not keep trying to live as a little girl and achieve all those wonders I wished I had achieved at a younger age.

I stared at the clump of red in the toilet, disgusted and afraid.

» » »

I finally confessed to my mom, through an email, yet again, that I was ready for the help she had offered to get me seven months ago.

A few days later, we drove together to an eating disorder support group.

I cried on the way to the meeting, wondering if I would walk into a room of anorexics and that my problem would be nothing compared to theirs. My food problems didn't seem "bad enough," and I believed I would just have to suffer with this "in-between" disorder.

We arrived, and I entered a small, stuffy room to find a group of about ten women, silent and tense in their seats. I felt relieved to see there were some women my size, if not bigger. There was even a man in the room, sitting next to a woman with curly hair. I took a chair in the corner of the room near them, afraid I would start crying again at any moment.

Don't cry, Rachael. Just do something about this.
Don't be upset. Just take control of your eating.
Be strong, Rachael. Don't let anyone see you're upset.
Just eat two pieces of toast instead of five.

Karen, the leader of the group, looked around and flashed a crooked smile. Her eyes were soft as she said, "I see we have some new people here."

But I was the only one who nodded. Karen continued to smile and asked if I'd like to explain why I had come.

"Um . . . well, my name is Rachael," I began. "I just wanted to check this out."

And before I could stop it, I began to cry. The room stayed dead silent, save for my outburst, and the curly-haired woman handed me a box of tissues.

This is a mistake. I am not supposed to be here.

Wiping my eyes, I found a moment to blurt out my reasons for coming.

"I . . . restricted for a few years, and now I'm eating too much and gaining too much weight. I hate it." The tears ran down my face, and I tried to wipe them away quickly. "I feel like everyone is watching me eat and I'm scared to eat, but I feel out of control."

Everyone was silent before Karen said, "Can anyone else relate to Rachael?"

There was another pause before a young woman spoke up. "I know exactly what you mean about feeling like everyone is watching you eat."

"Yeah." Other women nodded.

"And feeling out of control."

I looked down at my hands, still clenched into fists in my lap.

These hands have ruined me. These hands have taken all the food and put it into my mouth.

They have made me fat.

» » »

When we drove back home that night, I told my mom more, more secrets, more shame. We talked about the hundreds of pages on which I had documented all the food I had eaten, on which I had recorded all the calorie counting, the measuring, the feelings and emotions.

My "raw food journal" now seemed more like the face of the sickness.

Yes, I had an eating disorder. No, it did not include being fed intravenously in the hospital. No, I had not gone down to eighty pounds. No, I was not throwing up my food.

And no, the bingeing was not a lack of discipline after all.

I had restricted. I had binged. And I knew now that I had been too thin at my thinnest, but not *that* thin, not thin enough to be alarming. It was possible to dismiss it. I just looked like a very disciplined runner who found she could run faster at that weight.

But living with the constant thoughts, the obsession? It had taken over my life, my happiness. At this point, I felt all I had to live for was thinness and running fast.

It was self-destructive and life-consuming. And that, more than anything, made it a disorder.

» » »

When we returned home that night, I sat on the steps leading up to my bedroom. I had given my mom permission to tell my dad everything, and I waited to hear what I could of his response.

I have an eating disorder.

I have an eating disorder.

Mom, I don't know if I want you to tell him now . . . Mom, I don't know if he'll believe you . . . I don't know if this is really happening . . . Mom . . .

I heard her talking quietly to my dad as he watched TV. It was difficult to make out exactly what she was telling him over the noise of the baseball game, but I heard "eating disorder," "January," and "group meeting."

"But how has this been happening? Are you sure? Why hasn't she told me?"

I could hear the faint murmurs, the outlines, jagged pieces of words drifting in and out of the fog, as I sat on the steps and cried.

Food for Thought

1. Why do you think it took so long for Rachael to confess to her dad about what's going on?

2. Rachael didn't turn to the support group until she realized she couldn't "fix" herself the way she had hoped (through a certain diet). But Rachael isn't ready to let go of her eating disorder yet; she just wants to stop the bingeing part of it. Why might this not work the way she hopes?

3. "I just looked like a very disciplined runner who found she could run faster at that weight." How might this phrase reveal how tough eating disorders may be to see in sports? What "excuses" may many athletes make to deny an eating disorder?

Mile Markers: Digging up Denial

1. Reread the quote at the beginning of this chapter. Have you found your turning point yet? Or are you still anticipating your turning point?

2. What would happen if you stopped dieting to "fix" your problem? What would that mean for you?

3. Have you attended a support group? What are the pros and cons of doing so? Take a few minutes to look online for a support group in your area and challenge yourself to attend this group in the near future.

Chapter 36

Coach and Confessions

"DO YOU THINK YOU should tell your coach about what's been going on and how you feel?" Jennifer asked.

Jennifer—Jennifer, my therapist.

"Well, yeah, my coach knows what's going on . . . through the online running log we have," I said. Indeed, I had admitted to some of my food issues on the log, but Woj and I never discussed it in person. "But it's not like I reveal a whole lot about it on there."

Jennifer tilted her head. "Do you think it would help to talk to him in person?"

I hesitated. It would be mortifying.

Talk about weight, especially now that I'm fat?

But just as I had revealed my disorder to my mom, I sent Woj an email about what I had been dealing with the past few years and emphasized that I didn't want it to affect how I raced for the upcoming cross country season. I wrote that I was working on things and just needed him to know how much I struggled with food.

Days later, with an invitation from Woj to talk in person, I found myself sitting in his office. I felt exposed as I sat across from him, but at least I had already disclosed the basic facts. I didn't have to try to explain anything unless Woj asked.

As usual, Woj began with some lighthearted talk about how good cross country camp had been the week before and how he thought we were going to have a great team. I agreed, smiling and finally feeling myself relax.

"So the email," he began.

I sank in my seat and looked down into my lap.

"I honestly think you look so much better now," he said. "I look back at those pictures of you as a freshman and just don't see 'healthy.' I think you can accomplish a lot more with this new body. It may take some time, but your health is more important."

I nodded. But I couldn't shake the fear that Woj would now see me differently, even consider me a danger to the team because I might blurt out all this random nutritional information to everyone, because I might encourage them to lose weight to run fast.

After all, once anyone knew the secret, wouldn't they go for it?

As if he had read my thoughts, Woj reminded me about the time I had taken care of his baby daughter. "I trust you with Cecelia!" He seemed to be saying that if he trusted me around Cecelia, he trusted me to be a good influence on the team.

He also reassured me that I was still a good person. He told me that I still mattered, that times were not the important part of being a runner for Aquinas College. No matter what happened in the upcoming season, I would still be the Rachael he had chosen for the team when I had finished first at my high school race, and he told me how much he appreciated that I went back to cheer on the others.

"I'm just scared I won't run as fast as I did my freshman year," I admitted, choking back tears.

Woj looked at me for a moment, his eyes gentle.

"You don't have to."

Food for Thought

1. Again, Rachael writes when she *first* confesses about her eating disorder, this time, to her coach on the online running log. Do you see why it might be difficult for Rachael to talk in person when she thinks, *"Talk about weight, especially now that I'm fat?"*

2. What does Woj emphasize about Rachael that is an important part of her recovery?

3. Rachael didn't have any crazy expectations when she joined the cross country team her freshman year. Why do you think the eating disorder worsened her sophomore year? How much does comparison factor in eating disorders?

Mile Markers: Beyond the Numbers

1. Get a group of friends, and give each person a sheet of paper. Everyone writes their name on this paper.

2. Pass this paper around in the group. Each person can write up to three great qualities about the person who is written on the paper.

3. When everyone gets their papers back, have everyone go around and read their favorite quality about themselves out loud. Focus on one quality each day of the week to emphasize its importance over the number on the scale.

Chapter 37

A New Start

"What cannot be said will be wept. "
~Sappho

MY JUNIOR YEAR OF college began a week later, and I felt excited about training and racing with the team. It was my chance to start over after the madness of the year before, and I felt sure I would recover quickly from the eating disorder since I thought my situation was minor.

Moving into my own apartment with just one roommate gave my enthusiasm another boost. Brooke was one of the three girls I had lived with a year before, so she had witnessed the drama of my love affair with raw food. In fact, Brooke inquired about my new diet the moment we began arranging our kitchen and storing food for the next few weeks.

"Are you not vegetarian anymore?" she asked as I placed frozen chicken breasts in the freezer.

"Yeah, I just figured going back to meat was a good idea," I said, not wanting to elaborate on my dieting disasters.

"Well, that's good," Brooke said. She seemed relieved.

Having a kitchen for only two put me in major control of my food. No more school cafeteria food plans with dinners full of unknown ingredients. After I had filled my summer with learning how to cook steak (thanks to Pete), chicken (props to Dad, sans oil), fish, and even rabbit (which, I realized, wasn't worth the trouble since there was barely any meat on the bones), I couldn't wait to get started on my optimal meals.

Still focused on the Paleo diet, I avoided carbs like bread and, believe it or not, even fruit. These restrictions, of course, led to bingeing on carbs in the form of peanut butter and granola bars. In reality, these weren't the worst things to eat, but being that they weren't Paleo, and they were considered only treats in my mind, they were forbidden.

And they weren't *mine*.

I had stolen bits of Brooke's food in the first binge a week after school started. For some reason it hadn't occurred to me that running a large workout in the morning, then eating only a large bowl of steamed vegetables just wasn't going to cut the hunger. With only two hundred calories in my stomach for the day, I still found it surprising that I binged on the "wrong" foods later that night.

Brooke was gone. I initially just wanted a bite of her sugary Jiff peanut butter, just a taste of one of her Nutri-Grain bars. And then I wanted a spoonful of her Hershey's chocolate syrup, a nibble on her apple fritter, a jab at her leftover pasta and tomato sauce.

With these small bites here and there, I figured my thievery wouldn't be obvious.

The guilt raged in my mind that night as I lay curled up in my bed in tears. I had already eaten a large dinner, and now I thought about all the calories I had eaten on top of that. How could I fix this? How could I live with myself? Why was nothing working?

And then, like each revelation I had over those years, it hit me; I could ask for help this time. I could actually confess what had happened, and *ask someone for help!*

Alina was one of only two of my friends who knew. With my permission, she had told Elizabeth. But, like my dad, I had never talked to Elizabeth about it.

I called Alina, only to sputter her name when I had her on the line. I had never confessed to someone like this in the moment it had actually occurred. I didn't know how to explain that I stole food, didn't know how I could enunciate the word "binge."

And I couldn't; I just broke down.

"Rachael! What's going on?" I could hear the fear in her voice. "Do you need to come to my place?"

I told her I did.

The moment I reached Alina at the steps of the Sherman Shire, I collapsed into a mess of tears. I was horrified by what I had done, but I knew I had to open up, because as much as it hurt to admit what was going on, the pain of loneliness was worse than any pain of confession.

I still found it difficult to explain what had happened that night. I couldn't even walk inside the house, afraid she would see my bloated stomach. So we sat out on the dark porch, where I hung my head to avoid her eyes.

Alina stayed with me in the darkness as my body shook with tears and frustration.

» » »

Alina continued to support and comfort me that year. She urged me to contact her whenever anything went wrong with food, and the more I grew accustomed to seeking her help, the easier it felt to talk about food.

The binges began to lose their power as I came to fear them less.

Not only was Alina there for me mentally, but also physically. As I had anticipated, my running times for cross country that fall were not as fast as they had been my freshman year. But that meant I ran beside Alina, and the two of us led the team.

It wasn't easy to accept these slower times. Grieving the loss of the runner I had been and realizing how badly I still wanted to be that runner had me clinging to wanting ultimate control over food. Woj never looked down on me for my slower times, but it was more difficult to impress anyone and stand out as a very successful runner when I was right back in the middle of the racing pack, just as I had often been throughout high school.

At home, the mirror of the apartment bathroom mocked me. But I couldn't stay away. I squinted at it as I tried to make out my body, as I tried to understand what other people saw. And as I looked into the mirror, I shifted blame from that piece of reflective glass to the lights. It was obvious: the problem was the lights.

Why can't they shine in the right way?

Why can't my eyes see the truth, let me know?

I observed my reflection, stared at my legs.

You're big.

I pulled at my thighs to make them look thinner.

Then just eat less.

But I don't want to eat less.

You don't want to run fast?

I do! But I don't want to be hungry. I did that already. I don't like it anymore.

I don't like this game.

You don't like success?

I do! But at that expense?

If the mirror seemed too confusing, then the scale felt like the only way to judge anything. But the scale had become my new demon. Even when I hid it at the back of a shelf in the bathroom, it continued to peak out at me, taunting. I only weighed once a week now, but whether limiting the use of the scale was out of fear or a step in the right direction, I did not know.

As I visited Alina more and more to spill out my worries and frustrations, Elizabeth was often left forgotten, quietly sitting in the corner as I mumbled my downfalls to Alina. I felt bad for leaving Elizabeth out, but she had lived with me the summer of raw food (when I had begun bingeing), and I was afraid she would think me a fraud.

You don't have an eating disorder.

I saw you eat just fine.

Even now, I was still unable to call my eating problems by name, insisting they were not a disorder, but something in me, a character trait, that was severely broken.

Food for Thought

1. "Grieving the loss of the runner I had been and realizing how badly I still wanted to be that runner had me clinging to the food." What might this indicate about how Rachael can recover from this eating disorder?

2. The voice of a healthier Rachael is now talking to the voice of the eating disorder (*"Then just eat less. / But I don't want to eat less."*). Write about this dialogue and how you think it's a sign Rachael is moving in the right direction.

3. *"But I don't want to be hungry. I did that already. I don't like it anymore."* What might these thoughts indicate about how Rachael wants to live her life? Do you think she was really "living" when she had the eating disorder?

Mile Markers: Action Plan

Make an action plan for the next time you are about to binge. Remember, what works for one person during a binge may not work for another. This is the plan that began to work for me as I incorporated a variety of whole foods into my diet again without restricting macronutrients:

1. If you've already bought binge food (assuming it's low-nutrient, processed food), throw it away in a place you cannot access it again.

2. If you feel it would work for you, grab one of the binge foods to save for your treat, but make sure no more is available/within your reach. This may help reduce the feeling of complete deprivation.

3. Encourage yourself to slow down for a moment and choose whole foods that you are less likely to overeat and foods that will keep you full and nourished. These should be easy to access, so prepare before you even have the urge to binge: chopped vegetables with hummus, oatmeal ready to cook, or leftover chicken, vegetables, olive oil, and brown rice in the refrigerator. Choosing these foods may be tough in the moment of desperation and knowing you will binge, but muster up the courage to take this new step forward. Do not force yourself to eat a certain whole food just because you feel it is the one you "should" eat; choose a whole food that sounds tasty.

4. If you are still craving the binge foods after you've eaten some whole foods, check in with yourself again to make sure you actually have eaten enough food. Allow yourself to eat some of the treat you may have saved and check in with your level of desperation to eat a large amount of this treat. Has it died down?

5. Keep experimenting with yourself and trusting the process. Come away from each binge with a new lesson to incorporate for the next time it occurs.

Chapter 38

Just One Drink

EVER SINCE MY BOUT with orange juice, I never drank my calories. Thus, when my twenty-first birthday arrived that September, I was sure I wouldn't even drink the calories from alcohol. I didn't want to spend my birthday feeling guilty, so I figured I would avoid it altogether.

But Alina, Carly, Abigail, and Elizabeth convinced me to celebrate with at least one drink that night. I gave in later that afternoon, only agreeing to drink if they set up a time and a ride to the bar so that I didn't have to do any of the work or planning.

As the evening approached, and as I sat in my American Literature class and munched through an entire plastic bagful of raw okra (a vegetable I had learned about in my raw food days from the famous blogger Steve Pavlina), I couldn't stop thinking about that one birthday drink and its calories.

Drink for your friends.

Show your friends you can have fun.

"Almost there," Carly texted when I walked out of my class that night. "GET EXCITED."

She pulled up in her Ford Explorer with Elizabeth, Abigail, and Alina hanging out the open windows. I couldn't help cracking a smile when I saw that they were wearing birthday hats and blowing noisemakers. It was then that I realized how special this night was supposed to be. And *they* were making it that way.

I just had to get as excited as they were.

It was a Tuesday night, so it was easy to find a quiet bar. We sat outside on a balcony decorated with white Christmas lights, where a warm breeze drifted around us as we sat together and talked. This was exactly the atmosphere I craved for the night.

"So what are you going to get?" Elizabeth asked, her party hat sitting lopsided on her head.

I looked at the long list of martinis, all of them half-price. What *would* I order? I knew nothing about alcohol, not having drunk at all before, not even at the college scene.

"No, thanks," I used to say to the pleading looks from Dustin and Stephen at the cross country parties. They were just as eager to see me drink as they were to see me eat junk food. I tried to laugh it off, and they weren't too pushy.

But now?

Now, I ordered a pomegranate martini.

Five minutes after having my ID checked for the first time, I found a tall glass of sugary alcohol sitting before me. I felt a mixture of fear and pleasure at my first sip.

I loved it.

Sweetness. You know that means it's overflowing with empty calories.

What was it that Jennifer had said at my last appointment?

"When you look back on your birthday in ten years, are you going to worry about the calories or think about how much fun you had?"

"Whoo, you flew through that, girl!" Abigail said, laughing as she took a picture of me and my empty glass.

I laughed, too, wondering what the alcohol would do to me. I hadn't felt anything yet but curiosity. What *would* it feel like to be drunk?

I peered at the menu again, just to check it out, of course, and found the chocolate martini.

"Anything more for you ladies?" the server asked.

I looked around the table.

Ten years, Rachael. What are you going to think in ten years?

"Uh . . . yeah, I'm going to get the white-chocolate martini," I said, grinning at my friends. They raised their eyebrows; Alina and Elizabeth's mouths curled into smiles. "But you guys have to help me drink it!" I said quickly.

They nodded.

» » »

The first sip of that chocolate martini tasted thick and rich in my mouth. I could feel the alcohol burn down my throat with each gulp of the sweet drink.

Stay in control.

Let them drink the calories.

Don't drink it all, Rachael.

"I'm going to order the next drink for you," Elizabeth said, holding up the menu.

I cringed.

Another?

Elizabeth ordered a Bloody Mary. In all my inexperience with drinking, I didn't see this as an unappetizing combination after the chocolate drink, only that I was able to sample these different drinks for the first, and what I planned on, last time.

By the time we were ready to go, there were about two gulps worth of the Bloody Mary left, but I didn't want to add any more calories to the night.

"Come on, suck it down, girl!" Alina said, laughing.

It'll be fine.

I gave in, hoping to impress my friends while the fearful Rachael inside me screamed.

"I told Woj I would condone this kind of behavior!" Alina laughed as we stood up to leave. And as we walked out of the bar, I noticed I felt dizzy. Was this *drunk?*

Since it was a Tuesday night and we had cross country practice early the next morning at the soccer field, the five of us decided to call it a night. However, circumstances changed on the way back to campus when we thought it would be a great idea to sleep in the middle of the field so we'd be up and on time for practice. Carly, Alina, Elizabeth, and I were eager, so we dropped off Abigail, then stopped at Carly's house so she could grab her sleeping bag.

I waited with Alina in the kitchen until Elizabeth and Carly came down the stairs with more than a sleeping bag.

Two paper sacks clanked with heavy bottles.

"Happy Birthday!" Carly said handing me what could only be more alcohol.

My eyes widened as I pulled out a bottle of thick, brown wine.

"*Chocolate* wine?" I asked in awe. "And raw Kombucha beer?" I laughed as I pulled out the other bottle. "Nice nutritional touch." We stood there for another moment. "But you guys, you know what this means," I said, looking at the alcohol. "We have to drink these tonight. I told you, I'm not drinking any other night after this."

My friends stared. "No, no, they're yours!"

"No, you guys don't understand; we have to drink this now." Desperation set in. They really *did* have to help me drink up these calories. Because I had already had more than my allowance of alcohol calories, this became the night to let it all go, the only time I would allow myself this carefree celebration. Here it was again: all or nothing. I would make this the biggest, baddest birthday party of my life. Then never do anything like this again. Ever.

My friends, of course, agreed to do their part (it was my birthday, after all), so we grabbed some mugs from the kitchen and walked into the living room where we found Kelsey, from the cross country team, sleeping on the couch.

"Oh, no, no, it's fine," she said, laughing as we apologized for accidentally waking her up. "I'd like to see how this unfolds."

Other team members who lived in the house, Jackie and Lesley, heard all the commotion from their rooms and decided to join in. All of a sudden it was looking like a party.

Alina popped open the Kombucha beer and started filling the mugs.

As we (or mostly I) drank and talked, I could taste the lure of the alcohol. I felt warm, open, and eager to be the life of the party. It was as if I were wearing a cape of protection and could do anything and everything without guilt or worry. It was a delicious feeling and entirely unfamiliar.

"Am I going to be able to run tomorrow?" I asked my friends, standing up from the couch. I stumbled across the room, attempting a jog.

"Rachael, be careful!"

I swayed mid-jog, almost hitting the dinner table.

"Yes, you will be good to run by tomorrow morning," Lesley said, erupting into a fit of giggles.

"Woj is gonna hate me!" I said, falling back onto the couch. "Woj is gonna kick my ass. He's is gonna kick my *ass!*"

Rachael, the good girl, come to practice *drunk?*

"You'll be fine," Jackie said, laughing harder. "We have six hours before practice."

After another hour of talking, crawling up the stairs where I pulled off my sandals because they felt "too heavy," decorating the chandelier with toilet paper, and writing "Woj is gonna kick my ass" on the white board in the living room, Alina, Elizabeth, and Carly insisted we head over to the soccer field and get some sleep.

Once on the field at about 3 o'clock in the morning, we unrolled our sleeping bags, and my friends instantly drifted off. But I lay wide awake, staring at the sky and giggling as the stars spun in circles. The warm night air eventually caressed me into a light sleep, while my mind turned over and over as if I were swinging in a rhythmic, soothing hammock.

The next thing I knew, my alarm beeped next to my cheek. There must have been a light rain that night, because my sleeping bag was damp. I looked around at my friends lying next to me and then at the small group of people gathering at the soccer benches.

Practice was about to start.

Although my worries about falling over while running were eased by the fact I no longer felt dizzy, I felt giddy and was still in a slightly drunken state as I ran across the field to meet my teammates. I seemed to have shed the major problem and retained the pleasant buzz of the alcohol.

"Nice night, Rach?" Crysta asked as I bent over in a random fit of laughter. The freshmen stared at me with crooked grins, and Woj just patted me on the back and smiled.

The night had been worth every calorie.

Food for Thought

1. Rachael wants to avoid a night of calories. How has weight and food warped her perception of holidays or events? How might this hold her back from living life and finding happiness beyond the eating disorder?

2. While drinking is probably not the answer to Rachael's happiness, it does allow her to feel hours of bliss away from guilt and perfectionism. Why might you see some people using alcohol or other drugs based on their experiences with any kind of disorder?

3. Rachael believes that "[t]he night had been worth every calorie." What does this mean for her? What kind of revelation does it bring?

Mile Markers: Letting Go

1. When have you found a time to "let go"? Was it easy to do something fun for yourself?

2. Without using drinking or any destructive means of "letting go," brainstorm something daring and fun to do with friends.

3. Write about the experience and your emotions throughout the events. Does this experience give you hope?

Chapter 39

The Meal Plan

I DIDN'T WANT TO see the dietitian.

In our weekly sessions, Jennifer had encouraged me to see Trina, the eating disorder dietitian in the same office building— Trina, who I was sure would bombard me with facts I already knew, Trina, who would most likely not like my intention to eliminate wheat and dairy.

It was after my fifth refusal to see her that I finally consented. Jennifer promised me that if I didn't like it, I wouldn't have to go back. So it was worth a try, right?

But how would I explain the Paleo diet to an eating disorder dietitian? How would I convince her that we don't really need to eat dairy or that I didn't want anyone to make me eat from all the food groups?

"So would you feel good with a meal plan?" Trina asked a few minutes after she had introduced herself in her office.

I pursed my lips, fearing the worst. "Honestly I feel like I already know what foods to eat," I told her. "I've done a lot of research."

Trina tilted her head. "You said you've been bingeing, right?"

I nodded.

"Bingeing on what food?"

"Sugary peanut butter. Sugary granola bars and such."

Trina nodded, scribbling something on her notepad.

"What are you eating for your carbs?" she asked, peering through her glasses at me. She had a small, pointed face. I envied her tiny body. But her body reassured me, too, that if she was thin, perhaps she didn't indulge or push anyone else to indulge. I had also heard she was a triathlete.

"Onions . . . berries . . . eggplant . . ."

"Is that it?"

"On rare occasions, tortillas."

During my binges, more like.

"Would you be willing to add some more bread in there?"

I pursed my lips again. "Well, I'm trying to do the Paleo diet. You know what that is, right? And on the Paleo diet you don't eat bread, for health reasons."

"What if I told you that it would take away the bingeing to include more bread?" Trina said.

I paused. She couldn't be serious, could she? Wasn't bread the *cause* of bad cravings? At least, that's what I had learned from the Paleo advocates.

Next Trina recommended structured meals, which included dairy and a large amount of starch or carbs, just as I had predicted. I refused to bring dairy back in and told her so, but starch in the form of bread was something I could consider.

As I looked down at my new meal plan (once Trina had privately calculated the calories I normally burned with my college running regimen), I considered the possibility that she might actually help me.

"Lunch and Dinner: 3 starch, 1 vegetable, 2 protein, 1 fruit, 1 other."

A portion sheet came with the meal plan, showing how a portion of starch equaled a potato the size of a computer mouse; a protein source, like chicken, the size of the palm of your hand; and an "other," a 2x2-inch brownie or a thumb-size pat of butter.

Looking at the portion sheet was horrifying.

Only half a cup of vegetables, and it's not even an option in the meal plan for breakfast? One measly egg is a serving of protein? And I'm only supposed to have one serving of protein for breakfast?

I suddenly felt even more like a pig. Trina seemed to be proving that I was as gluttonous as I always thought I was.

She would be appalled by how much I really eat.

I couldn't face telling her, but I told myself that I had to eventually move past that self-consciousness if I wanted her to help me get the eating under control.

Food for Thought

1. Rachael says that she's eating onions, berries, and eggplant for her carbs. Look up the number of carbs in these food items. Do you think it reaches her recommended daily carb intake? How might this contribute to her bingeing?

2. "I couldn't face telling her, but I told myself that I had to eventually move past that self-consciousness if I wanted her to help me get the eating under control." What kind of strength does recovery require? What does Rachael need to keep asking of herself in order to move forward?

Mile Markers: Conjuring Courage

1. Name a fear you have about food, either a particular food or a specific situation.

2. What goal do you have in mind for addressing this fear? Could you discuss with your dietitian what goals you could set?

3. What are some positives you may find in eating this food or being in this situation? Can you use these positives to start to think differently about your fear? Work on finding a way that sticking to this new goal will benefit *you*.

Chapter 40

Blog Beginnings

"For too long eating disorders simply haven't qualified as serious diseases that merit funding and treatment. They have often been dismissed as faddy diets or food hang-ups; self, silly, female concerns."

~*Emma Woolf*, An Apple a Day

150 POUNDS

THE CROSS COUNTRY SEASON that fall didn't give me much to feel excited about individually since my times were almost a minute slower than my freshman year. But I was still a strong runner for the team, often finishing first or second for Aquinas since Alina and I raced next to each other.

I continually berated myself for the slower times, while I fluctuated between bingeing and restricting. The night after the national cross country meet in November (in which our team took seventh, and individually I took fortieth), I sat holed away in the hotel room shoveling in vegetables dipped in peanut butter while my teammates celebrated together.

I felt alone and trapped.

When I returned home, I finally told Elizabeth the details, and she and Alina tried to support me as much as possible that winter. I came to them in tears at least one night a week, furious and frustrated with my body. The torment and guilt over bingeing alternated with the euphoria of restriction, and I didn't know how I'd ever get out of it.

One of the worst nights involved a bike ride to the campus café where I bought five large granola bars and ate them all in the bathroom stall. And, despite my stomach bursting at the seams, I bought five more and ate those, too.

The cravings for this sugar fix had been so intense that I felt powerless to stop it as I ate. My stomach felt like it was ripping with the strain.

There was no way to get comfortable. I couldn't even climb back on my bike, let alone walk to my apartment without wanting to shriek in pain. I lay as gingerly as I could on a cushioned bench in the basement of the academic building, frozen with fear that if I moved in just the wrong way, my stomach would tear. The jacket I had won from a huge NAIA race my freshman year, a jacket I had worn like a dress at my lowest weight, now stretched against my protruding stomach as I prayed to God to release me from the discomfort.

I wondered over and over how I could possibly be bingeing this much when I ate protein and vegetables, everything I thought would fill me up more than just fruit. I tried to stick to Trina's meal plan, but I always ate more than she recommended, which led to terrible guilt. I felt ashamed of almost everything.

You're broken.

I had no way of knowing that my body had grown afraid of starving and was protecting itself in the only way it knew. The body has its own wisdom and will fight to survive. And so my body fed itself.

I continually tried to fight back as I worked with Jennifer and Trina. At this point I was bingeing so much that even when I thought about going back to a raw or fruitarian diet, I knew that the cravings would be unbearable.

I couldn't even stick to a "normal" diet.

» » »

I binged again in December. The belief that I had done something shameful combined with my helplessness to stop the constant thoughts about food prevented me from concentrating on any homework, so I browsed the Internet. Not only did the eating disorder rob me of the precious time I spent bingeing and calculating calories, I then wasted hours, sometimes days, dealing with the emotional aftereffects.

It was like a part-time job with no pay.

Resting my chin on my hand, I scanned through various blogs and went back to a blog that Todd, a young man I had met earlier that summer through a Paleo group, had created about whole foods. I had been emailing Todd back and forth about possibly starting a blog of my own, but I wasn't sure when or if I would actually follow through with it. Todd had given me helpful advice about choosing a domain name ("make sure it's the one you want, as it's permanent!") and suggested the site where I could start the blog.

I began to think that possibly others might be interested in reading many of the journal entries I had written for myself about raw food. If I could explain myself to the world, could put the tedious hours of research and obsession to some sort of use, maybe I wouldn't have to look back on my life and see all those hours just gone. I could make this eating disorder into something; I could tell my story. I might be able to make a difference, just like listening to the stories of the people in that support group had made a difference to me.

And then, I wondered, would it also help me to see how everything led up to this point? I hadn't read through the past raw food journal entries since writing them. Maybe I could figure out more about myself, why I felt so lost and confused about food.

I could understand when and why it all started.

I tried to imagine the people who would be able to see this, who would read it, and what they would think of me. But I knew I had to take the chance. That's what writers do.

I had been running in silence for too long.

Food for Thought

1. Even though Rachael had a "revelation" the night of her birthday with friends, she has fallen back on her "safety" of food when she doesn't celebrate the national cross country meet with her teammates. Why might it be so difficult for her to let go of the eating disorder? How might being at the national cross country meet make this even more difficult?

2. Describe all the possible ways in which "running in silence" speaks about Rachael's experiences. How might it speak for yours?

Mile Markers: Discipline vs. Disorder

1. Write what you think is the difference between "discipline" and "disorder."

2. How might Rachael's bingeing qualify as a disorder rather than a discipline? How might your own eating experiences constitute a discipline or a disorder? Why do you believe this?

3. "My body had grown afraid of starving and was protecting itself in the only way it knew. The body has its own wisdom and will fight to survive. And so my body fed itself." What might this tell you about eating disorders in general in relation to discipline and disorder? Do you think someone who simply lacked discipline would have found him- or herself like Rachael at one point, barely able to move on the couch and in extreme pain?

Chapter 41

Running in Silence

*"Sometimes what we're most afraid of doing
is the very thing that will set us free."*

~Unknown

WHEN I FIRST CREATED runninginsilence.com, I debated whether to present it on Facebook. I worried it would be difficult to admit I even had an eating disorder.

What if no one believes me?

I never looked thin enough.

Everyone will think I'm trying to get attention for it.

I knew I hadn't reduced my food to an apple a day and a lettuce sandwich with mustard. I had teetered on the tip of anorexia, had balanced on the very edge. As an athlete, I knew I had to eat just enough to compete well, but my preoccupation with food and the obsession with losing weight to run faster carried me in the direction of anorexia athletica.

But no one will believe you.

I could already imagine friends finding my post on Facebook and rolling their eyes, thinking, *God, Rachael, you don't really have an eating disorder.* If anything, I wanted to explain why I had gained so much weight and that it was not because I was ignorant and lazy. It was not because I didn't know about calories.

I wanted to show them that I knew *everything* about calories.

As the background image of the blog site, I chose a picture of my freshman self, running at the NAIA national cross country meet. Then I wrote two blog posts about what went on in my mind through the eating disorder and what the blog would entail. I decided that every few days, I would post an early journal entry from when I began recording my experiences with raw food.

I posted a link to my blog on Facebook and avoided the Internet for an hour, nervous about what I might see in response.

I finally logged onto Facebook.

"Rachael, this blog is awesome," one girl wrote, a runner from my high school conference, in fact. "Good for you. I just read both posts, and I am blown away by your honesty. Sharing your experiences will do nothing but help other people. Keep it up!"

And then Amanda, a friend from Albion had commented, "I agree with everything Alissa said! You're such a talented writer, too, which just makes this blog even more awesome!"

And Woj: "Good stuff, Rachael. I admire this venture. Keep it up."

I kept scrolling through the comments as they popped up within that next hour, my heart racing, my mind reeling. I wasn't doing any harm? They didn't think me a fraud? I began to see vulnerability as a positive thing, rather than something that caused me to shut down and keep my silence.

"I'm loving this blog of yours. You are a fantastic writer!"

"You have been extremely transparent. Know this will help you to sort your motives and feelings. A great step ahead!"

Even Margaux Drake, leader of the Rawluck group, commented on my blog, "Thank you for sharing your struggles AND accomplishments. You BRAVE girl!"

Brave? I couldn't believe people were saying this about *me*. Margaux's words kept echoing in my mind.

"You BRAVE girl" . . .

» » »

Over the Christmas break I continued to receive more responses from my peers about the blog, including many who struggled themselves. By speaking up, I no longer felt so alone.

My denial over the eating disorder began to leave me for good.

I hadn't realized how many people dealt with eating disorders or disordered eating for that matter, preoccupations with food that could lead to an eating disorder. These preoccupations could include struggling with self-worth or self-esteem, feeling overweight even though they are at a healthy weight, over exercising, obsessive calorie counting, and anxiety about certain foods or food groups. Worries like this have the potential to develop into an eating disorder when they become more frequent, severe, and take over their day-to-day thoughts and activities (*Eating Disorders Victoria*, 2015).

Word got out to the athletic director at Aquinas, however, and I found out at the next indoor track meet for Aquinas when Coach Wood, the head track coach, approached me.

"There's a woman who emailed the athletic director about your blog," he said. "She's worried about us having eating disorders on the team and that you need help immediately."

I felt heat rise to my face.

"But I'm not; those are past journal entries I've posted from years ago!" I said.

Coach Wood smiled, nodding, and Woj walked in on the conversation. I looked to Woj.

"I'm so sorry, I didn't mean for you two to get involved with this," I sputtered. I hadn't even wanted Coach Wood to know about my blog.

"It's all right, we are sorting things out with her," Wood said, smiling. "We know where you're at."

Mrs. Wilson, a family friend, contacted me about my blog as well.

"You are doing great helping others, but you should read what you wrote in your blog and figure out how to help *you*," she messaged.

She was right. After all, I had wanted to figure out how I got obsessed with food by looking back at these entries myself. "It's not about the raw food diet at all," she typed. "That's a piece, of course, but when you go back and read it, why were you not happy with *you?* How did the restriction start? When did it all begin?"

I felt I already knew the answer to that one.

"My sister. I already know that part. She lost weight, and I wanted to do the same."

"But really think," Mrs. Wilson typed. "Stop and think."

I stared at our Facebook message conversation, trying hard to understand what to look for in my past.

A rush of everything, the comparison to my sister at the doctor's office, talking to my mom about weight, it had all started as disordered eating.

When had it turned into the eating *disorder?*

And then it came to me.

Food for Thought

1. What helps Rachael's denial about having an eating disorder to fade? How might sharing our struggles contribute to owning our experiences and conquering them?

2. Margaux emphasizes Rachael's bravery. How might that make Rachael feel valued? How does this give Rachael a new definition of success and pride beyond fast running times and low weight?

Mile Markers: A Blurry Line

1. Rachael talks about the difference between disordered eating and eating disorders. Write down ways in which you or someone else may have experienced one or both.

2. Write about when disordered eating may have morphed into an eating disorder in your life or that of someone you know. Did something trigger it? Or if you don't believe yourself to have a full-blown eating disorder, what could you do to stop one from developing?

3. Answer Mrs. Wilson's question for yourself: "Why were you not happy with *you?*"

Chapter 42

High School Track, Senior Year

"In order to understand who we are, we must understand who we were."

~Unknown

I WOULD ALWAYS REMEMBER Coach Jenson's sly crooked smile and the way her large brown eyes looked up at me from a little over five feet.

But Coach Jenson stood like she was six feet tall.

"We're doing quarter mile repeats today. If you have to puke, then puke, but you're not stopping. In fact, you *should* be puking by the end of this."

The high school sprinters exchanged looks of defeat and injustice. The freshman and sophomore distance girls shifted next to me. I could already see the thought going through half the fifty-member team; they were quitting tonight.

Coach Jenson was a young woman, a new coach during my sophomore year of high school, and she wasn't about to let anyone get away with a half-assed workout or effort. If you didn't give her everything, she questioned your dedication to the team. Coach Jenson was everything Nicole embodied.

Nicole was a grade ahead of me. By the time she graduated and left for college, she held four school records, including the mile with a 5:05, the half-mile in a blazing 2:13, and the two relay records she shared with me in the 4x4 and 4x8 relays. With her bright blue eyes and blond hair, Nicole looked sweet and innocent until she got to that start line. I didn't dare talk to her before races, as her upturned lips and furrowed brow could make even her closest teammates cower. Nicole won most races before they even started, just with that look of determination.

That scowl that matched her aggression in the race made her one of the top runners in the state. She ran with more guts than anyone I had ever known. And Coach Jenson was a godsend for Nicole. Since she was everything Coach Jenson admired, it was a no-brainer that Nicole won instant stars. And puking after workouts and races seemed to show even more how tough she was, so much so that I yearned to barf just to prove I was her equal.

No one stepped on Nicole's toes. During a 200m workout one day, two of the sprinters dared to spit, "Fuck Coach Jenson" as they struggled down the straightaway.

In front of Nicole.

I was shocked, looking at the girls in disbelief when we finished. But Nicole got to them first, wheeling around to release her wrath.

"Don't you *dare* say that about Coach Jenson!" Nicole yelled, pointing her finger in their faces. "Don't you dare insult her like that again, *ever!*"

Things as simple as mentioning the name of her greatest rival sent Nicole reeling, too. I had innocently mentioned Arianna Smith during one of our workouts when I heard a deep-throated growl, "*Never* say that name on this track."

Arianna was a short, muscular runner who held every middle distance and distance record at her high school. Her ability came from hard work, yes, but she was gifted with extraordinary talent that Nicole simply didn't possess.

Nicole, her face burning, pushed herself to the limit just to stay on Arianna's shoulder. Meanwhile, Arianna ran serenely around the track, her small, round face calm, and her tight, curly hair bouncing gently in the wind. Never mind that Arianna had the potential to go to the Olympics, nor that her parents were nearly Olympians themselves. It didn't matter who beat Nicole, because Nicole didn't, and wouldn't, lose.

I wanted to be Nicole. After racing in Nicole's shadow for three years, I wanted to show the same aggressive speed, to show I was just as indestructible, *just as good* as Nicole for my senior year of high school. I wanted to prove to Coach Jenson that I had always been like Nicole, just second place instead of first, that who I was only seemed insignificant because Nicole always finished before me.

And then, something changed; my weight dropped.

Without realizing the connection between losing weight and running faster, I first saw the jump in performance at an indoor track meet.

"Are you sure Emily should be in this heat?" Mrs. Elliot asked, eyes wide. We were about to start the indoor mile, and blond, bushy-tailed freshman Emily Elliot jogged around the inner turf.

"Sure, sure," I replied, smiling again to reassure Mrs. Elliot. "The times they announced for this first heat are just an estimate. No one's going to run anything close to a 5:10 today."

And I wasn't lying; running a time that fast in January for the indoor track season wasn't common.

I knew I would be thrilled with a 5:20-5:30.

I gave Emily's mother one more reassuring glance and motioned Emily to jog to the start with me. My legs felt light and loose in the featherweight spikes, and I grinned at the other nervous girls.

Emily and I stood at the line, Emily rubbing out her legs and me relaxed and trying to talk to my competitors. I knew it was a low-key meet, and I wanted to keep it that way.

From the shot of the gun everyone blasted from the start, battling each other for position. I tucked myself behind the first girl, but as the others sped up from behind me, I found myself boxed in. I breathed deeply, twelve years of competing wisdom whispering at me. My long stride shortened as runners slowed down in front of me. I moved further out to the right and felt Emily's small presence next to me, hanging onto her spot as I held onto the pace. It felt fast, but comfortable.

"Seventy-five seconds!" a timer shouted at a quarter mile.

I was still boxed in. *They're doing all the work,* I reassured myself. But the front three girls began to pull away to form a new pack, and I knew I belonged up there with them. I had no choice but to find my exit and speed around the girls slowing me down.

Emily followed me as we approached the front pack. The explosion of speed depleted my reserves for a few seconds, but I eventually fell into the rhythm of the new, faster pace. It comforted me to see all the tight shoulders and lurching strides while I waited patiently to use what I had left.

We crossed the half-mile mark in 2:35, and I felt like I was still in first gear. At that moment, a voice deep within urged me to try something new, to go beyond the limits I had always imposed on myself as a middle-pack runner, as someone who saw herself as the girl behind Nicole, Nicole, who was no longer here to compete against me. Nicole, competing for the college that hosted this meet, watched from the sidelines.

I decided this was it. I pulled up to third place, found the pace almost too easy, and passed second. With a quarter of a mile to go, my adrenaline exploded. I pumped my arms harder, pushed off my heels, and lifted my knees.

One second I decided I would win, the next I decided I would win magnificently.

I thrust my body forward and glided away from the pack, widening the gap between second place and me. With the clang of the bell to mark the final lap, I tore around the bend of the track. I felt the grace in my long, powerful legs as I raced the last 300 meters. I could almost hear the gasp from the stands, the cheers of "Go Cheetah!" from my mom, and as I looked around in my relaxed, comfortable state, I took in the stares of people watching.

I rounded the final curve where Coach Jenson urged me to go on, even if it hurt. I wanted to laugh, to show her that this didn't hurt, that in those moments I wasn't like Nicole after all, but like *Arianna Smith,* racing to a win in the most serene, relaxed manner in the world.

With one hundred meters to go, a man shouted, "4:52!"

I could barely make sense of what he just said. It had to be wrong. Although a distance runner, my limited sprinting technique was enough to hurl me toward the finish with a new personal best of 5:09 flashing before my eyes.

Time slowed down in those final moments when I crossed the line and turned back to watch the others come barreling in after me. I witnessed every girl I beat cross the line in exhaustion, and suddenly the rush of the crowd clapping reached my ears. I looked up and realized it was *my* turn now. I was finally getting the recognition I deserved, was getting the results I had worked for so hard.

"I think it's all the strength training I've been doing!" I told my dad when he came to hug me afterward. What else could it be? I figured the hard work had paid off at last.

Coach Jenson walked up to me moments later. "Great job, kiddo!" she said, giving me a big hug. I felt my heart swell; I felt like her new little star. "So it's your senior year!" she said, looking up at me. "It's your year to choose what events to run for outdoor track."

If I thought the elation from the race couldn't send me higher, I was wrong.

My dreams are coming true.

"Well, I'll run all four distance events if we need points in the earlier meets," I said, smiling. Not only did I enjoy the distance running, but I also loved the idea of racking up points for the team, building up a base, then finally showing everyone what I had with just one or two spectacular performances at the end of the season.

"It's up to you. Nicole got to choose her events last year, and you deserve it this year as a senior. We can save you to specialize in your favorite events near the end, just like we did with Nicole."

» » »

About a week after the indoor mile race, something clicked in my mind. As I wondered with awe and pride how a 5:09 indoor mile could feel effortless compared to the grueling 5:13 outdoor mile less than a year before, I suddenly got it. Yes, weight training may have been part of the equation, but weight *loss* was what really did it for me. I knew, thanks to a recent doctor's appointment, that I had lost seventeen pounds by restricting my food after Angela's weight loss revelation. But I never thought the weight loss would actually make a difference in racing, never thought it would help me to improve this much.

I didn't realize I had seventeen pounds to lose for that matter. I just wanted to make my stomach look smaller, to feel thinner, to look "right." I didn't even know back then what fat really looked like on me. I had never seen large thighs, love handles, or a hint of a double chin on my body. I never had to buy new clothes in high school because I was outgrowing my old ones. Because everyone had pointed out my large stomach for most of my childhood, I just got the impression that I always had a few pounds to lose from there.

But seventeen? Seventeen. That was when I began to look more closely at the nutrition label on the box of Raisin Bran. That was when I found another world beyond just cutting back on food.

There were *calories* to count.

Since my stomach still looked the same to me, I clearly had to keep dropping weight. After all, the number on the scale proved it was possible.

I just wanted to see it in the mirror

» » »

While Coach Jenson mostly oversaw the twenty sprinters run 200- and 100-meter sprints down the track, Coach Mac assigned our six-girl distance team to pound out 400m repeats at nearly every practice, making it difficult to recover enough for the two to three track meets we had each week.

But when Emily (our superstar freshman) sailed away from me in the mile and broke the school record in the two mile at the first meet of the outdoor season, Coach Jenson watched my performances with a critical eye. After all, I had not shown the same speed I had in indoor track.

"You're not trying hard enough," Coach Jenson said to me when I had finished the mile in 5:38, depleted. "You are just as fast as Emily; in fact, when you two are racing, you are going the same speed. You just need to make up those few feet separating you and then stick with her."

I didn't see how that mattered at this point, as we were still earning the same number of points for the team no matter whether Emily finished in front of me or I finished in front of her. And I always had the 800m to run soon after (my third race of the evening), while Emily had time to rest before we both ran the two-mile.

But if I couldn't get my body to do what Coach Jenson wanted in running, then maybe I could get it to do what I wanted in eating. I could ignore its pleas for food, just as a runner did its cries for rest in a race or workout. It was all about pushing yourself beyond your limits. So on top of the splits, the personal records, the number of steps in a minute with running, calorie counting entered my daily thoughts with full force. I could not let my body overtake my mind, could not let my body fall back just as it fell back from Emily in the races.

Run as fast as Emily? Watch me get as small as she is.

I never saw my discipline with food as actual restriction. I thought I was finally eating like a normal human being, finally imposing the order I felt I had always needed, because without it I would someday be overtaken by a beast of destruction, would gain an absurd amount of weight.

I did not pass out in the hallways. I did not count the ribs in my chest or post "thinspiration" photos on my bedroom wall. I felt like an embarrassment to the world of food and running, too ashamed to explain to others how much control I had to force onto my body and too ashamed to let anyone know what a gluttonous runner I had become.

I hated that it took this much willpower to simply eat like everyone else did. I hated that forcing myself to eat "normal" amounts of food left me feeling so hungry. And where was all this fatigue coming from? It had to be something wrong with my thyroid. And how come I couldn't see the weight come off? It must be a thyroid problem.

I am the only runner who has a weight problem, the only runner who has to force herself not to eat so much.

I am broken.

I took many bathroom breaks throughout the day, my stomach sloshing with the water I had forced down in an effort to tame the hunger that raged inside. I would count to three before pulling my heavy body up from the classroom seat, walk across the room wearing my large, flowing sweatpants, and walk down the hallway with my hands in my sweatshirt pockets.

Nothing passed through my mind as I roamed those hallways except the thought that I must make it to the bathroom, that as much I wanted to stop and rest, to curl up against the wall and sleep forever, I had to make it down this hallway.

The spring sun shone through the large windows of the school, but the light only blinded me, mocked my deep, all-consuming grief.

I couldn't even muster the energy to talk with my friends or speak up in class.

» » »

Near the end of track, Coach Jenson handed out a sheet that showed how many points each person earned for the team throughout the season. I felt pleased to see that although I finished behind Emily more often than not, by competing in so many events (running four miles worth of races in each meet), I had racked up the most points for the team. That, I thought, showed my dedication. I had sacrificed excelling in my best events by running in so many distance races. I also felt that it secured Coach Jenson's promise that I could just race my most cherished events in the final few meets: the mile and two-mile.

Even our distance Coach, we called him Mac, was on the same page.

"Do you really want to race the 800m tomorrow?" he asked the day before the regional meet. Mac wanted to devise a way to help me qualify for the state meet. If running all four distance events wore me out, then maybe just two would help lessen the fatigue.

"If you don't qualify in the mile, you'll at least have a better chance in the two-mile if you skip the 800m," he said.

I agreed.

Mac and I stood for another moment before he said, "Well, you haven't had the best season."

I looked at the ground and shrugged. Mac's words felt far from encouraging, but he was right; it had not been the season I had hoped for after my outstanding indoor track performances.

"Have you been eating enough?" Mac asked.

I looked up, surprised. This was the last comment I expected to hear, especially from him. *Eat enough?* What was he talking about?

"It looks like you've lost weight."

My heart hammered wildly in my chest. Me? Lost weight? *I didn't know this could actually happen to* me!

The weight on the scale wasn't enough to convince me. For someone to say something like this, for someone to *notice,* felt exhilarating. I hadn't seen the difference, but apparently Mac had.

"Oh, I eat a lot."

My parents had always laughed at how much I ate.

But a wild joy pulsed through my body at Mac's words.

» » »

The next day Emily shook with nerves in the heat of the afternoon as I reassured her that everything would go well. But I felt just as nervous; we had ten minutes before the start of the Regional mile race where, to qualify for the state meet, we had to run a sub-5:13 or finish first or second.

The sun blazed in the middle of the afternoon as we took our places at the start. Nearly every seat in the stadium was filled, while the field was littered with jumping, sprinting, stretching athletes and their coaches.

The starter raised the gun, his arm hazy in the heat. I breathed my last scared, full breath and jumped at the bang.

I took the lead immediately and felt relieved at how light and loose my legs felt as I lifted my knees and blazed around the first curve. About halfway around, I fell into a more comfortable rhythm, allowing Emily and a tall gangly girl in black and orange to pass me.

The pace slowed slightly as we barreled into the second lap. I caught up to Emily again, her twig-like arms swinging from side to side. Krista, wearing black and red, moved in beside me. Her strong thighs and hips propelled her body forward as we finished lap two, the pack of four of us together.

The positions didn't change much in lap three as we stayed on each other's shoulders, but going into the final lap, the group thinned. Emily passed me and joined black-and-orange girl. Krista shot forward as well. I was left about a foot or two behind the group, but still within reach of the lead.

Coach Woj had come to watch the meet and stood near the 300m mark with my parents outside the fence. His words from before the race echoed in my mind. "Don't worry about time; just race."

He was right. I couldn't think about qualifying for the state meet by time. If I raced these girls, if I focused on beating them, everything would fall into place. With that in mind, I knew that there was only one thing to do.

I *had* to beat these girls.

As the bell clanged to signal the final lap, I continued to focus on the pack of girls ahead of me. This was the decision moment. This was what would build or break me.

I had over a minute left of the race.

With half a lap to go, I was still behind. Deciding this was it, I used a final surge of energy to circle around Emily, black-and-orange girl, and finally, Krista. I circled around the final bend of the track to lead the regional mile race until Krista put on her last explosion of speed and caught up to me again. Neck and neck, she began to pull ahead. We reached the final straightaway where I stuck to her shoulder, the screams from the stadium a deafening thunder to my ears.

Krista continued to pull away from me to finish first. I finished a moment behind her, my time a mere half-second away from Nicole's school record. I was an automatic state qualifier by place, and since Emily finished only a few seconds behind my time of 5:06, she also qualified.

I turned around and hugged Emily, relieved. I was even more relieved to know I only had one race left and plenty of time to rest up for it.

Unfortunately, I didn't have as much time as I thought I would. Minutes after my mile cool down run with Emily, two teammates ran up to me, gasping for breath.

"Coach Jenson has been looking everywhere for you. She seems upset," they said.

What had I done *now*?

I found Coach Jenson sitting high in the stadium with the

sprinting and hurdle coaches on either side. Climbing up the metal bleachers, I approached her.

"You wanted to see me?" I asked.

Coach Jenson nodded. "I don't mean to discredit your great mile race, but why aren't you racing the 800m? I have been looking all over for you."

I sat there, stunned. Hadn't Mac talked to her about dropping the 800m?

"Mac and I agreed that I could scratch it," I explained. She couldn't be mad at *me* for that, could she? After all, Coach Jenson and I had discussed that by the end of the season I could focus on my best events, anyway, which were the mile and two-mile.

"Well, *he* didn't tell me that," she retorted. "Rachael, you have to look at the big picture. We need the points. You aren't thinking about the team."

I stared at her, dumbfounded. I understood her disappointment in not knowing about my dropping out of the race, but *need the points?* This far into the meet, we were nowhere near finishing in the top as a team. And my position in the 800m wouldn't rank us any higher. I would score better by placing in the two-mile, where I was stronger as a distance runner. And with fresher legs, I had an even better chance of finishing well.

But what hurt me the most, what really hit me, was that she thought I wasn't thinking about the *team*.

"I'm disappointed in you," she said.

It took me a moment to collect myself as the finals of the hurdle race took off below us. The stadium erupted in cheers, and I stared off into the infield, her words like a sickness in my chest.

Don't cry, don't cry.

I wanted nothing more than to hide under a dark blanket. I felt scared to even look at Coach Jenson. No one had ever said they were disappointed in me, and to a perfectionist, that was like a slap in the face.

"So do you want me to run the 800m then?" I asked in monotone as I forced myself to look back into her eyes. I hoped to satisfy her, clung to the last bit of hope that she would see I was trying my best, even if it meant toeing the line of the 800m race to trash my legs yet again before the two-mile.

"It's too late now," she said, looking away.

The 800m started in ten minutes.

It stung to feel she had given up on me, to feel she no longer cared, especially after everything I tried to do to please her.

"Okay," I replied. I sat up and turned away. Tears welled up in my eyes as I lumbered down the hot metal bleachers with the *clang, clang* of my heavy, worn steps.

I was not Nicole. I would never be a Nicole, but I wanted to make an impact somehow. Had I failed the only thing I had left? But I *did* care about my team, didn't I?

I thought about all the parents who had told me what an impact I had made on their daughters, all the encouragement I had given to even the slowest runners on the team. I wanted others to succeed. Couldn't Coach Jenson see that? Didn't she understand how much the sport meant to me, not just for my own speed and success, but also for the others?

I made my way to the other side of the track, a new energy burning within me. I had disappointed Coach Jenson to the point of no return, so I didn't have to please Coach Jenson anymore, did I?

As I walked across the infield and reached the fence on the other side, Woj was there to coach me for my final race of the day.

» » »

I walked to the front of the room crowded with parents and track members when Coach Jenson announced my name at the track banquet. I walked up excitedly, assured that I had earned my spot as a strong runner for the team when I capped off the season with an eighth-place All-State finish at the state meet in the mile, as well as qualifying for the two-mile. I felt like a new woman and, most importantly, that I had proved my determination and grit to Coach Jenson.

I stood beside her that night, smiling as she began to describe me: how I loved to run, how I had worked hard that winter. She looked at me and said I would be missed.

She did not hug me like she had the year before.

What about my All-State finish? What about how I had led the distance team?

I am more than someone who just works hard!

I watched as Coach Jenson called up the other girls, her clan of sprinters, giggling as she gave them warm hugs and described their "funny, snarky attitudes" that couldn't be controlled sometimes, but of course they were good girls and teammates anyway.

Emily won the "Outstanding Distance Runner" award that evening. I clapped, feeling something die in my chest. It made sense though, didn't it? She had beaten me in many of the distance races.

And then, a crazy thought burned in me; if I hadn't won that award, did it mean I might get anything else? I had to have earned something for running all the races I did for the team, for racking up the most points, for being a captain and leader. Yes, Coach Jenson and I had had a few hard moments, but she couldn't deny that I still made a positive impact. After all, she hadn't mentioned that I achieved All-State when she talked about me in front of everyone. Was she saving this announcement for something bigger?

The awards continued to be distributed, including an award to recognize two girls who had puked after their races, of course.

Having not yet received an award, I felt suddenly aware that I might hear my name at the announcement of the beloved, the holy, the cherished *Bulldog* award.

Nicole had earned the Bulldog award the year before. Coach Jenson made it clear at the beginning of each track season that this was the award of all awards. I remembered the look in Nicole's eyes, the tears that welled up as she moved to the front of the room to receive her prize. I remembered her parents, how proud they had been of their daughter. I watched the way Coach Jenson looked upon her precious athlete with pride and a love that belonged just to Nicole. I had wanted that from the moment Coach Jenson described how important the award was, how it epitomized the true bulldog athlete: hard-working, dedicated, team-oriented. I had watched with a hope, a deep yearning to be there the next year.

Coach Jenson held that final plaque in her hands, and looked around the room.

"And *obviously* the Bulldog award goes to Becky."

I could hear the emphasis on "obviously," and to me it was

if she were pointing in my face and laughing at my dedication, laughing at what I thought had been a strong effort, laughing at my failed attempts to be a team player. And Becky, who had just earned the Outstanding Teammate award as well, walked to the front of the room in tears of shock and joy.

I could understand Becky's overwhelming happiness. I could understand why she was popular among the sprinters. I could also see why Coach Jenson wouldn't give me the award after everything we had been through. But after not having mentioned any of my accomplishments, after everything I *did* do for the team had gone unnoticed, I couldn't help but feel a rush of loss pull at the pit of my stomach.

I was glad to be in the back of the room so no one could see my face. I tried to hold it together the best I could, but forcing a smile was not easy. These final moments solidified everything in my mind; I was not worth much to Coach Jenson this year, if at all. And it hurt. It hurt to know I had disappointed someone, especially a coach, and a coach for a sport I had loved since childhood.

My hands clapped as Becky grabbed the large plaque. And as Coach Jenson described Becky's "caring, encouraging attitude towards her teammates" and "dedication and hard work," my heart dropped. *I must be conceited, self-absorbed.* This yearning to be recognized, this need to be reassured that I was doing the right thing, these were not part of the perfect Rachael I wanted to be.

Before I knew it, the room erupted in cheers from the sprinting group gathered on the right side of the room, and Becky's dad came up to give her a hug. This had only been Becky's second year of track, while I had competed for the team for four long, hard years.

Running for a team had meant *everything* to me.

I awoke to what was going on around me. Coach Jenson was about to end the banquet, and I still had to walk up front and give out the coach's gifts.

I stood up and felt myself float across the room from my seat at the back where I had sat with the young distance girls. I forced a smile that I hoped looked genuine as I faced the entire room of athletes and parents.

"Um . . . I have a little something to say before we all leave here," I stammered. The sprinters murmured and laughed in the corner, caught up in their own conversations as I talked. I worked on my smile again as I held four envelopes in my hand, one for each coach. Unfortunately, the team hadn't done a great job handing in their money on time, so my parents had to cover most of the cost of the gift cards.

I wondered if they regretted it.

I tried to hold it together and not to cry as I turned to face the one woman who forgot or ignored what I had done that season. Only, at this point I wondered if I had done anything at all.

I pulled out the cards to give to the coaches and tried to explain what an influence and inspiration they all were for our team, how they had pushed us through thick and thin. But words failed me. A fake smile passed my lips, and my voice broke. I ended my speech weakly.

Everyone clapped, but the applause seemed far off as I presented the coaches their gifts. The assistant sprinting coach, with whom I had always been on good terms, gave me a hug. With a smile she said, "Thank you for everything you've done this season."

I rushed back to my seat a minute later and picked up my belongings. I wanted to vomit everything I had just eaten at the banquet. The vast array of desserts we had consumed was no longer food; it was calories, horrible calories all over again. I couldn't wait to run to my car, to get away, to cry it out. I had to give myself time and space to think things through.

"Rachael, Rachael! We need to take pictures!" Parents held up their cameras just as I had nearly made my escape, but I turned back.

I smiled in a picture with Emily as she held her plaque. I put my arms around the girls who had labored with me through the tough workouts. I tried to fake joy, to not look the crabby fool who was upset about not getting an award.

» » »

"I'm sorry about that awards banquet."

One week later the mother of one of my freshman teammates had come up to talk to me at the spring sports academic awards ceremony. "Those awards last week . . . you should have received recognition," she said.

I wanted to hug her, to cry into her arms and show her how much I needed to hear that. My parents had been distraught for me, but because they were my parents, I didn't know if what I felt, abandonment, frustration, resentment, was justified.

All I could tell Mrs. Fisher was, "Thank you."

» » »

I began training for my first college cross country season that summer. The intensity with which I trained and concentrated on food meant that I rarely saw my high school friends. In fact, I had already begun to lose any real connection to them my final semester of high school, what with my lack of energy and sole focus on running faster and losing weight.

Thus, that summer I slaved away at the computer, tried to find answers to nutrition on the Internet because there was no good answer for what happened at the end of track. There were, of course, the larger issues.

Was I really going to let Coach Jenson's disapproval rob me of my self-respect? Couldn't my achievements and my integrity satisfy me? What was the matter with me?

The answers to these questions could not be found online, but I knew I could find answers to losing weight, could find ways to keep restricting food and feeling good about my body. Never mind the exhaustion I felt on my runs. Never mind the way I constantly dreamed about food.

6.22.10

> *I'm obsessing over food, and I need a way out. I'm so frustrated and consumed by weight loss. I guess it's finally the time to admit it; I don't want to think about food all the time. It's controlling my life. I want other things to make me excited and happy, not food! I know I'm not overweight, but I'm scared to gain weight, especially in college.*

For the rest of the summer, Coach Jenson's disappointment made me feel like a disappointment to the running world. With my parents' encouragement, I wrote her a long email explaining how I felt. I hoped it would help me to close this chapter of my life and move on. It was the first piece of writing in which I had ever exposed myself that much, and the two pages I filled gave made me feel naked and uncomfortable.

But I had done it. And as much as I cringed hitting the "send" button, I knew it was the best thing for me.

Less than twenty-four hours later, Coach Jenson responded.

> *Rachael,*
>
> *I've been here three of your four years, and I've watched you grow and mature as a person and athlete. I wish you continued growth in whatever you choose to do in the future. Thank you for your thoughts.*
>
> *Coach Jenson*

"Well, you did the right thing," my dad said when I read off her email.

It was time to walk away.

I didn't recognize the shadow that had been growing inside me until a triathlon I raced near the end of that summer. I felt a power, a new darkness lurking as I lost weight.

And suddenly, suddenly, I saw how I could seek revenge. I could beat the people I had always wanted to beat. I could run faster than Nicole, could prove to everyone the runner I had been for so long, just covered by weight. I would make my competitors feel my wrath in the easiest, most socially acceptable way possible:

I would beat them.

I hadn't seen the weight loss in the mirror, but the scale didn't lie. And now the pictures, the races, they proved it. Now I could see the tendons and muscles emerging from my legs, could see the abs defined more than ever, could see how my ribs shone more prominently through my skin.

Look at me.

See me.

Listen to me.

I could beat everyone, beat down and crush them with ease without lifting a finger or saying a thing. It was almost laughable, how much I improved. I could make my competitors work hard, could make them suffer as I floated away from them like a ghost.

"You're just not trying hard enough."

I could change that now. I could make Coach Jenson eat her words.

I shocked my high school teammates who heard about my performances that next cross country season, shocked my high school cross country coach who commented on how "toned" I looked.

And I shocked Woj. He was proud of my performances, and I felt his excitement. He gave me side-hugs, high-fives and clapped enthusiastically during my races. I was earning praise at last, and I thrived under it. Never mind the raging hunger. Never mind the daily war with food. This praise ruled over any of that. I hungered for success, recognition, and love, and I got it all.

I thought I had moved past everything after my strong, record-smashing cross country season at Aquinas. I had received the Spirit Award from Woj and was recognized not only for my achievements as a runner, but also for my contribution to the team as a person.

But something still lingered. I could not walk away unscathed. I walked through the small wooded Aquinas campus thinking about food, continually counting calories, fighting a losing battle with the occasional binges, finding myself hanging over a toilet one night after stuffing myself with pizza, wondering *how much longer can I keep this up* as I walked into the cafeteria each morning, wanting nothing more than to eat a large waffle with syrup and peanut butter.

If I stayed at a low weight, ran fast, and ate perfectly, I wouldn't have to deal with failure.

I don't ever have to fail.

The illness had overtaken my mind:

I have more weight to lose.

It was not until I surrendered to the punishing rules of raw food that I realized I had lost more than weight.

I had lost myself.

Food for Thought

1. Rachael's response to this public rejection by Coach Jenson is hurt, humiliation, doubts about her own worth, great sadness. If you were Rachael in this situation, what do you think you would be feeling? What are your reactions as you read about it? If you could, what would you say to Rachael?

2. Why do you think Rachael is so keen on pleasing her coach?

3. Rachael writes, "I had lost myself." What do you think this means? Did the eating disorder really fix the hurt that she felt?

Mile Markers: Past Feelings

1. What are some instances in your past that may have led to your eating issues or addiction? It is often a combination of factors, so feel free to write a few ideas.

2. Read over what you've written. What feelings do these memories bring up? Do you feel you have fully embraced these feelings yet?

3. Brainstorm ways in which you can forgive, talk to someone, or work through the situation you have been through.

Chapter 43

You Can't Keep Doing This to Yourself

"Sometimes the only reason why you won't let go of what's making you sad is because it was the only thing that made you happy."

~Unknown

I HAD THESE NEW realizations about my past with the eating disorder, but now I didn't know what to do with it all. How could understanding the problems with food work in other areas of my life? For example, if I couldn't believe I was worth something unless others praised me, how could I escape from that kind of thinking? Where did I go from here?

Nothing changed about my eating patterns. I felt the thrill of restriction yet again that Monday and the guilt and rage when I ended up bingeing on a jar of peanut butter that Friday. And that night just so happened to be the eve of our next indoor track race.

I was supposed to race the 5k with Catie and Ranae and wear the new uniform top I had gotten from Woj earlier that week.

"I lost my old one," I had written in an email to him.

It was a lie.

"Medium or small?"

Definitely a medium.

I felt self-conscious as we walked to the locker room to grab the new uniform with Woj. And now here I stood, days later at the line of the purple indoor track, my thick, round stomach bloated beneath the looser-fitting top.

"If you hit 43s, you can qualify for Nationals."

Woj had told me this all week. He thought I could hit the qualifier.

Any day but today, Woj.

I eyed a girl in maroon in lane one.

She will win this.

I knew, because she had stick-thin legs. She had a space between her thighs, a mockery of mine years before. Her arms looked lithe, and I felt my jealousy bubble over.

That was you years ago.

I dragged through the first mile of the 5k.

"Right on pace, Rach, you gotta keep this up!"

Keep this up? No way in hell.

"Come on, Rach!" Nicole yelled out to me. Nicole, who had transferred colleges after a few years of injury. Nicole, the runner I had always wanted to be. It felt good to see her again, and ironically, after I had just been thinking about my past with her. But I didn't want her to see me like *this*. Nicole cheered for me, but I would have given anything for her to turn away.

I circled around the track lap after lap with Woj cheering me on and telling me to "keep your arms low," "hold onto the rhythm," and "relax your shoulders." But it felt too difficult because I couldn't even ask my body to eat right without feeling it would resist me, without feeling it would abandon me. Why care anymore if I knew I would just binge again?

Maroon girl, with her arrogant thighs, lapped me two times near the end of the race. I could just see God mocking me as she passed, laughing as she blew by, and I watched her matchstick-thin legs glide while mine rubbed together.

I was done. I didn't want it anymore, didn't want any of this.

Too tired to keep pushing.

No chance of making it to indoor nationals.

Don't care.

Hate this.

I felt my body, seemingly worse off than even my high school body, drag the good Rachael down.

You are so much slower than the old you.

The words slammed over and over in my mind. I knew how to run and race, but I didn't know how to fight back against thoughts this strong and relentless. I tried to stay relaxed, but inside my mind screamed.

Pathetic.

Slow.

Failure.

The words dripped with hate.

This is your fault. You're the one who put the food into your mouth. You're the one who gained all the weight.

Catie and Ranae caught up to me near the end of the race, finishing just a few seconds behind me. I had nothing left to give. There was no fire, no sense of urgency. I crossed the line, and all I wanted to do was curl up in a ball and cry.

"It's just a race, Rach," Catie told me afterward.

But it wasn't the race that hurt me; I could deal with bad races due to other circumstances, circumstances that I could change. But how the hell could I change this? How many more times would I have to endure a binge that made me feel so heavy, that made me hate running? Running, racing, even, used to be my escape. Now it just reminded me of how trapped I felt in my own body.

Woj approached me after congratulating Catie and Ranae on their strong performances.

"I'm only mad because I know you're mad," Woj said to me, his hand on my back. "What happened out there?" I stared at the ground, shaking my head. How was I supposed to explain this? "We'll talk later," Woj said.

He walked away.

» » »

I feared putting *anything* in my mouth that afternoon. I knew I would just keep eating and eating. So, I rationalized, if

I didn't eat at all, I wouldn't have to worry about overeating. I wouldn't have to worry about losing control. Because once I started eating, I couldn't seem to stop.

No calories, no stress, no worry. No eating. To eat normally, I felt, would be to give up. I could not just give up. I had to keep *trying.*

It was then that the thoughts I had pushed down for so long bubbled up.

What is the point of living if I have to go through this hell every day?

Running and food are the only sources of happiness in my life.

They have backfired on me.

I don't have much else to live for.

I hate hunger, but I hate fullness.

I hate bingeing, but my body craves it.

Trapped.

I knew that even while I felt happy that I could run and thankful for great friends and family, food dominated all of it.

Eat too much, run too slow.

Don't overeat in front of your friends.

Hide your eating from your family.

I felt guilty for even *contemplating* ceasing to exist. I knew I wouldn't take my own life, but what hope was left for me? I didn't see anything worth fighting for anymore. I felt as if I were facing a black wall, a wall I would never be able to climb. Everything in my future simply stopped.

When I thought about continuing to live with the eating disorder, all I could see was each day in my eternal hell, waking, thinking of food, eating too much, hating myself, hiding as I ate late into the night, trying to puke and failing, only to grow heavier. I knew I probably wouldn't become obese, but as a runner I would feel obese, and no one would understand, and I felt that I couldn't even label what I had as an eating disorder, so how could I explain myself? That I just ate too much now? That I just ran slowly, but I used to be fast and the only problem was food?

That's it, they say? That's *it?*

You feel hopeless because of *that?*

But I tell you, this is no way to live. I cannot keep doing this, and I don't know how to stop.

» » »

Woj approached me later that afternoon, and we sat together on the side of the track.

"I'm mad because I know you're mad," he said again, sitting down next to me against the wall. "What's going on?"

I looked down at the floor.

You have to be more open if you want help. You have to be brave.

"It's food," I said.

I couldn't believe I was confessing this.

"Rachael, you know if you don't eat enough food, you're not going to fuel your body to run well. You won't have the energy."

I remained quiet. He thought I hadn't eaten *enough*; how funny. I almost laughed in spite of the situation.

You have no idea how badly I wish I could do that now and hold onto it.

"It wasn't restriction. It was . . . the opposite."

I didn't know how else to explain it without feeling more exposed than I already felt. I kept my eyes on the ground, shame flooding me. I had never told Woj anything like this, nothing so close to the time of the binge itself. It was one thing to post on my blog about my bingeing experiences from years ago (especially when I had been at my lowest weight), but to talk about what was happening right now, now that I thought I was fat?

Woj fell silent for a moment. "You can't keep doing this to yourself."

What else *could* he say?

But I wanted so badly to turn toward him and shake him, to run out screaming and pulling my hair.

Do you know how much I want to stop doing this to myself? Do you know how much this tears me apart not just during the races, but every minute of every hour of every day? I wish you could know how much I want to stop. I wish I didn't have this awful relationship with food.

Food for Thought

1. Rachael is telling her coach about a bad experience with food very close to the time it actually happened. How difficult do you think this was for her to do? Think about where she has come since her first text to a friend in Chapter 17.

2. Reread the quote at the beginning of the chapter. How might this apply to eating disorders? Why are eating disorders a double-edged sword? In what way did the eating disorder make Rachael happy?

3. Rachael has been running since she was a young girl. Why might the eating disorder's connection to running make it so difficult to give up the eating disorder?

Mile Markers: Breaking the Black Wall

1. Rachael understands the underlying reason for her eating disorder now, but it's still difficult for her to get out of the cycle of restricting and bingeing. Look over what you wrote about what may have led to your eating issues or addiction. Write down what steps you could take to work through those issues that caused you to use the eating or addiction to cope.

2. Coach Woj tells Rachael, "You can't keep doing this to yourself." Have you heard comments like this from people who don't understand your addiction or eating disorder? What makes addictions or eating disorders so difficult to "just stop"?

3. When have you felt that "black wall" of hopelessness blocking your view of a happy future? Remind yourself that even though it feels like you have no idea where to go or how to get around it, that black wall *will* move with time. You are not alone.

Chapter 44

Elizabeth Speaks

I FINISHED THE REST of the indoor track meet by convincing myself to eat again (a can of green beans I had brought) and cheering for my teammates. I put my distress to the side until I saw Elizabeth and Alina later that night, and days later I fell back into my routine of fearing food and finding ways to overcome it with Jennifer and Trina.

And then I noticed Elizabeth had begun to pull away.

She seemed withdrawn, quiet, and irritated with me. I was convinced she thought I was making up the eating disorder or that I was exaggerating my distress.

And a week later, when it was just the two of us, Elizabeth finally spoke up.

I jumped down from my seat on the couch in the living room and joined Elizabeth in the dining room, where she had been sitting at the table doing homework. Crawling onto the floor, I looked up at her and smiled. I was in a wildly giggly mood, which at that time was a drastic change from my somberness when I binged. Lately my emotions quickly went from depressed and distraught to spunky, talkative, and energetic, which I realized now was partly due to the diet pills I had started taking. The diet pills that were laced with caffeine.

"What's up?" I asked Elizabeth.

Elizabeth shifted in her seat, facing me. "This is tough because I don't want to hurt you, and I don't want you to take what I say out of proportion," she began. "I just want you to hear me out, I guess."

I nodded, feeling anxious. I just wanted her to get to the point!

Elizabeth took a deep breath. "It seems that whenever you're with us, you draw the attention back to yourself."

I felt my stomach clench and hoped my face didn't show how afraid I felt.

Was this about the blog? Was I making a fool of myself? I hadn't meant for it to come off as something I was trying to show off. I had been updating the blog every few days and wondered if I was just bombarding people too much. I suddenly wished I hadn't updated my blog that day, wished I had never said much at all about the eating disorder in general.

She's telling you the truth. Just take it, Rachael.

"What do you mean exactly?" I asked, my voice shaking.

Don't cry, Rachael, don't cry. Hold it together.

"Like, you make snarky comments. When I said something nice about Alina's pants the other day, you said something like, 'What about *my* pants?' I just don't want you to come off that way. I'm starting to wonder if it's the eating disorder, like sort of a self-esteem issue."

I stared at her.

What?

"And it seems like your personality is all over the place," Elizabeth continued.

"Like you said something at Carly's birthday party, and I responded with, 'It's *Carly's* night, Rachael.' You didn't even notice, but Alina gave me a look because I kind of stepped over the line, I guess, but it's been getting out of hand, Rach. You just don't have . . . you don't have much balance right now."

Don't cry. You need to hear this.

Don't cry.

"As Woj says constantly, balance in life is key," Elizabeth

said. "I don't think that you have that, and that may be what bothers us. I personally feel like if I want to talk about running or nutrition, I can talk to you, but other than that, there isn't really much else I can talk to you about. Running is an idol for you, to be honest."

The tears came before I could stop them.

"No, no, Rach, I'm sorry," Elizabeth said, sliding off her chair to sit down on the floor with me. She gave me a hug, but I couldn't hold back any longer and cried harder. I already felt alone and out of control with food, and now my friends had been talking about me? They had been *annoyed* with me?

It scared me to think that when I wanted so badly to be with my friends, I had been pushing them away by acting self-centered. I felt glad Elizabeth told me how she felt, but now I didn't know *how* to act around them anymore.

» » »

Later that night I texted Carly to ask her about the situation because I found out she was in on it, too.

"Yeah, it feels like you've been a little 'overbearing' lately, like you seem too energetic and just say or do anything, even when the setting or timing is not appropriate," she wrote.

I stared at the message and felt my stomach drop. I could see what she meant. One minute I was over at the Sherman Shire in a torrent of tears, the next on a high of giggles and jokes. My emotions were all over the place.

I knew I wanted to erase the mopey Rachael because I felt ashamed to have behaved so low around my friends. I didn't want the eating disorder to define me, and suddenly I felt like it had.

"Maybe you should try to feel comfortable being alone," Carly suggested.

I felt my stomach drop further.

Alone?

They didn't want to be with me. They were annoyed with me. And now, after reading that, how could I want to hang out with them? How could I want their company if they didn't want mine?

But I need you guys.

I really need you guys right now.

I had begun to see how valuable friendship was in my life.

I feared losing my friends, wondered if this was their way of telling me that I had changed too much. I wondered if this was the first step in breaking off ties, and I would be alone for good. I wondered if what I had done couldn't be fixed. My friends couldn't understand how much the eating disorder had warped my thinking, but I couldn't see how much running had warped my life. I had been so absorbed in the eating disorder that I didn't know how to be *me* without running and controlling food.

I want to take everything back. I'm sorry.

I could see why my friends had had enough.

Food for Thought

1. When Elizabeth starts this tricky conversation, why do you think Rachael instantly starts worrying about how much she has revealed on the blog? Do you think she shows a lack of confidence in speaking up?

2. Rachael's emotions have been up and down a lot with the bingeing. She mentions caffeine as being the culprit, but do you think there is more to this than caffeine?

3. "I had begun to see how valuable friendship was in my life." As difficult as this open communication is with Rachael's friends, what do you see happening here in terms of balance?

Mile Markers: Finding a Balance with Friends

1. Have you found any difficulty dealing with your eating disorder with your friends? Do they know what you struggle with? Write down ways in which they can be supportive.

2. Arrange a time to talk with your friends about what you're dealing with.

3. Let your friends know that you simply need their support. You could share your list of comments that may trigger the eating disorder. Remember that their best gift to you is their love, care, and support.

Chapter 45

Waterlogged

"People have a hard time letting go of their suffering.
Out of a fear of the unknown, they prefer
suffering that is familiar."
~Thich Nhat Hanh

I DID NOT VISIT the Sherman Shire for weeks after that. I wanted to have my friends back and wondered how I could take myself away from the bingeing all on my own. But I didn't dare ask to hang out again, afraid and horrified by my behavior.

After having been through raw food, Paleo, and even attempts to purge by vomiting (only to manage chunks here and there), I searched my past to find another way to cut weight, and it came to me at the drinking fountain one afternoon.

Water.

I used to chug bottles of water throughout the day as a senior in high school, my stomach sloshing as I walked through the hallways. It was another chance. If eating a certain way wouldn't help me lose the weight, maybe this was the fix for what I saw as my broken, stupid body. Maybe I just had to fill up on water until I felt *sick*.

Then, I thought, I could allow myself food.

After track practice for the next week I kept my head in the fitness center drinking fountain, as if an invisible hand were forcing my head down.

Drink.

Drink.

Drink.

It felt powerful to force more water into my body as I breathed through my nose. I kept the water running, even when I thought, *Maybe now I should stop, maybe now I should stop, maybe now I should stop.*

But those thoughts were countered by, *Just a little more, just a little further.*

And as I sat with my stomach growling for food in the library, I guzzled from my water bottle, determined to silence the cries of hunger.

Shut up, you stupid body, shut up!

You don't know the difference between hunger and thirst.

Since Alina had again become my sole confidant, I invited her to my next therapy session with Jennifer. She agreed to come out of interest and support. And there, I admitted my renewed obsession with water.

"How much do you drink?" Jennifer asked.

"A lot."

"When do you stop?"

"When I feel sick." I smiled after I said this, as if I were taunting someone.

I want my body to hurt.

"Did you talk to Trina about this?"

I paused.

I shouldn't have mentioned the water.

"I just feel like I should drink as much water as possible to push away any doubt that I may actually be thirsty and not hungry," I explained.

"Have you been following your meal plan?"

I fell silent. Had I? What *had* I been doing?

"Yeah, for the most part," I lied.

"So if you're following the meal plan, then you shouldn't have to worry about water, right? Because you're doing what the meal plan says?"

Good point.

But didn't I have to learn to listen to my own hunger? What if my body didn't need food, but my meal plan said I had to eat? What if eating according to the meal plan made me *maintain* weight when I could *lose* it?

"I'm going to see if Trina can see you tonight," Jennifer said, getting up from her chair.

Alina and I waited.

"Why do you still want to lose weight?" Alina asked quietly.

I looked up at her, exasperated.

"You *know* why."

It had come off harsher than I had intended, and I saw it by the way Alina jerked her head back. It was as if I had slapped her in the face.

Trina peeked her head into the room a moment later. "Come on in, Rach," she said. "We can chat for a few minutes."

I wanted to roll my eyes. Everyone was making this water issue a bigger deal than it should have been. I knew I wasn't going to do what Trina asked of me.

"You know you could get hyponatremia, right?" Trina asked as I sat down across from her at the round table in her office. "That you can die from it?"

"Oh, yeah, I understand that," I said. I just didn't think it would ever get to that point. I also knew that I would rather risk hyponatremia than risk eating too much.

"And you know, when your belly is full of water, it doesn't mean you're not hungry," Trina said.

I nodded.

I can't let my college career go to waste.

I have already wasted so much.

I want it back, I want it back!

I wanted to scream at all of them, scream and tear off the serious look on their faces. *They* didn't understand what I was going through, *they* didn't see this as my last resort, *they* hadn't known the praise I had received from my success, the attention I had had, the adoration from my coach, how good it felt to have something I never thought *I* would have deserved!

I deserved that, and I want it back!

I began to cry silently, and it was then that the tears showed the truth behind my anger. I was grieving, and it was difficult to let it all go. Dieting, any form of trying to lose weight, was trying to hold onto a past that I thought I could get back, a past that I felt I could control with food. I kept telling myself to leave the past behind, and Alina had always encouraged me to "focus on the *now*." But wasn't I focusing on the now? *Now* I hated my body. *Now* I couldn't stand the discomfort of a stomach with a roll of fat, thighs that could no longer fit into my jeans, and arms that were no longer thin twigs.

Now I wanted to just drink *water*.

"Can you help me lose weight?" I asked Trina, my voice shaking. I looked into her eyes, desperate, yearning for a way out of this. I hated that there wasn't a secret; water *had* to be the secret!

If you help me to lose weight, if you can somehow control my monster, I will stop drinking so much water. Give me a pill, something to suppress this.

Anything.

Trina remained quiet for a moment, her eyes soft as she looked into mine. "You are not in a good place to lose weight yet. You still are engaged in disordered eating patterns."

I sat there, fuming.

You're supposed to fix this. You're supposed to help me.

"What qualifies as 'disordered eating'?" I asked icily.

Trina looked at me, her eyes sad. "Well, Rachael, abusing water would fit in that category."

Food for Thought

1. Reread the quote from the beginning of the chapter. Do you think Rachael fears the future? Life? Why might suffering with the "familiar" be easier for the time being? In what way is this simply *existing* rather than *living*?

2. What would giving up the eating disorder mean for Rachael's *running* future? What might be scary for her if she isn't as "successful" in running as she had been her freshman year of college?

3. Rachael is completely isolating herself from coaches, from teammates, from friends, parents of friends, her therapist, her dietitian, her own parents, often by choice, by her actions, or just in her own mind: "They didn't understand what I was going through." Why do you think this is happening? Why is Rachael cutting off any source of help while also believing people should be helping her: "You're supposed to fix this. You're supposed to help me"?

Mile Markers: Grieving

1. As destructive as the eating disorder is, what makes it so difficult to recover is that most people with eating disorders don't want to let go of them. There is something that holds or "roots" them to the eating disorder. Think of these things that "root" you to the eating disorder. Why might you be so afraid to break away?

2. Write down what you will grieve in letting go of the eating disorder.

3. Give yourself time—it may be a matter of days, weeks, or a few months—to grieve. Once you

have met this set time, prepare yourself to move forward in your life, but keep in mind that it is okay to feel sad and grieve losing a part of yourself you have used to cope for so long.

4. Refer to **GRIEVING: The second step in mental recovery** in Appendix B for more.

Chapter 46

Scaling Back

"Sometimes the process of growth looks a lot like destruction and pain. But you'll realize with time that you're not breaking; you're healing."

~Brittany Burgunder

I EVENTUALLY CUT BACK on water, but it wasn't the meeting with Trina that scared me into doing it. Instead, the hunger roared back into life full force and, as with all my other methods of trying to lose weight, I binged.

That had been it for me. I surrendered to the idea that there was nothing left, no way to get out of where I had fallen. I still tried to lose weight, tried to stick with whole foods, but after each binge, I cared less. I still felt guilty. I still felt out of control.

But like that final indoor track race I ran, I had nothing left to give.

In fact, that race became one of my last races that year. I approached Woj weeks later to tell him I had to take a break from competition, that it was for my health, that I needed time away from the races to figure out my body.

That I was exhausted from the emotional struggle.

When I talked to Jennifer about it, she said it was up to me whether or not I wanted to step out of competition.

"Because you're not clinically at an unhealthy weight where it would compromise your safety to compete," she said.

But when I look back on it, my safety was potentially compromised by continuing to compete. With wanting to lose weight being so closely tied to running, to remove running from my life was a relief for me.

Without the prospect of competition anytime soon, I wasn't as desperate to lose weight as quickly. I wasn't comparing myself to other runners and feeling demoralized over and over again, ready to restrict, and only to binge.

As my friends had advised, I did finally sit with myself. It was uncomfortable. Food didn't fix itself. And I continued to binge here and there. But I also took the time to grieve at last. I grieved the loss of a body I had worked so long and hard to achieve, grieved the past that I might never get back. I said goodbye to the dream of perfection, and I didn't know if I could face this new Rachael and like her.

It seemed like such a silly "death," the eating disorder. It was not something you should love, appreciate, or want to keep, but I had success tied to it. And running? Did I even love running anymore? Was it even worth it to compete that upcoming fall for cross country? But in our conversation in his office, Woj and I agreed that cross country 2013 would be my next focus. I had to ready myself mentally for that season, and I had that spring and summer to get my life back together.

But I wondered if, without the prospect of running as fast as I used to, I could still be happy competing. I wondered if I could ever accept myself at my current weight.

》　》　》

That spring, as I continued to run some workouts with my teammates and cheer them on in their races, Trina agreed to weigh me without showing me the number so I would stop getting on my own scale each week. It was a step in the right direction, but the mirror still revealed the changes in my body.

Each time I looked at my reflection, I found something new.

It felt as if I were seeing myself for the first time, and it both fascinated and terrified me to realize how much my body was affected by all the commotion in my head.

I saw a fuller face and rounded cheeks. And when I pulled in my chin even just a little, I could see the second chin forming behind it. I saw creases in my skin; creases that marked how the skin folded over when I bent my arm. Each time I pulled my knees to my chest, I watched as thin, horizontal flesh lines appeared on my thighs. I even found these same lines on my wrists when I watched them bend.

"What will happen to Rachael's scholarship if she gets hit by a bus?" my mom had asked Woj before I joined the team my freshman year.

"She keeps it."

Maybe this eating disorder was the bus that hit me.

I had witnessed how something as simple as the desire to control food had changed me not only physically, but also mentally. And even though I knew what I needed to do, my view of food had become so warped that I was powerless to do it.

» » »

The bingeing episodes began to lose their power that spring. I realized that I had to eat larger portions than Trina had recommended for me in my meal plan. She had been right that whenever I craved sugary foods (like pie, chocolate, granola bars), eating whole food carbs would reduce those cravings.

I just learned through personal experimentation, and perhaps a dose of advice from 30BAD, that I had to eat more of them.

So I ate. It might have been more than Trina recommended, but I allowed my body to take in what it asked for, and that in the end was her main message: trust the body.

I filled myself with potatoes, bread, oatmeal, and fruit, so at least I wasn't bingeing on a thousand more calories of dessert or other forms of high sugar foods. I ate protein to feel full and fat to stay satisfied and add flavor.

While my meals weren't perfect and I may still have been bingeing on whole foods, there was less guilt associated with it. I did realize how similar this method had been to the 30BAD method, that I would just eat more carbs to avoid bingeing, but this time I didn't have to eat only one kind of carb (fruit), and I had fewer wild, intense cravings overall.

Thus I confronted each incoming binge with less fear and distress because I knew how to tackle it. I knew what was going on. I kept up with the vegetables, too, of course, always maintaining the title of "Veggie Queen" bestowed on me by my cross country teammates.

» » »

Summer arrived, and I continued to write about food: how I felt, what worked best, what I feared most. I made direct connections with more readers of my blog, reassuring those who struggled that we were never as alone as we had thought. I admitted that my recovery from an eating disorder was ongoing and involved hard work, but I offered hope and suggestions along the way.

And then I had the urge to weigh myself.

The last time I weighed had been six months ago, and suddenly I yearned to know, needed to see those numbers.

I stepped on the scale and saw 157 pounds.

It still scared me to see such a high number, but I also felt a sense of relief that it had not gone any higher. In fact, it was the same number I had seen in January.

I had made it through half a year maintaining my weight.

» » »

I stayed home alone that summer afternoon of the personal weigh-in, still compelled to type the numbers and an account of the day's eating into my food journal. Staring blankly at my laptop, caught in the old familiar worries, I sensed a sudden heaviness in the air and noticed that the light in the room had changed. When I looked up, I saw the sky had turned from bright, radiant sunlight to an eerie grey-green.

A deep thunder rumbled in the distance. I watched through the windows as the thicket of trees that surrounded our house thrashed violently in the wind. The rain, a pitter-patter minutes before, became thunderous pounding outside the screen door behind me, and I turned to watch as sticks and branches fell onto the deck outside.

I opened the screen door to step barefoot onto the wooden deck. Something about the suddenness of this storm made me want to get out there.

The rain drenched me within seconds, and despite the midsummer's heat, I felt a chill. I walked to the center of the deck and watched mist rise from the wet wood. And then, out of nowhere, I felt prompted to grab it.

The scale.

But the Rawchael inside pulled at the pit of my stomach.

Don't.

I did not want to destroy the scale, I told myself. Not yet, at least. It wasn't the right time. But I also knew I couldn't be free of the eating disorder while I harbored the monster that measured what I saw as my worth.

I didn't know it was the last time I would use you, I thought as I recalled the morning weigh-in. This wasn't just any scale. It had gained a personality, had been through so much with me. Deep down, I knew a part of me kept it as a trophy to remember I had stepped on it at my lowest weight.

One hundred and eighteen is the maximum temperature that food could be cooked.

It was also the number I thought would propel me to a national cross country title.

I had told myself months before that I would get rid of the scale when the time was right. But would the time ever be right? Everything pointed to this moment, home alone, the storm, my final weigh-in.

It must happen now.

I ran to my room and forced myself to grab it, the scale I had stepped on for years. Gripping the plastic edges with both hands, I walked back out into the rain.

I approached the porch railing. The rain continued to pound as I stared at the exact spot where I would strike the scale. I raised the contraption, raised this friend turned enemy, into the air and at the rumble of thunder smacked it onto the ledge.

My right hand stung with the impact, and I bent down, dropping the scale to hold my fingers. I had hurt myself more than the damn scale! The scale only had a sliver of a scratch, barely a dent in the plastic, while I sat there ready to howl into the wind.

It was hard not to laugh at the absurdity of the scene.

My hand wasn't even bruised, and I smashed the scale with a little more force, the sound barely audible beneath the pounding of rain and rumble of thunder. I continued to slam the scale over and over against the wood, realizing what melodrama this was. I had hoped this ritual would lead to a revelation, would, like the storm, wash everything clean. I had dared to believe I would walk away as some sort of renewed woman.

After the final crack of the scale against wood, with my hair soaking wet and my clothes drenched, I shoved the three large pieces of broken scale under the tarp lying outside and walked back into the house.

The upper half of the scale lay face down on the ground, its digital numbers hidden from the world.

Food for Thought

1. Rachael feels broken, tired, and somewhat hopeless. She hasn't given up, but she's no longer fighting to stick to a diet. How will this gradual "letting go" allow her to heal?

2. Why does facing this "new" Rachael scare her so much?

3. Do you think the fact that Rachael realizes she has maintained her weight will help her trust her body more? When do you think this trust was lost?

Mile Markers: Rituals

1. Has there been any event in your life for which you have created a ritual of some kind—maybe the burning of letters when a relationship ends, or the planting of a tree at the birth of a child? This does not have to be a major event.

2. Write about this event and the ritual you used to honor it.

3. How did this help you to move on?

Chapter 47

Stuck

*"No one warns you about the amount of
mourning in growth."*

~Te V. Smith

I HAD HOPED THE rain would wash out the numbers. I had hoped the ghost of the scale had departed. But something felt eerie to me, having done this. Had I angered the scale? Now that it was broken, I wasn't sure if I liked this at all.

"You don't have to like it; you just have to accept it," I told myself as I removed my drenched T-shirt and shorts to put on a fresh pair of clothes. I looked into the mirror. "You just have to sit with it."

I observed my stomach, the way my hips rounded over my shorts.

"You have to adjust; it's done. You've done it. No going back."

I had taken the time to grieve, and knowing that this was the end, that I couldn't look back, scared me. It was the discomfort of knowing I had to move forward now at this weight, with *this* person.

» » »

When I returned home from a run later that night, I walked out onto the damp deck. As the sun set behind the trees, I turned the wet scale over with my right hand and saw the digital triple-zero-period-double-zero glare up at me.

The scale was still alive, although just barely.

I thought about what to do next. I couldn't bury it, as any lingering piece of the instrument could haunt me from its grave.

The zeros continued to stare, waiting.

Weighting.

I grabbed a hammer from the shed and carried the broken pieces of the scale to the front of the house near the garage. Squatting on the ground, I stared it down, stared down at the screen where I had seen the 118 pounds years ago. Had it been *years* already?

I could remember every single number I had ever seen on that scale: 120, 123, 124, 125, 127, 130, 132, 137, 139, 140, 141, 145, 147, 150, 152, 157, each one distinct and memorable, each one an image of a particular time and place. These numbers had all gathered to play and mock me.

You have to make it through this.

And before I could think about it, before I could stop myself, with one little tap of the hammer, a crack split the glass, and some sort of dark Etch-A-Sketch-like ink poured like blood through the crevices.

No screaming, breaking, mutinous yelling necessary. That evening, Rawchael was sucked into the black abyss of my past with the tiniest clink of a hammer on glass.

» » »

Woj posted an article about perfection on our cross country Facebook page later that week.

"If you feel like you are losing yourself because every fiber of your being is dedicated to perfection, give yourself credit on the effort, rather than the result" (Chen, 2013).

I texted Woj soon after reading it.

"Awesome blog article to post on our page," I wrote. "It couldn't have come at a better time."

I spent some time checking my email before I saw that Woj had responded.

"Sweet. Sometimes God knows just when to put out awesome blog posts. Keep winning your battle."

Winning. I didn't have to fight as much anymore. I was *winning*.

Food for Thought

1. "I had taken the time to grieve, and knowing that this was the end, that I couldn't look back, scared me. It was the discomfort of knowing I had to move forward now at *this* weight, with *this* person." Rachael still feels very uncomfortable where she is, so we can see that acceptance is not easy, and it doesn't mean she will automatically love her body. Do you see acceptance as an act of courage? What other feelings do you have about Rachael's decision?

2. "Rawchael was sucked into the black abyss of my past with the tiniest clink of a hammer on glass." Why is this moment so enlightening? What does it say about finding a way to break free of the eating disorder?

3. Rachael is beginning to see perfection in a new light, as something that is taking the soul out of her body to the point of apathy, hopelessness, and exhaustion. How might focusing on the "effort" of an activity become her new way to view success? How might this help her to accept herself more?

Mile Markers: Acceptance

1. How do you feel about your body right now? What would acceptance mean to you?

2. Write down what you will gain in your life with acceptance.

3. Acceptance is being content with imperfection. What are some areas in your life where you feel like you "must" be perfect? Why?

4. Refer to **ACCEPTANCE: The first step in mental recovery** in Appendix B for more.

Chapter 48

Rachael

"It is not the strength of the body that counts,
but the strength of the spirit."
~J.R.R. Tolkien

LATER THAT SUMMER ON a warm Friday evening I met up with a few teammates for our first cross country workout. Woj stood at the bottom of the first downhill while a few of us women and ten guys worked through three one-mile repeats. I ran on my own at a 6:20 pace, while the other ladies formed a group at a 6:40 pace.

Dashing out into the open grass from the baseball field, I turned sharply around the orange cones, sped between the trees, pumped my arms up the small grassy slopes, and let my legs fly on the way down.

I still felt large as I ran that evening. I still felt far from ideal in my body. But I ran that workout with serenity, the same way I was learning to approach food. I had no one to compare myself to, no times to judge against, and no wild expectations.

I had no raw food to "fix" my eating, my running, or my life.

I wondered if I could find a new way of participating in the sport, wondered if there were something besides running faster and being the best in the nation that could keep me happy. I wondered if running could ever be as freeing or as much fun now that I knew I might never lose the weight, now that I might never run as fast.

As much as I hated the "dark side of running" with the eating disorder, I also realized that it was how I approached running that made it "good" or "bad," just like how I approached food. I had transformed running into something so defining, because all my life I depended on it for my own popularity, for my escape, for my voice.

But now, I myself could define a great race. I did not have to measure a race performance by time, but by effort and drive and determination. It sounded silly to think this way, so naive, I thought. But if I could win by effort, then the effort I had put into the races that past year by far beat the effort I put into the races I had run as an All-American freshman.

I finished the mile intervals that evening a few minutes before the rest of the ladies, so I jogged around the sunny park and eventually stood with Woj to cheer on the team.

"Can I run with them?" I asked suddenly, giving Woj a sly smile as the women dashed past. It felt so *like* me to want to go do that. Woj nodded (I thought I caught a slight eyeroll of amusement), and I tore off through the trees after my teammates.

I felt, despite the fatigue in my legs, that I could stretch them again. And in this new body, I was the same old Rachael I had been before. Except this time, I felt stronger, wiser, and yes, heavier. But I still felt the same joy and freedom in running that I had had ever since I first began, before competition, before weight and food had ever invaded my mind.

Food, and my life, for that matter, was not "perfect," but I understood that it didn't have to be.

I was not fixed. The eating disorder lingered, and the desire to lose weight was still there. But I fought for the growing, strengthening part of myself that told me to accept where I was now. And that acceptance would have to come before love and happiness could (hopefully) ease their way in.

Perhaps, in this journey to self-love, I would find something beyond running to keep me happy and balanced. Because I knew, deep down, that running would not save me.

Rawchael would not save me.

Rachael would.

Food for Thought

1. Rachael's journey isn't quite finished, but she has come to the point of reckoning. What do you think the next year has in store for her?

2. Look at the title of the first chapter and this last one. What kind of growth happened in between the transition of Rawchael to Rachael?

Mile Markers: Redefining Success

1. Reread the quote at the beginning of this chapter. What does it tell you about what we are remembered for? How might this affect what you do in this life?

2. Rachael redefines success in running. In what ways could you redefine success if you have previously measured your success and worth by the number on the scale? What would success look like for you?

3. The next time you strive for success and feel disappointed that you hadn't reached "perfection," remember to congratulate yourself on the effort and the mental strength it took to get where you are.

Gallery

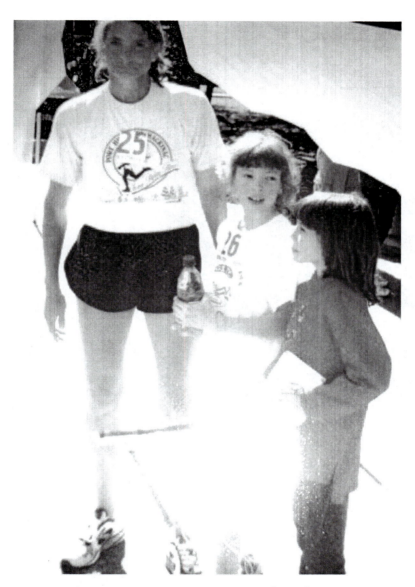

Running at a very young age—my first 5k at age 8.

9 years old, running at my future college track.
September 2001.

Exhausted and emotionally and physically depleted. I'm ending a season under head track coach Jenson. June 2010. Photo credit Peter Draugalis.

Tired and hungry. It's a strained smile. Summer 2010.

My first college cross country race—fast and afraid.
September 2010.

I'm enjoying the lead and on the way to an effortless win at the conference cross country meet. Things would be very different in the next two years. November 2010.

My first raw food pie I made with Jill. April 2011.

The night at the Olive Garden with my teammates. I was afraid they would see how preoccupied I was with my food and weight. April 2011.

A few weeks into the raw food diet. May 2011.
Photo credit Mary Reyna.

Eating raw food with Elizabeth. June 2011.

The triathlon I participated in soon after seeing 124 pounds on the scale. I'm racing as if my life depended on it.
June 2011.

A turning point—the night I decided to end the raw food diet.
January 2012.

Running after the first 10-pound weight gain. I was so worried about how "big" I looked while running. Spring 2012.

Attending open houses after the recent weight gain and very clearly feeling uncomfortable with my "new" body. I'm about 15 pounds heavier here from my lowest. June 2012.

Racing at the National NAIA cross country meet with Alina where I took 40th and our team took 7th. I ended up bingeing that night alone in the hotel room while my teammates celebrated together. November 2012.
Photo credit Jim Cherry.

*Tired from a night of bingeing and embarrassed
about my weight gain. February 2013.
Photo credit Mark and Linda Heston.*

*Speaking publicly about my experiences
with the eating disorder. Summer 2016.
Photo credit Kristina Bird.*

Appendix A

Glossary of Terms for Running

Cooldown: in running, a relaxed, easy run or walk to loosen up the muscles after a tough effort.

Long slow distance runs (LSD): a workout often completed once a week, usually at an easy pace for a distance greater than the running distance in a typical day of training.

Orthotics: "Devices worn inside running shoes to help treat or prevent injuries. Orthotics can be hard or soft, and of varying length, depending on what injury they're trying to address." (*A Guide to Common Running Terms*)

Pace: "How fast you're running, usually expressed in terms of minutes per mile." (*A Guide to Common Running Terms*)

Personal records/personal best: the fastest running time in one's career, depending on the distance/event.

Spikes: lightweight shoes most often used for racing, with pointed protrusions screwed into the bottom.

m (meter): the measurement used to distinguish distances in a track meet.

Warm-up: in running, a relaxed, easy jog or walk to loosen up the muscles before a tough effort.

Glossary of Terms for Eating Disorders

Amenorrhea: the absence of menstrual period, often due to low body weight or not eating enough calories.

Anorexia: an emotional disorder characterized by an underweight BMI, loss of menstrual cycle, preoccupation with losing weight, and restricted calorie intake.

Anorexia Athletica: an emotional disorder characterized by the obsession with losing weight for one's sport, or over exercising to lose weight.

Bingeing: an emotional disorder characterized by eating a large amount of food very quickly with very little feeling of control and results in extreme guilt.

Body Mass Index (BMI): an estimation of body fat to determine whether or not your weight is healthy. BMI is derived by comparing your height to your weight.

Bulimia: an emotional disorder characterized by eating a large amount of food in a short amount of time and self-induced purging the food through vomiting or exercise.

Disordered eating: "refers to a wide range of abnormal eating behaviors, many of which are shared with diagnosed eating disorders." (*F.E.A.S.T.'s Eating Disorders Glossary*)

Eating disorder: a mental illness that may be in the form of anorexia, bulimia, binge eating disorder, or EDNOS, and is characterized by the preoccupation with food, poor body image, and commonly associated with changes in body weight

Eating Disorder Not Otherwise Specified (EDNOS): "an eating disorder classification for individuals who don't meet the DSM-IV-TR criteria for anorexia nervosa or bulimia nervosa yet display severe eating disordered symptoms." (*F.E.A.S.T.'s Eating Disorders Glossary*)

Forbidden foods: also known as fear foods, forbidden foods cause anxiety for eating disordered individuals, and the list of these "forbidden foods" will vary between those with eating disorders. Forbidden foods can also include a whole macronutrient group like protein, fat, or carbohydrate.

Female Athlete Triad: "refers to a combination of three conditions in female athletes: disordered eating, amenorrhea, and osteoporosis. A female athlete can have one, two, or all three parts of the triad." (*F.E.A.S.T.'s Eating Disorders Glossary*)

Meal Plan: a regulated amount of food often suggested by a dietitian to guide someone with an eating disorder to have established meals for recovery. It may challenge the patient or reduce anxiety, provide nutrition, and be a model for future meal choices chosen by the patient post recovery.

Orthorexia: emotional disorder characterized with the preoccupation of the "purity" or "cleanliness" of food, not yet recognized by the DSM-V-TR.

Paleo: a diet based on the types of foods presumed to have been eaten by early humans, consisting chiefly of meat, fish, vegetables, and fruit, and excluding dairy or grain products and processed food .

Purge: to get rid of an unwanted food through exercise, laxative use, or vomiting.

Triggers: a person, place, thing, event, or emotion that is upsetting or leads someone to engage in eating disorder behaviors.

Vegan: "A person who eats only plants, excluding all animal products including milk or eggs. In an individual predisposed to an eating disorder, a decision to become vegan or vegetarian may signal a developing eating disorder and a means of restricting caloric intake." (*F.E.A.S.T.'s Eating Disorders Glossary*)

Vegetarian: "A way of eating that excludes meat products for cultural, ethical, or health reasons. Often, a sudden decision to become vegetarian contrary to family food preferences can be a way to limit intake of calories or to avoid food in social settings." (*F.E.A.S.T.'s Eating Disorders Glossary*)

30 Bananas a Day (30BAD): a community led by Freelee and Durianrider who promote eating 2500-3000 calories from fruit and vegetables each day, with limited fat and protein intake (at most, 10 percent of calories from protein and 10 percent of calories from fat). They advise eating this much to avoid bingeing on cooked, non-vegan foods, as well as to stay 100 percent vegan.

Raw till 4 (RT4): A 30 Bananas a Day method to help members transition to a vegan lifestyle by eating raw fruits and vegetables until 4 p.m. and then consuming cooked vegan food for the rest of the day. This method was merely a suggestion in the days I was a 30BAD member and is now heavily encouraged today for 30BAD members.

80/10/10 Diet: diet promoted by Dr. Douglas Graham that encourages the consumption of only raw foods in the form of fruits, vegetables, and limited nuts and seeds, with eighty percent of daily calories from carbohydrates, ten percent from protein, and ten percent from fat.

Appendix B

Recovery Worksheets

If you think you might have a problem with food

or

If you know someone who struggles with food

If you are dealing with your own eating disorder, you are going to be facing much more than just problems with food. Once you decide to commit yourself to recovery from this illness, you will be confronted with your own emotions and the reactions of those who care about you. Because of that, these worksheets address both food and feelings. I have included information, suggestions, and tools that have worked for me. I understand that different methods work better for different people, but I hope the tools I provide here will work for you!

If you care about someone you believe might be in trouble with food, you will need to read what I have included in these worksheets for them. The more information you have about this illness, the more effectively you will listen, understand, and support. Part of your job as a friend or family member will be knowing what to say or do and what not to say or do. Sometimes silence and a hug are the best support you can offer.

You will make mistakes. Don't worry about them. Bring your genuine concern and your honest commitment to be of help, and mistakes won't matter. The recovering person will make plenty of them!

Welcome to recovery!

For my readers who are concerned about someone they fear might have an eating disorder

Points you need to keep in mind:

1. An eating disorder thrives in secrecy.

2. You can't always *see* an eating disorder.

3. An eating disorder is not a matter of discipline. If they could fix it with information, willpower, and good intentions, they would have done it already!
    <u>Disorder</u>: a state of confusion or chaos; a medical condition (physical or mental) that isn't normal or healthy
    <u>Eating Disorder</u>: a serious, sometimes fatal, illness that causes severe disturbances to a person's eating behavior and personality

If someone talks to you about an eating disorder:

Having to explain an eating disorder to a loved one is probably one of the most difficult tasks in the journey to recovery. While you may not completely understand, try to listen with an open mind. An eating disorder is just that: a disorder. It is a condition that leaves the person with an eating disorder feeling afraid and helpless. It is not a way of living someone decides to adopt.

You can't:

Fix an eating disorder

You can:

1. Read books on the subject

2. Spend more time listening than advising; this goes for anyone who is not a therapist or dietitian. Your place as a loved one is to offer support and

acceptance. Those with eating disorders may repeat themselves; be patient. I had many "ah-ha" moments as I talked through everything with my mom. Encouraging someone with an eating disorder to keep communicating will help them make sense of what's happening to them and can begin the journey out of shame, loneliness, and isolation.

3. Read the Recovery Worksheets for the problem eater so you are familiar with the triggers that activate the disorder.

Discussing the Disorder

When I first told my mom about the eating disorder, she seemed to make the wrong comments about my food and body (based on *my* perception, since my perceptions of food and my body were skewed). One such question was in Chapter 24 ("Two Toasts to Twenty Bananas"): "All right, how about you get on the scale?"

Knowing what to say to someone who is afraid they have an eating disorder is not about thinking what the person "should" or "shouldn't" let affect them, but about finding ways to help them navigate through their situation more easily. And remember, this mostly involves listening with an open mind.

Understanding the biological aspect of eating disorders will allay some of *your* confusion and fear about the disease as long as you know that it still doesn't mean you should give advice. My parents were both very confused by the disorder, and when I finally understood why my mind and body felt and acted like they did around food, I was able to answer some of their questions.

Two questions I think that are very important:

How can you physically keep stuffing in more and more food?

Binge foods are often foods high in sugar and fat and low in nutrients. We may crave these types of food because our bodies can quickly convert this into energy in our bloodstream. And if someone has starved him- or herself enough, his or her body will yearn for the quickest way to get energy again to survive. With the body in that desperation mode, those with eating disorders often stuff themselves until they are uncomfortably full, even if it hurts. They often may still feel hungry despite this. This is because, while their stomachs may be *filled,* their bodies are not *full* (especially if the foods are low in nutrients!). The body will do anything in its power to get the calories, even if it means shutting off your brain to it or overcoming "willpower."

Why can't you just eat normally? Just stop restricting so you don't binge! Just stop bingeing so you don't restrict!

Those who want to support people with eating disorders may wonder why they either restrict or binge. Many people with eating disorders have the "all or nothing" mentality that I mention in Chapter 38 ("Just One Drink"). You get a "high" either way, a bingeing high when you eat everything you've ever been holding back on, or a restriction high, when you feel you are growing closer to your weight loss goals. Balanced eating doesn't achieve either of these highs. Just as I never wanted to be an "average" runner, I felt I could not eat in an "average" way for fear of becoming nothing more than "just Rachael." Also don't forget the physical component of these highs. Sugar certainly generates an immediate rush, as does fasting or purging. You alter your body chemistry when you alter what you put in your body.

The best way you can better understand the person you care about who suffers is to allow them to be as open as possible with you. Avoid criticizing eating disorder "decisions," which are often out of their control and which are certainly not a measure of willpower. It is a difficult disorder to understand, but if you are there to support, listen, and make small changes in how you react to their decisions, they will find recovery with you to be less stressful.

For my readers who are facing their own eating disorders, perhaps for the first time

SUPPORT

Laying a foundation

In Chapters 24 and 25 ("Two Toasts to Twenty Bananas" and "A Moment More with Mom"), I seek help for the first time. It doesn't go as well as I had hoped, but my mom doesn't let the difficult topic go until she feels she has a better grasp on this.

Whether you encounter loved ones who try to support you or fail to support you, you will want to find someone who will be a part of that inner circle. So write a list of resources! Examples include therapists, a dietitian, family, friends, phone apps, and a journal. Make a list of this support team specifically by name so that you know where to turn when you need help in specific situations. You might even put a few people on speed dial on your phone!

1.

2.

3.

4.

5.

Understand that it takes time and patience to work through tough situations with food. It's a decision you have to make for yourself. Your support team will help, and might make the road easier. But . . .

You are the most important person in your recovery.

Your goals are: becoming aware of what triggers your eating disorder, learning tools to avoid destructive behaviors, and working towards bettering, accepting, and eventually loving yourself.

Bringing up the eating disorder to a loved one:

Having to explain your eating disorder to a loved one is probably one of the most difficult tasks you will face in recovery. While your listener may not completely understand what you are going through, the biggest thing people who care about you can offer is support.

Things to consider before you confide in someone:

1. What comments might they make that would be uncomfortable for you? Write these down and discuss them before you begin talking about your eating.

2. What are some things you want them to know about your eating disorder? What can they do to help you at each meal? Each day?

3. When might *not* be the right time to bring up the eating disorder?

4. Remember that you might not get the response you want from everyone. Believe that your recovery does not depend on those responses.

You have depended on food; now you get to discover that you can depend on yourself!

WRITING IT DOWN, THINKING IT THROUGH

Reaching the small goals to keep you moving forward

Writing about your situation with food is a great way to put your thinking cap on and begin to develop ideas to make you feel more comfortable eating in a way that will benefit you and break the eating disorder habits. I know that when my dietitian or my therapist suggested something to help me in my recovery (See Chapter 39, "The Meal Plan"), I often resisted, but after writing about all the pros and cons, I was at least willing to try it. But it had to be *my* choice in the end for me to make that change. Now it's time to find a way to make those good ideas *your* choice.

Here are two examples from my own situation:

1. Re-Introducing

    a. I didn't want to eat pasta. My dietitian Trina asked me why I was eating so much oatmeal when whole-wheat pasta was not all that different. I didn't agree with Trina at first, but I let it sit with me. Trina's comment violated one of my internal "rules," and I had to find a way to not feel like I had to follow that rule any longer.

    b. I began to write about it. Writing allowed me to really look at all the ways of thinking about her question. I realized that whole-wheat pasta had fiber, it had about the same number of calories as oatmeal, and it would add some variety to my meals so maybe I wouldn't binge as much.

    c. I began to eat pasta and found I no longer felt as guilty eating it.

    d. It became a part of my normal routine. I no longer viewed eating this food as binge food.

    e. I moved on to another whole food I feared. It was one food at a time with this method.

2. Counting Calories

    a. I wasn't sure how to avoid counting calories so often.

    b. I set a goal: Stop counting calories.

    c. Even after making it a priority to stop counting calories, I continued to count calories! I was trapped in that way of thinking, but I tried to be patient with myself in working through it.

    d. Writing about the patterns in my eating allowed me to see what was going on. When my calorie count at the end of the day was lower than I expected, I sometimes binged as a "reward" and probably because I was simply hungry; when it was over my limit, I binged because I was miserable and felt like a failure. *Writing helped me see just what a terrible cycle this was.*

    e. In the new cycle of listening to suggestions, then writing about them, I learned that for each meal, instead of counting calories, I could eat what I wanted (to avoid feeling deprived and reduce the chance of a binge) and focus on getting the macronutrients my body needed. If my fear meal was ground beef with vegetables and bread, I would remind myself that the beef was full of protein to keep me full, the vegetables added fiber and thus more fullness, and the bread (a carb) helped me to avoid eating too many processed carbs later. I focused on foods that would keep me full and tasted good rather than foods that may have been lower in calories but didn't keep me full. Thus calories didn't become as important in the end.

Your Turn!

Write down small, manageable steps toward reaching the goal of eating a fear food or eating in a frightening situation. One tip is to choose a fear that is within reach, something that you feel you could tackle eventually at this point in your recovery. Don't try just setting a goal, then jumping toward it all at once. I can tell you that never worked for me!

1.

2.

3.

4.

5.

When you reach this goal (and you will!), continue to work on it. When you feel comfortable enough and have moved past it, find something else that scares you about food and work on these same steps to overcome it. Writing about each of your fears in your journal may help. This will help you to trust you and your body more, giving less power to the eating disorder.

Believe in yourself. Trust the process. Eventually you will be able to enjoy your food so that you can enjoy your days.

RETURN OF EMOTIONS

Your Journey into Recovery

"I am thawing."

This powerful quote from Laurie Anderson's book, *Wintergirls,* expresses what most of us feel in the midst of our eating disorders, frozen, with little emotion or feeling. We often become robotic perfectionists, often not someone most people are excited to be around.

Chapter 42, "High School Track, Senior Year" describes a cold, numbing restriction of my food, and in Chapter 44, "Elizabeth Speaks", as my bingeing intensifies and my emotions become erratic, my friend confesses that she doesn't enjoy being around me.

At this point, when do you feel the most emotion? When do you feel the least? Is it possible that the disordered eating is deadening your feelings?

_____

_____

_____

Thawing out, opening up to mistakes, working on that recovery process, did not feel good for me at first. I didn't understand what was going on. Here I was working on *recovery*, and I was feeling worse, not better! My goal for recovery was to gain control again and immediately be happy with my body. As I stated in Chapter 45 "Waterlogged," I wanted a quick fix, a pill, something to cure everything immediately. I had no idea how to accomplish something one step at a time. I didn't know how to love myself, how to deal with the emotions, or how to enjoy life except when I was running fast.

If you are in that "thawing" stage, what are some emotions you may be feeling? How do you cope with anger, sadness, hurt, or fear?

_____

_____

_____

I turned to my journal and wrote about my past: my childhood **humiliation** when others made fun of my stomach (Chapter 12, "Stomaching the Realization"), my **anger** with my mom for not understanding eating disorders (Chapter 24, "Two Toasts to Twenty Bananas" and Chapter 25, "A Moment More with Mom"), and the terrible **insecurity** of feeling unappreciated as a high school runner (Chapter 44, "High School Track, Senior Year").

And gradually I came to understand what led me to the eating disorder and to embrace the emotions I never fully allowed myself to feel.

ACCEPTANCE

The first step in mental recovery

An important warning: Accepting your body as it is in the moment does not mean staying either dangerously underweight or dangerously overweight. Rather it means accepting the reality of who you are, whether you like it or not. Acceptance demands being honest with yourself because it is only if we see <u>what is</u> that we can work toward <u>what might be.</u>

This is tougher than it sounds. Even when I reached the stage of acceptance (when I smashed the scale in Chapter 46 "Scaling Back"), it was difficult to let the old Rachael go. It took me months to fully accept where I was.

Say this to yourself:

I want to live my life. In order to live my life to its fullest, I have to be okay with who I am right now, without dreaming about future weight loss or hating myself for gaining the weight in the first place.

What are some areas you can work on in your life to be happy that have no relation to weight or food?

1.

2.

3.

If you find benefits to these areas in your life over the "benefits" of the eating disorder, you will find more motivation for acceptance and thus recovery.

I had to overcome the fear of being who I was in the moment, full of mistakes and imperfection, but with lots of potential for new relationships and activities ahead of me. I accepted that I would never be perfect with food.

GRIEVING

The second step in mental recovery

Friends may tell you to simply "just let go" or "just stop." Unfortunately, just as it is with losing a loved one, you are losing a part of yourself! Time is the key here. You will have days when you feel free of the disorder and other days when you don't want to let it go. Make sure you are writing in your journal a little bit every day so you can see those changes in your thinking and take pleasure in your achievements as you reach one goal after another.

During the tough days, what can you do to remind yourself of those goals, of your plans for reaching them, and of the person you are becoming as you work toward them?

_____

_____

_____

What are the things you look forward to doing in the future without the eating disorder? Some examples for me included traveling without fear about food and going out with friends and enjoying the food that was there.

_____

_____

_____

What will help you *want* to recover? That is the key here. Recovery begins when you take the step to get help.

_____

_____

_____

Write down a goal for each week. Everyone's eating disorder looks a little different, so your goals may not be the same as mine.

1.

2.

3.

4.

5.

Here were some of my goals:

"You have to be okay with this." (my mantra)

"Give your worries to God." (if you are religious)

"Eating differently for the sake of great experiences is better than eating perfectly and missing out on great experiences." (to encourage myself that life without the eating disorder would feel more fulfilling)

DISCOVERY AND SELF LOVE

The third step in mental recovery

Here comes the fun, and yes, still challenging, part of recovery. My book ends where I don't quite love myself, but I have accepted my fate and I'm ready to move forward. Your task is to continue this process; how do you move forward after acceptance? What are your goals at this point? Who do you wish to be beyond what you weigh? What do you want out of your life?

We must find activities, hobbies, and other modes of happiness to replace the eating disorder, motivating you to want more out of life than this illness.

Keep a journal and make a bucket list. What are some things the eating disorder has held you back from doing?

_____

_____

_____

For me it was traveling. I was always worried about going out with friends even for the weekend for fear that I didn't have the "perfect" food with me. I skipped events because I worried about how guilty I would feel if I ate the "wrong" things. I even worried so much about getting the right amount of sleep every single night that I missed out on a lot of experiences that in the end would have made me feel better than if I had gotten a full night's rest. It's about balance.

Start with an attitude that gets you into the world. Sometimes it takes someone to push you out of the nest. Let them.

Once you're out here, try out different activities to discover what you love and are passionate about. Begin to define yourself by something other than your weight.

Taking chances means risking the possibility of getting hurt. But it also means you are willing to live rather than just exist. You have already practiced this when you started "unthawing" and accepting emotions. It's time to go out and live it.

What can you identify as your potential talents or strong points? What activities might allow you to explore those strengths?

_____

_____

_____

How do you learn to love yourself? By taking all these steps:

1. Find your supporters (including yourself!).
2. Apply the recovery tools to your daily life.
3. Learn to embrace emotion.
4. Begin to accept yourself.
5. Give yourself time to grieve.

You will risk mistakes; yes, you may fail. But learn to get comfortable with the discomfort of imperfection. What are some mistakes you are afraid of making?

_____

_____

_____

MOVING FORWARD WITH FOOD

Bingeing can be a result of emotionally filling a void, as well as the body physically needing more food. I know now that it wasn't a matter of "discipline" that made me go for the foods I binged on (usually high-calorie, processed food), but more because I was restricting them completely, I wasn't eating enough food in general, and because many of the heavily processed foods that I binged on can be chemically addicting and gave me a "high" when eaten in large volumes. These "highs" distracted me from the emotional pain of feeling like my running (my definition of success and worth) was going out of control.

I am now aware that if I eat enough whole, filling, nutritious foods throughout the day, I no longer crave and cave into the heavily processed food to cope with my emotions. It is easier to resist a binge to fill an emotional void when my body is physically getting enough nutritional food. I have taken care of my physical body so that I can deal with my emotional stress in a less destructive manor.

A turning point for me came when my dietitian suggested that I was not eating enough whole food carbs. I was bingeing on heavily processed foods and feeling very out of control with them. So I needed to eat more whole food carbs in the form of:

- oatmeal
- potatoes
- whole-wheat or rye bread
- whole-wheat pasta
- quinoa
- brown rice
- other grains
- fruit

The more you eat of these starting early in the day, the less likely you are to binge later. This is a very similar concept to what the 30 Bananas a Day community was advocating; eat more food in the form of whole food carbs. But if there is one thing I learned from my mistakes on the 30BAD diet, it was that I never felt satisfied eating only carbs. I still had intense cravings, and

I was still bingeing. If anything, I might not have been eating enough food on that diet, but eating was already taking up most of my day at that point.

Thus protein and fat are also factors in keeping you full, so I know that it's important for me to have protein and fat in each meal. From the Paleo diet I learned to focus on obtaining foods from sustainable sources (like grass-fed beef, free-range chicken, wild-caught fish, etc). If you have the money to eat more sustainably, I urge more of us to take this route, which not only pays for better treatment of animals, but it also means we are buying food with a higher nutrient profile.

Protein:
- red meat (great source of iron!)
- tofu
- chicken
- eggs
- beans
- fish

Fat:
- avocado
- nuts
- seeds
- coconut oil
- olive oil

And, of course, including vegetables helps to keep meals lower in calories while also keeping you full and providing nutrients that will reduce intense cravings. I know calories shouldn't be counted, but I found it was easier not to count calories if I included plenty of vegetables in my meals. Meals shouldn't be made up of *just* vegetables (you read how this didn't work for me; cue the bingeing episodes!), but they are important in adding fiber and minerals to your diet.

Eating these whole foods does not mean you shouldn't have treats. You just don't want to *binge* on treats, and you are less likely to feel like doing this if you are eating more whole foods that make you feel full and satisfied. Once I began eating more whole, filling, nutrient-rich foods with the occasional treats, I no longer felt as deprived, I no longer had intense cravings (or at least I knew how to handle them rationally when they came), and I was finally maintaining my weight, which allowed me to trust my body more. I understand that eating whole foods is not the only key to my recovery, but it was a big part of it.

If I am tempted to eat an entire pie after having one slice, I know that I need to eat more whole food first until the craving goes away or lessens. By doing this, it is no longer a fight or struggle to "avoid" the whole pie. I don't even have the craving to eat more than a slice.

My life is no longer a daily struggle with food.

Eating whole foods is not always an easy change or transition. While I have certainly found a big part of the "cure" in eating more whole foods, I understand the psychological component of bingeing as well. Addressing internal issues are very important factors in bingeing, but we cannot ignore the physical effects of what or how little we eat may cause us to binge.

For many of us, the toughest part is getting ourselves to eat enough if we are still actively trying to lose weight. We will be tempted to restrict our food intake, which in turn often leads to bingeing. This is why it is so important to take time to grieve and find acceptance, so that it is easier to encourage ourselves to eat more again. Keep in mind that you will probably consume more calories if you restrict and then binge on highly- processed food than if you were to incorporate more whole foods throughout the day, leaving you feeling satisfied and without the yearning to binge.

This is a *process.* Everything that worked for me may not completely work for you. But be willing to keep an open mind, write down pros and cons of what you are trying, and forgive yourself for the mistakes you make on your way to understand you and your body better.

MY MEAL PLAN AT HOME

Since I am no longer exercising as much at this point in my life, I'm not as hungry as often as I used to be (since I'm not burning as many calories). The amount of food below may look either like a lot or a little to some of you, but to me, I feel full, satisfied, and comfortable. It maintains my weight. I rarely have intense cravings. Use this as a guide if you so please, not as something that is "perfect." Do not use it if you think it might be triggering to your eating disorder.

Breakfast	2-4 eggs with vegetables Oatmeal with Himalayan pink sea salt *This meal gets in all my macronutrients—protein and fat from the eggs to keep me full, carbs from the oatmeal to avoid cravings, and fiber and bulk from the vegetables.*
Lunch	Whole-wheat tortillas with turkey deli meat or tuna, avocado or hummus, and lettuce 1-2 apples A peanut butter sandwich if I'm still hungry Or I might have a wrap made at a local café that I make sure has lean protein, vegetables, and a healthy fat.
Snack	Meal bar
Dinner	Crock pot meal including chicken or red meat with vegetables like carrots, corn, tomatoes, beans, and broccoli. Or I may go out to dinner and order a dish with a protein source (like fish or chicken), vegetables, and carbs in the form of pasta or potatoes.
Dessert	If I'm craving anything, I'll have some dark chocolate, another meal bar, or I may not even want dessert because I'm satisfied from how much I've eaten throughout the day. I indulge when it sounds good, but I don't let it turn into a binge, and I don't make myself indulge when it doesn't sound appetizing.

EATING WHEN I TRAVEL

Ever since learning the meal plan given to me by my dietitian, the first thing I think about is including a macronutrient in each meal: carbs, protein, and fat (plus vegetables).

Carbs

I find that oranges often work best if I do bring any fruit; they are less likely to get squished. Rolled oats in a bag are great, especially if you have access to a microwave or you can find a coffee shop and ask for hot water. This is an easy option, but sprouted whole-grain bread is even easier. I usually buy Ezekial whole-grain bread because you can find this in many grocery stores in the freezer (you don't have to seek out a health food store), and it's easy to grab-n-go.

Protein

Canned tuna. I try to find the cans with a pop-open seal so that I don't have to bring a can opener, too. Jerky is a fine option as well and easy to get at almost any gas station.

Fat

Coconut oil is a great nutritional fat to scoop into a small container. I usually eat my tuna with coconut oil on sliced bread for a small meal.

Vegetables

Keep it canned if you don't have access to a refrigerator, but beware of the increase in pressure on airplane rides. I found this out the hard way.

Emergency Snacks

I have pre-made peanut butter sandwiches prepared for me to grab, but if those aren't available, I get a meal bar.

There is no right or wrong way to travel with food, but this is what I do to feel most comfortable. These foods keep me full and satisfied and help prevent binges. Please allow yourself wiggle room and be forgiving if things don't turn out the way you expect them to. I always keep in mind that if I'm eating all these healthy, whole foods, then I get wiggle room for "unideal" circumstances with food. That way, I no longer have the black-and-white thinking, too.

I never refuse to eat with friends at a restaurant just because I have my own "safer" food with me to eat instead. I try to challenge myself to buy a snack I may not normally eat to change things up and practice overcoming my fear. I also know that a few days on vacation with newer foods out of my "safe" zone are not going to ruin me, but I also realize that a complete "free for all" would make me feel too uncomfortable at this point. It's about taking small steps that push you a bit out of your comfort zone, but not so much that it would cause you to try to compensate with destructive behaviors.

Your Time, Your Journey

Recovery is an ongoing process. No one recovers in exactly the same way, so be patient with yourself and you will find what works best for you. Acceptance is not easy, grieving and embracing your emotions are difficult, vulnerability is uncomfortable, and taking risks will make you feel the unease of imperfection. But when you use your recovery tools, face your fears, apply your meal plan, and continue to open up about your pain and your story, you will eventually find peace and a life that is happier, more fulfilling, and more fun than a life consumed by food and weight.

It's your turn to stop running in silence.

Acknowledgments

To my best friend, Jackie Archer, who noticed when things weren't right before anyone else did; to Ashlee Santiago and Kathy Middaugh for their support of this book in its early stages; to Rachel Luehm and Carly Plank for encouraging me to find my worth and value beyond running.

To Paige Boldt for discussing the female athlete triad and eating disorder prevention to our cross country team. She became a wonderful friend and supporter.

To "Mrs. Wilson," who guided me through many stressful bingeing episodes and encouraged an exploration of my past to understand how my disordered eating morphed into a full-blown eating disorder.

To "Papa" Dale Bales for being there at my fastest and my slowest and for cheering me on as I made my emotional comeback.

To Tim Zindler, Hossein Sadat, Jennifer DiGennaro, and Bri Goodyear Luginbill. Thank you for your tremendous generosity in supporting the publication of my book.

To the wonderful Dr. Jeri Kessenich for her support and advice to my parents and me.

Thanks to Dr. Gary Eberle for his guidance in seeking publishers, and Dr. Jennifer Dawson, Dr. Michelle DeRose, and Pamela Dail Whiting for their positivity, encouragement, and enthusiasm in all my literature classes at Aquinas that allowed me to gain confidence in my writing.

I'm forever grateful to Jennifer Wisniewski, my therapist, Karen Holmquist, the eating disorder support group leader, and Trina Weber, my dietitian.

A huge thanks to Alina Dhaseleer for handling the worst of me. She continually listened, sympathized, and sacrificed her time to be there in my darkest moments.

To my dear friend Sheri McCormack for her tremendous, unwavering support and advice in creating this book. She went above and beyond in supporting me through the entire publishing and marketing process. Thank you from the bottom of my heart.

A special thanks to Coach Woj, who always emphasized the value of my character over my speed. I enjoyed our adventures in racing fast (big smiles and all!), and I will never forget how much he supported me when I was at my lowest.

Thank you to Dr. Brent Chesley, who created a "kinship" with me the moment we met at Aquinas College in the spring of 2010. He was integral in helping me to gain confidence, "make connections," and embrace the "person of quality" he believed every one of his students to be. Brent played a major role in the early editing process and helped me to transform my raw food journal into a manuscript.

A huge thanks to Wendy Marty for finding any way she could to spread the word about my book, as well as for connecting me with my second editor, Dean Robertson. Dean spent countless hours reading my manuscript over the phone, by herself, and with me in her lovely home in Virginia with Isaac the cat. Her advice, insight, and wisdom made my story into the polished book it is today.

Thanks to Doug Pilley, Joe Coccaro, and John Koehler of Koehler Books for their fine editing work and leading the way in the publication of this book. I am forever grateful for what they've done to bring my story and thoughts on recovery to life. John, a big thank you for your advice and support from the beginning of my book publishing journey. You have gone above and beyond as a publisher.

Thank you to my parents for reading and learning as much about the eating disorder as they could just to try to better understand what I was going through, for supporting me in both my good and bad races, for encouraging me to cry when I needed it most, for holding me when I felt weak, for listening when I needed to speak and heal. I wouldn't be in such a good place today without their support, and I wouldn't have had the time or opportunity to follow my passion in writing without all they have provided for me.

And to the readers of my website from the very beginning, thank you for sharing your stories and encouraging me to continue to share my own. As I've learned from you all, we are never as alone as we think. Many of the positive steps I made in the last half of this book were due to knowing you would read it someday and that everyone was rooting for me to win the race of my life.

Reference List

Chen, Catherine. (2013, August). *The Difference Between Perfection and a Healthy Pursuit of Excellence.* Retrieved from http://www.huffingtonpost.com/catherine-chen-phd/the-difference-between-perfection_b_3490442.html

Eating Disorders Victoria. (2015, June). Retrieved from http://www.eatingdisorders.org.au/eating-disorders/disordered-eating-a-dieting

Factors That May Contribute to Eating Disorders. (n.d.). Retrieved from https://www.nationaleatingdisorders.org/factors-may-contribute-eating-disorders

F.E.A.S.T.'s Eating Disorders Glossary. (n.d.). Retrieved from http://glossary.feast-ed.org/

Freelee the Banana Girl. (2011, November 7). *How to get rid of Cooked Food Cravings 10 tips* [Video File]. Retrieved from https://www.youtube.com/watch?v=43QXpCTz5jo.

Freelee the Banana Girl. (2012, April 20). *Weight Loss on Raw Food Freelee 30 Bananas a Day.* [Video File]. Retrieved from https://www.youtube.com/watch?v=3kZ9R3_2tTA

Healthfoodjunkies. (2008, February 6). *Health Food Junkies.* Retrieved from https://www.youtube.com/watch?v=aTec K6odDoc&list=PL24C6C87240EDA2CC

Jamie Oliver. (2010, May 21). *How To... cook steak, with Jamie Oliver's mate Pete*. [Video File]. Retrieved from https://www.youtube.com/watch?v=h5gcJjOSDv4

Pavlina, Steve. (2007, December 31). *Raw Foods*. Retrieved from http://www.stevepavlina.com/blog/2007/12/raw-foods/

Russo, Ruthann. *The Raw Food Lifestyle: The Philosophy and Nutrition behind Raw and Live Foods*. Berkeley: North Atlantic Books, 2008.

Van Allen, J. (2016, July 20). *A Guide to Common Running Terms*. Retrieved from http://www.runnersworld.com/start-running/a-guide-to-common-running-terms/slide/1

Wrangham, R. (2009). *Catching Fire: How Cooking Made Us Human*. New York, NY: Basic Books.

Contact the Author

I love connecting with my readers! I speak publicly about eating disorders to share my story, create awareness, offer tools for recovery, and bring hope. I am available for phone, Skype, or personal consultations. You can find me here:

www.runninginsilence.com
runninginsilence@gmail.com
Twitter: @RachaelSteil, #RunninginSilence
Facebook Page: Running in Silence
YouTube: Running in Silence
Snapchat: runningNsilence

Please take a moment to rate this book at amazon.com!

CPSIA information can be obtained
at www.ICGtesting.com
Printed in the USA
FFOW05n2024011116

9 781633 933408